THE BIBLICAL CANON

A Theological Account

MATTHEW Y. EMERSON

Baker Academic
a division of Baker Publishing Group
Grand Rapids, Michigan

Published by Baker Academic
a division of Baker Publishing Group
Grand Rapids, Michigan
BakerAcademic.com

Printed in the United States of America

Library of Congress Cataloging-in-Publication Data
Names: Emerson, Matthew Y., 1984– author
Title: The biblical canon : a theological account / Matthew Y. Emerson.
Description: Grand Rapids, Michigan : Baker Academic, a division of Baker Publishing Group, [2026] | Includes bibliographical references and index.
Identifiers: LCCN 2026021018 | ISBN 9781540963017 paperback | ISBN 9781493455942 ebook | ISBN 9781493455959 pdf
Subjects: LCSH: Bible—Canonical criticism | Bible—Canon | Theology, Doctrinal
Classification: LCC BS521.8 .E44 2026
LC record available at https://lccn.loc.gov/2026021018

Baker Publishing Group publications use paper produced from sustainable forestry practices and postconsumer waste whenever possible.

26 27 28 29 30 31 32 7 6 5 4 3 2 1

"Scholars have frequently pursued quests for the historical canon, attempting to understand the process of its formation, literary composition, and ideological function. Emerson paves the road less taken, drawing systematically on a wide range of doctrines to provide a theological account of the canon's divine origin, unified christological content, and ecclesial function. The result: a valuable account of both what the canon is (a theological rule) and how it should be read (in a theologically ruled manner)."

—**Kevin J. Vanhoozer**, Litfin Divinity School, Wheaton College

"Stephen Chapman has rightly noted that 'the church's concept of a canon lay precisely at the fault line between history and theology.' Emerson explores this fault line by testing the implications of bringing together what canon is (theology) and how the canon was formed (history). His synthesis, a form of ruled reading beholden to Scripture's ontology, should be considered in its own right as a positive contribution. Modern historicism, along with theological amnesia, has complicated exploration of this fault line, but work like Emerson's is a healthy step in the right direction, avoiding both. I can think of fewer more pressing issues than the need for a dogmatic account of canon and its implications for Christian reading of the Bible. I am grateful to Emerson for moving the conversation toward a more rigorously dogmatic account of canon."

—**Darian R. Lockett**, Talbot School of Theology, Biola University

"Studies of the biblical canon often focus on questions of historical development or hermeneutical function, while theologies of Scripture frequently leave the question of canon underdeveloped. Emerson brings these conversations together with impressive theological and exegetical skill. Situating the canon within the broader framework of Christian doctrine, he offers a constructive account that engages the best of contemporary canon studies while illuminating the theological significance of Scripture's shape and scope. This volume fills a gap in current scholarship and provides a thoughtful contribution to the study of Scripture and canon. Recommended without hesitation!"

—**Ched Spellman**, Cedarville University

"For too long, the question of canon has been subjected to modern empirical inquiries that jettison basic theological assumptions. In this timely volume, Emerson reminds the people of God that they hold in their hands a precious canon given by the triune God as the rule for all matters of faith and practice. His compelling theological account of what canon is and how it is formed offers a needed framework for understanding Scripture rightly. Drawing from the wisdom of the premodern tradition, especially Irenaeus of Lyons, Emerson charts a better path forward, one that envisions Scripture as one book, given by one author, and centered on one subject and story, and he teaches us how to read it accordingly. This is an important and engaging book that deserves a wide readership."

—**Stephen Presley**, Center for Religion, Culture & Democracy, Southern Seminary

"The sheep hear the voice of their shepherd and follow him, for he knows them. But how can they know his voice? How is it disambiguated from every other voice? Because they recognize it is intrinsically holy, unique, and set apart from every other voice. Put another way, Christ is the Lord of his church and rules it through his Word, but that Word itself has a particular shape, a rule, a *canon* whose contours distinguish it—and therefore must distinguish our approach to it—from every other text. Emerson lays out that shape with clarity and discriminating judgment, not just by treating the canon as a problem of historically discerned lists or marks (important as those are), but by situating it dogmatically in relation to the sweep of Christian revelation. The result is an illuminating study that I highly commend."

—**Derek Rishmawy**, author of *The Fire of Glory*

"A wide-ranging book on the Protestant Christian canon, one that considers matters like the ontology of Scripture, its phenomenology, typology, Christology, and eschatology. There are many works on the phenomenology of canon (lists, manuscripts, citations) but very few that consider the deeper theological and philosophical implications of canon. Here is such a book!"

—**Stephen G. Dempster**, Crandall University (emeritus)

Contents

Acknowledgments

This book has been percolating in my thought and my research for quite a while. In some ways it is the dissertation that I wanted to write but was not ready to write, one that wedded the academic insights of the "canonical approach" with the theological truth claims about the Bible as God's Word. In other ways it is the book that I wanted to give to certain ministers in high school when they told me that the literary and historical qualities of the Bible—that is, its quality as the product of human authors spanning millennia—meant that it could not simultaneously be inerrantly inspired by the Holy Spirit. And in yet other ways it is an outflow of gratitude toward those who, unlike those certain ministers from my childhood, taught me how to take the Bible seriously as Holy Scripture.

I am grateful for my mentors, spiritual and academic. During my graduate and postgraduate studies, they urged me to understand the Bible as God's Word and to read it as such. I have been indelibly shaped by their passion for Scripture and reading it as God's divinely inspired address to his people. I have seen that passion modeled by David Hogg, Steven Wade, Keith Harper, Tracy McKenzie, Bob Cole, Craig Bartholomew, Greg Heisler, and many others. I am indebted to Heath Thomas not only for teaching me how to read the Bible as Christian Scripture but also for showing me what it means to walk in the way of Jesus, following him wherever he leads. I owe Brandon

Smith and Luke Stamps for the many hours of conversation about the intersection of biblical studies and theology, about Christ-centered hermeneutics, about retrieving the interpretive resources from our Christian forebearers . . . and of course about college sports. I am especially grateful to Heath, Luke, and Brandon for continually speaking into this project and giving me feedback. Darian Lockett, Ched Spellman, and Patrick Schreiner graciously read an earlier draft of the book and gave valuable feedback. I owe Dave Nelson my gratitude for seeing this book proposal through to a contract with Baker. Likewise, I owe Bryan Dyer my gratitude for his patience and insight as my editor for the final phase of this project. The same is true for Tim West and the rest of the Baker editorial team who took this book from a rough draft to a publishable version. And I am thankful to Andrew Tucker, my erstwhile grader and now my peer and friend, for his help in finding and assessing early Christian sources that helped me in my research. Sometimes reading the Bible as one book really does just make you so excited you start to perspire.

Finally, to my wife, Alicia—you opened the Bible and showed me how to take it seriously, for life and for doctrine. Even when we were teenagers, you were pushing me to hear God's Word and heed it. You were the first to challenge me and encourage me to read Scripture for what it is—God's inspired, inerrant Word—and you continue to challenge and encourage me to read it and follow it two decades later. I dedicate this book to you as, I hope, the fruit of your labor in my life to point me toward the Lord through his Word by his Spirit.

Introduction: Entryways into Canonical Conversations

While writing this book, and for entirely unrelated reasons, I took a trip with my oldest daughter to the Black Sea. We stayed in Sinope, a coastal community in Türkiye populated largely by retirees and college students. What most of the current residents probably don't realize, and what I did not know until a colleague pointed it out to me at the beginning of my trip, is that Sinope was once home to Marcion, son of the bishop of Sinope. In Marcion's day, in the late first and early second century AD, Sinope was an important city in the Pontus region of ancient Asia Minor, known for its shipwrights and mariners. It had already been evangelized, perhaps by Priscilla and Aquila or the apostle Peter, by the time Marcion was born, as evidenced by his father's position as a leader in the churches of the region.[1]

It was not lost on me as I wrote portions of this book that I was looking out onto the same coast and sea that Marcion saw. I walked through ruined Hellenistic-era fortresses and on Hellenistic-era streets, ones that, most likely, Marcion knew well. I heard sounds that probably were familiar to Marcion—seagulls crying, waves crashing, ships signaling their entry into port. But while I shared

1. See M. Wilson, *Biblical Turkey*, 337–40.

common geography with Marcion for about a fortnight in total, I do not share Marcion's views of the biblical canon. Unlike Marcion, I affirm the biblical canon's fundamental unity—a unity rooted in the triune God, expressed in the human authors' writing of it, and acknowledged in the church's reception of it.

For those who have studied church history, and in particular the history of the biblical canon, Marcion's name should ring plenty of bells. He brought to the fore the question of biblical authority precisely by denying the inner coherence of most of Scripture. Instead of seeing the biblical canon as an inherently unified document, Marcion posited that the biblical material reflects a conflict between the true God and the Demiurge, who is evil and responsible for creation and its history as recorded in the Old Testament (OT). The true God, on the other hand, is revealed through the work of Jesus, who frees us from the material (evil) creation and brings us back (spiritually speaking, not physically) to God.[2]

In response to the claims of Marcion, as well as various Gnostics, Irenaeus, the bishop of Lyons, wrote his *Against Heresies* and *Demonstration of the Apostolic Preaching*. We will refer to Irenaeus and his work throughout the book, so we will not summarize his argument in detail here.[3] Suffice it to say that, contra Marcion, Irenaeus affirmed the inherent unity of Christian Scripture, a unity ultimately grounded in the triune God's revelation of himself to his people. Irenaeus marshals a number of arguments to demonstrate this profound unity of the Bible, chief among them the hypothesis, economy, and recapitulative patterns of Scripture. Each of these will be important in the current work. For now, it is simply important to note that Irenaeus (1) affirms the unity of the biblical canon because of its nature as

2. On Marcion's interpretation of Scripture, see, most recently, Young, *Scripture, the Genesis of Doctrine*, 44–73. Young relies heavily on the account of Lieu, *Marcion and the Making of a Heretic*. I do not agree with all of Young's or Lieu's conclusions, but theirs are the most recent treatments on the subject at hand.

3. For an introduction to Irenaeus's mode of biblical interpretation, see, e.g., Reventlow, *History of Biblical Interpretation*, 1:153–74, as well as O'Keefe and Reno, *Sanctified Vision*, esp. 34–40, and Presley, *The Intertextual Reception of Genesis 1–3 in Irenaeus of Lyons*, 1–45. Another of Presley's recent works, *Biblical Theology in the Life of the Early Church*, considers other early Christian thinkers besides (but also including) Irenaeus, but the latter remains a focal point.

God's revelation, and (2) demonstrates the unity of the biblical canon through its Christocentric content (hypothesis), structure (economy), and typological repetition (recapitulation).[4]

Irenaeus's articulation of Scripture's unity has been and remains influential in the history of Christian theology and biblical interpretation. From its role in shaping ancient and medieval Christian modes of exegesis to its influence on modern studies of canon, the Irenaean model for explaining the Bible's unity in light of its canonical shape can be described as foundational for Christian reflection on Scripture. This book seeks to follow Irenaeus's model, a model derived from Scripture itself, in considering the relationship between systematic theology, on the one hand, and biblical studies, on the other.

While these two areas of academic study are often pitted against each other in theory—the theologians are not exegetical enough and the exegetes are not theological enough, or so the trope goes—the reality is that they have always worked hand in hand to help us understand what Scripture is and how to read it well. In line with Irenaeus, I aim to show how a properly theological account of what Scripture is helps us explain and understand particular canonical phenomena. Scripture is an inherently unified document, and its inner, divinely grounded unity is demonstrable in certain canonical phenomena.

The Question of the Canon

When we use the term *canon* or refer to *canonical phenomena*, we are speaking broadly of questions that pertain to what is included and excluded from a particular corpus, literary or otherwise. Issues of canon in that sense aren't new to most of us. We just don't use the word *canon* when we talk about them.

Well, that's not entirely true. Hardcore *Star Wars* fans, for instance, invoke the word *canon* often in Internet debates about what truly counts as the "real" *Star Wars*. Maybe you didn't like Episode IX, for instance—"It's not canon, and I don't care who says otherwise!" Or, maybe you have an (understandable) aversion to Jar Jar Binks and goofy lines about sand being coarse, so you declare that the redacted

4. See Young, *Scripture, the Genesis of Doctrine*, 74–109.

version of the prequels, edited to remove the most egregious Lucas faux pas and combine the three movies into one, is "actually canon." On whose authority are these canonical decisions made? Your own? Some broader community of *Star Wars* experts? Dave Filoni? The "original author"? In that case, are we talking about George Lucas, Lucasfilm, and/or Kathleen Kennedy? Or maybe the authority rests with the owner and distributor of the "final form," the Walt Disney Company? These are questions of canonical boundaries.

But discussions about boundaries in contemporary culture aren't the only places canonical questions arise. We also see, for example, conversation about whether or not a particular author's works are conceptually coherent and unified. This is especially prevalent in literary studies, but it is not limited to academic settings. To cite another pop culture example, readers of the Harry Potter novels regularly debate whether author J. K. Rowling's extraliterary, public statements about her books' characters and events, whether in print or on social media or in interviews, are to be considered "canonical" information. And in that same vein, what is the "canonical" relationship of the Harry Potter movie franchise, including the Fantastic Beasts sequels, or of the other Potter-related books that Rowling has published subsequently, to the seven original novels?

These rather trivial examples are intended to show that the question of canon is not alien to contemporary discourse. Instead, these and other instances of canonical conversations show that our society is still invested in the issue of canon, even if some of the debates seem ultimately inconsequential.

When it comes to biblical studies, though, both the intensity and the importance of canon are multiplied exponentially.[5] Debates abound regarding some of the specific phenomena we will discuss in later chapters in the book—canonical boundaries, "final form," and "canonical criticism," for instance.[6] The canon's relation to bibli-

5. Most notably, see McDonald and Sanders, *The Canon Debate*.

6. Steinberg and Stone's definition of *canon* captures the state of the academic discourse: "Our definition of canon, then, is *a fixed or delimited collection of texts received and recognized as sacred (authoritative) by a faith community*" ("The Historical Formation of the Writings in Antiquity," 8). Their essay offers an overview of some of the canonical issues I bring up in this paragraph.

cal theology and its hermeneutical significance are central topics for the Theological Interpretation of Scripture movement. And recently, "noncanonical" texts, and especially their relation to the biblical canon, have become something of a hot topic within the academy.[7]

These and other academic studies of the biblical canon often revolve around the discovery, analysis, and interpretation of relevant observable data (such as manuscripts and lists). This empirical approach takes various forms, from manuscript discovery and evaluation, to debates about canon lists, to analysis of codex contents, to appeals to authorship and date, and, most recently to interpreting textual similarities and dissimilarities between so-called authentic and disputed books.

Sometimes, these canonical studies are undertaken within explicitly theological frameworks and in light of particular theological commitments. At other times, theology is eschewed in favor of a supposedly neutral epistemology, one in which the modernist tools of empiricism and reason are taken as sufficient to adjudicate claims about one aspect or another of the debates surrounding canon. This modernist approach, reliant as it is on logic and reason, has its advantages: The terms of debate are clear, and the objects of study and methods employed are accessible to scholars from various faith traditions or from no faith at all. The goal of scholars of all stripes in this model is to provide an empirically verifiable historical description of canon formation.

But while the advantages of an empirically and rationally driven approach are clear, that mode of operation sets to the side the question of Scripture's ontology. That is, a modernist approach attempts to defer judgment about what Scripture *is* while also making judgments about Scripture's scope and shape. To put it in epistemological and philosophical terms, modernist modes of canon studies focus their attention on the phenomenological realities of canon while infinitely delaying judgment about attendant ontological claims. This context is the impetus for this book.

7. See, e.g., Burke and Landau, *New Testament Apocrypha*, vol. 1; Burke, *New Testament Apocrypha*, vols. 2–3; Mrozek, "The Hegemony of the Biblical in the Study of Second Temple Literature"; Reed, "Afterlives of New Testament Apocrypha."

Far from being a topic relevant only to biblical studies and reducible to scholarly debates about empirical data, the question of the canon is an irreducibly theological one. What is this book whose scope and shape we are attempting to study? If, as the Bible itself and therefore historic Christianity have claimed, it is not merely just any book but is the Word of God, then this fundamentally shifts the mode of conversation. Understanding Scripture's dogmatic location—its place of consideration within Christian doctrine—can both shift the conversation away from exclusively focusing on empirical debates and also shed light on how to understand the oft-disputed empirical data.

I am certainly not the first to attend to the dogmatic location of canon or to the theological impact of Christian doctrine and practice on canon studies. John Webster has repeatedly made the point that the most obvious dogmatic location for the topic of canon is within the doctrine of Scripture. And with respect to the doctrine of Scripture, a number of profitable works have been produced recently, by Webster but also from other corners of Christianity. Many of these have, further, located the doctrine of Scripture in relation to other doctrines, most especially the doctrines of God, Christology, and pneumatology.

My goal is not to repeat or reproduce these recent studies, but rather to dig further in and argue that since canon is dogmatically located within the doctrine of Scripture, it is therefore also dogmatically located in systematic relation to the other loci of Christian theology. The primary metaphor I will use for canon is "rule," and in what follows I will demonstrate that in a number of different theological loci, the canon is both theological rule and theologically ruled.

I have in view at least two primary audiences. On the one hand, I am drawing on systematic theology and how we speak about what Scripture *is*, and so I hope to engage with systematic theologians about the doctrine of Scripture. On the other hand, I am engaging with what is often called "canonical approaches"[8] to biblical inter-

8. Paul House, for instance, defines the canonical approach as "analysis that is God-centered, intertextually oriented, authority-conscious, historically sensitive and devoted to the pursuit of the wholeness of the Old Testament message" (*Old Testament Theology*, 57). John Goldingay quotes this definition and goes on to explain his understanding of it, as well as categories (e.g., order, final form, intertextuality)

pretation. As we will see in the next chapter, one of the primary aims of "canonical criticism" is to demonstrate how the canon and its various components have been constructed in order to bring out its "final form" as one book.[9] And so I also hope to engage with those involved in biblical studies. For both of these audiences, I am essentially attempting to "connect the dots" between them.

Another way to put that is to say that I am attempting to help each group view their discipline from new vistas. Any time we view something from a different vantage point, we gain new perspective and, perhaps, insights regarding how to understand it. This is true for the hiker who trudges arduously through a valley and up switchbacks only to look back down from the mountaintop and see his path afresh.[10] But it is also true for understanding and knowledge; viewing our own disciplines from the vantage point of other fields can give fresh insight into our fields of study.

For the systematicians, then, I will ask: How are our theological formulations about the nature of Scripture connected to and impacted by the historical and material realities of canon formation? For the biblical studies scholars who specialize in canonical approaches, I will ask: How does the ontology of Scripture—that is, the nature of Scripture, what it *is*—help us to interpret and understand the canonical phenomena in front of us? At times, I may be asking either main audience to use the nomenclature of the other. While this kind of interdisciplinary exercise and dialogue may be challenging at times, I believe it is necessary and beneficial for the argument at hand.

That argument is, simply put, that the question of canon is a fundamentally theological question concerning the unity of Scripture. I need to be crystal clear at this point that this book is not an attempt

---

for pursuing such an approach ("Old Testament Theology and the Canon"). While I disagree with Goldingay's conclusions regarding the relation of the NT to the OT and of Christian theology to the OT, he does provide a helpful and heuristic overview of the canonical approach.

9. For overviews of canonical approaches to reading, see, as a representative sample and from a broadly Protestant perspective, Bartholomew et al., *Canon and Biblical Interpretation*; for a summary of Roman Catholic interaction with the movement as well as commentary from a biblical scholar, see Fitzmyer, *The Biblical Commission's Document*, 68–74.

10. I am indebted to Heath Thomas for suggesting this analogy to me.

to "prove" the unity of Scripture—as though that were even possible (as with Jesus, so with Scripture: Blessed are those who do not see and yet believe [John 20:29]). Instead, it is an essay on the theological context for considering the question of canon, a context that helps us to understand the unity of Scripture. This pervasive biblical coherence is theologically grounded in the ontological unity of the Godhead and is seen and demonstrated in the various canonical phenomena.

We will explore the issue of canon from a variety of theological contexts, in relation to the various systematic loci, but we should not forget the primary theological claim of the book: that canonical questions are questions related to the unity of the Christian Bible, and so their answers are fundamentally rooted in the reality of the triune God, who reveals himself to us in Holy Scripture. In this sense, this book brings our confession regarding Holy Scripture into dogmatic conversation with Christian doctrine's various loci in order to construct a theological approach to canon. In this approach, we will at various points give special attention to premodern interpreters' conception of Scripture in relation to issues of canon. The premodern interpreters approached the questions of Scripture and canon in ways analogous, although not identical, to the way I approach those questions in this book, and thus they provide us with helpful historical and conceptual precedents for some of the conclusions of the various chapters.

The Shape of This Book

The first chapter surveys the academic history of canon studies to demonstrate that, while some have attended to the theological location of canon and to the impact of theology on canon studies, the field has been dominated by empirical and rational approaches. That, in turn, will help bring into sharper focus the need for this kind of book.[11] At the end of the chapter, I set the stage for the rest of the book, arguing that canon should be viewed from its dogmatic location, along with being studied in light of observable phenomenon related to its formation.

11. This is not a new claim; Michael Kruger makes a similar argument and surveys the field in *Canon Revisited*, esp. 27–124.

The rest of the book can be split into two parts: chapters 2–4 and chapters 5–8. The first part addresses what the canon *is* theologically speaking, and then the second part attempts to understand particular canonical phenomenon in light of that theological reality.

As Brevard Childs and Christopher Seitz have noted repeatedly, the most fundamental reality of the Christian canon is its two-testament character—the fact of the Old and New Testaments being joined together into one book.[12] In the first part of the book, I address this reality and the question it raises, exploring what canon *is* from a theological perspective and *why* we have a two-testament Bible. The second part of the book addresses this reality and question theologically as well, but with an eye toward *how* the two-testament Bible is one book. In other words, in chapters 5–8 we will examine the material phenomena of canon[13] from within the theological perspective articulated in chapters 2–4. Key to the overall shape of this book is the claim that, while the material (historical and empirical) phenomena of canon are fixed, our interpretation of those phenomena is dependent on and located within broader theological categories and assumptions.

With respect to the theological foundation for canon, I argue in chapter 2 that the study of canon is situated theologically in the doctrine of Scripture, and as such has its ultimate dogmatic location in the doctrine of God. Scripture is divine revelation, and the canon is the boundary marker for what serves as divine revelation and what does not. I argue that a Christian understanding of canon will see it first and foremost as the rule for divine revelation, a rule governed and given by the triune God.

A primary implication of locating the canon in the doctrine of God is that the canon, like all of God's revelation of himself, is ultimately christological. Thus, chapter 3 argues that the canon's

12. Seitz, *The Character of Christian Scripture: The Significance of a Two-Testament Bible*. See also, e.g., Stuhlmacher, *Historical Criticism and Theological Interpretation of Scripture*, 26. And, for Childs, see *Biblical Theology: A Proposal*, 38–55.

13. I mean features such as textual sinews, ecclesial reception, eschatological ordering, and illuminated reading. Each of these terms will be defined in later chapters (see esp. chaps. 7 and 8 for those features mentioned here).

unity is grounded first in this Christocentric nature of revelation, and especially in the story told by the canon of Scripture, which finds its climax in the person and work of Jesus. In this light, the chapter argues that extracanonical books are so precisely because they do not fit into the larger Christocentric character and story of the canon. This final section also discusses canonical books that are frequently charged with not fitting into the "metanarrative" of the Protestant Bible.

Chapter 4 builds on chapters 2 and 3 and argues that the canon is Christocentric due to its inspiration by the Spirit. The Spirit's economic mission (in keeping with the divine processions) of testifying to the Son entails that his work of inspiration is centered on the Son.[14] This theological insight will be applied to our understanding of the canon, specifically with respect to canonical boundaries and intertextuality. I will argue that the inner-biblical allusions in Scripture are (1) a function of divine authorship; (2) the primary means by which the Christocentric nature of the canon can be discerned; and (3) the product of authorial intent, both human and, ultimately, divine. The nature of authorship and its relation to canon will be discussed here as well, and particularly the notion of "final form."

As a revelatory document, the canon is both from God and not God. It is, in other words, a creature and not the Creator, and so chapter 5 explores canon in relation to the doctrine of creation. As I argue in chapters 2–4, canonicity is first a function of God's trinitarian mission to reveal himself to his creatures, but it is secondarily a function of the order of creation. The interpretive means by which we see the canon's Christocentrism—intertextuality, typology, and allegory—are possible because creation itself is Christocentric, or *Logos*-centric, to paraphrase Maximus the Confessor.[15] All of creation derives its being and orderliness from the eternal Word, the Word that the Father speaks and breathes by his Spirit at creation.

14. This and other chapters rely on language from systematic theology. While certain readers may be unfamiliar with this terminology at this point in the book, the individual chapters go into further detail and definition regarding them (and the same is true for canonical "lingo").

15. Maximus the Confessor, "Ambiguum 7," esp. 54–61.

The canon exists as a unified textual document because it participates in the orderliness of creation and in the *Logos*, who gives and maintains order.

Chapters 6 and 7 continue to consider specific phenomenology (observable features that can be analyzed) of canon, and ones that so often dominate conversations about the canon, in light of Scripture's ontology. The discussion of lists (chap. 6) and order (chap. 7) is now couched in the broader ontology of the canon outlined in chapters 2–4.

Chapter 6 considers manuscript inclusion and canonical lists and argues that the proper dogmatic location of that discussion is the doctrine of ecclesiology. Canonical lists, like canonical orders, are products of the community of faith that receives the canon. Ultimately, the church is the creation of the Spirit of God in Christ, and so canonical decisions, evidenced in lists and manuscripts, are subject to evaluation via the ontological criteria given in chapters 2–4. Differences between canonical lists and manuscripts, in other words, are not evidences of different canons in an *ontological* sense. These phenomenological differences must be measured, or ruled (an intentional allusion!), against the trinitarian mission that serves as the source and context for the canon.

Another major phenomenological concern in canon studies is that of the shape or order of the canon, and chapter 7 argues that it is a function of the canon's Christocentric purpose. The canonical order, in all its variety, always evinces what John Sailhamer refers to as eschatological and messianic hope.[16] This chapter also returns to the concept of "final form" and relates it to the ontology of the canon outlined in the first half of the book. Finally, this chapter shows that canonical order is related to the community of faith that receives, passes on, and interprets the content of the canon.

The final chapter discusses how to read canonically. Here, the rule of faith will be discussed, and the focus will remain on its Christocentric content. Irenaeus's tools of hypothesis, economy, and recapitulation will be explained and put forth as proper tools for reading the canon in a Spirit-illumined, or ruled, fashion.

16. Sailhamer, *Introduction to Old Testament Theology*, 154–55.

In sum, this book attempts to address the phenomenological reality of canon from an expressly dogmatic, or systematically theological, vantage point. Before moving on to these dogmatic concerns, however, we need to return to canon in modern biblical studies and describe the current discourse.

ONE

Canon and Canon Formation in Modern Biblical Interpretation

The topic of canon is addressed and debated often in modern biblical studies.[1] Questions about the textual boundaries of the Bible, the conceptual unity or disunity of biblical texts, canonical shape and final form, and other such issues abound.

Canon studies have largely followed two different lines.[2] Some approaches emphasize empirical, historical, and material concerns, in some cases going on to raise hermeneutical questions but largely leaving aside the theological context for such concerns. Other approaches do attempt to relate those empirical, historical, and

1. This book, by and large, focuses its attention on English-speaking scholarship regarding the issue of canon. For entry points into canonical criticism in German scholarship, see Baldermann et al., *Zum Problem des biblischen Kanons*, and, more recently, Janowski, "The Contrastive Unity of Scripture." For an entry point into the conversation in French, see Auwers and de Jonge, *The Biblical Canons*. The latter text also includes English and German scholarship. For an up-to-date treatment of the field that spans German, French, and English scholarship, see Nicklas, *The Canon and Beyond*.

2. See Kruger, *The Question of Canon*, 34–45, for a similar demarcation, although he uses slightly different terminology.

material concerns to broader categories not only of hermeneutics but also of theology.

Of course, this distinction is not hard-and-fast. Some who focus on empirical matters are also attuned to related hermeneutical and theological issues. And those who focus on theological matters don't ignore the empirical and hermeneutical issues. Nevertheless, this distinction between empirical and theological approaches is helpful, especially in relation to the aim of this book, which is to argue for the necessity and the primacy of a theological approach.

I am not suggesting that the historical, empirical, and material questions and data points are unimportant or irrelevant. But they arise from and are addressed within particular theological contexts, regardless of one's own faith commitments. To take just one example, the question of the boundaries of the biblical canon is inherently theological because the Bible is a religiously authoritative text. And the answer to that question is developed within the theological framework of the canonical critic. For the atheist or agnostic, supernatural factors related to canonical boundaries, such as divine inspiration, are intentionally laid aside, whereas for devout Christians, the theological commitments inherent to their faith require them to acknowledge that reality. Both of those are theological contexts for understanding canon, even if they diverge in assumption and method. Further, a truly Christian approach to canon will consciously and faithfully attend to the theological context of these questions while reckoning responsibly with these empirical realities.[3]

In this chapter, I will distinguish the empirical and theological approaches to show how they address the questions at hand and will argue that theological context is crucial in conversations about canon, and in a variety of ways. This will lead to our consideration of various theological loci in relation to the topic of canon in the rest of the book.

3. See Kruger, *Canon Revisited*, esp. 160–287, for consideration of historical and empirical data in light of theological context.

Empirical Approaches

Study of canon in the modern period—roughly, the last two or three centuries—has often rested squarely on empirical matters.[4] Questions about authorship, date, original audience, and the like are at the forefront of scholarly attention in biblical studies. This empirically focused line of scholarship asks questions such as:

- Which canon list is older or better attested?
- When were the disputed books first attested as Scripture in the devotional and liturgical lists of the people of God?
- Which order of the biblical canon (or some subcollection) is older, or better attested, or has better textual evidence in its favor?

Sometimes, empirically focused studies go on to raise hermeneutical questions, questions of interpretation:

- What is the interpretive significance (if any) of canonical order?
- What canonical order (if any) is most important with respect to its impact on biblical interpretation?
- Is there a "final form" of individual biblical books, distinct biblical corpora, individual testaments, and/or the Bible as a whole? If so, what is its impact on the interpretation of the different parts of each of those collections?

Even what is known as the "canonical approach," while consciously attending to theological questions, often focuses heavily on empirical issues.[5] This discipline is more narrowly attentive to issues of redaction in relation to the final form of the text with an interpretive aim. Canonical approaches ask: Given evidence of redaction in

4. On some of the questions I raise in this section, see Bockmuehl, *Seeing the Word*, 27–74.

5. On the historical realities related to this shift, see Legaspi, *The Death of Scripture and the Rise of Biblical Studies*, esp. 3–26. See also the theological assessment of modern hermeneutics and its birth from the modern biblical studies movement in Maier, *Biblical Hermeneutics*.

particular biblical books and/or corpora, how do we understand that book and/or corpus as a coherent unit?

Ultimately, this question applies to the entire canon of the Old and New Testaments. In fact, as Christopher Seitz has repeatedly noted, the discipline of the canonical approach is concerned first and foremost with the reality of a two-testament Bible.[6] Similarly and influentially, Brevard Childs insists that biblical theology is primarily concerned with this question.[7] How do we read Christian Scripture as a whole book, when the first testament of that book originally was written and read by the people of Israel?

We will return to Seitz's approach, as well as this fundamental question, later in this chapter and in the remaining chapters of the book. Here, we simply note that the canonical approach is a particular mode of biblical interpretation that gives special attention to the final form of the biblical text, both at the level of the individual book and at the levels of distinct corpora and, ultimately, of the entire canon.

In focusing on final form, those who follow a "canonical approach" have various aims. Most fundamentally, though, the aim is interpretive. How do we understand the biblical text (book, corpus, canon), given its final form or shape? This question necessarily depends on identifying both the contents and the evidences of redaction (e.g., "seams" [see chap. 5]) that gave rise to that final form.

The end goal is interpretation, and so those who take the canonical approach often proceed by first considering the empirical evidence for a number of material realities. These include (1) historical data related to the canonicity of a particular book or books within a corpus; (2) empirical data related to the ordering of a particular book, or, more likely, a particular corpus; (3) sociocultural data related to understanding the original audience at the time of the final form; and (4) literary data related to identifying instances of canonical shaping, typically via intertextuality.

6. This topic is explored again and again in Seitz's corpus; perhaps the best place to start is the book named in reference to this question: *The Character of Christian Scripture: The Significance of a Two-Testament Bible*. See also, e.g., Stuhlmacher, *Historical Criticism and Theological Interpretation of Scripture*, 26.

7. Childs, *Biblical Theology: A Proposal*, 38–55.

Of course, any one of these questions can occupy studies of canon, but sometimes the aim is limited to answering the empirical questions more than it is to interpreting the text once those questions have been satisfactorily answered. But whether consideration is limited to empirical data or goes on to the hermeneutical task of attempting to interpret the text in light of that data, works self-identified as taking a "canonical approach" often tend toward the empirical rather than the theological,[8] and canon in those cases is seen primarily as an *empirical* rule.[9]

In an empirically oriented study of canon—whether or not it falls into the "canonical approach" category—the question of canon remains one of authority: Which books have authority over the church's life and practice, and why? And those questions and related ones are answered in a predominantly empirical fashion. Differing lists and manuscripts are examined in order to either prove or disprove a particular canon, understood as an authoritative list of books. Particular texts are exegeted in order to prove or disprove instances of intertextuality, or to approve or disapprove of later biblical authors' use of earlier biblical texts in relation to modern hermeneutical rules. Ancient quotations about and lists of the order of the canonical material, whether at a macro-level or with respect to a subcorpus, are rigorously scrutinized in order to prove or disprove the importance and historical priority of a particular canonical shape, or to approve or disapprove of the acknowledgment of a canonical shape for biblical interpretation.

In the end, the basic questions that modern canon studies attempt to answer from an empirical standpoint are "What *is* the canon?" with reference to lists and manuscripts, and sometimes then "What

8. See, e.g., Knox, *Philemon Among the Letters of Paul*, esp. 92–93; D. Smith, *The Canonical Function of Acts*.

9. This is not true of every work that self-identifies as an example of the canonical approach, nor am I claiming that it is endemic to the canonical approach as a whole; several works in that category will be cited positively both in this chapter and throughout the rest of the book as examples of attending to the theological contexts of canonical considerations. Rather, the point is that even works within the canonical approach, which generally attempts to be self-aware of the interrelation between empirical and theological categories, can focus attention on the empirical, without much attention given to the theological.

does the canon *mean*?" with reference to intertextuality, figuration, and order or shape.

To be sure, each of these questions is important, and there is good reason for these issues to have occupied so much attention in biblical studies over the last five decades or so.[10] We should not denigrate this important work in canonical studies, but it is equally important to recognize that the questions above are not exclusively historical, empirical, or material.[11] Nor are they exclusively hermeneutical.[12] Answering these questions requires attending to other, more fundamental considerations.

Theological Approaches

We cannot answer questions about canon if we attend to the material data available without asking more fundamental questions about what the canon *is*.[13] The issues of canon and biblical interpretation are both ultimately theological in nature.[14] In saying this, I am not coming to novel conclusions. There are many in past decades who have labored to relate biblical studies and theology, and particularly in relation to the issue of canon.

10. See most of the essays in McDonald and Sanders, *The Canon Debate*; Barr, *Holy Scripture*; Gallagher and Meade, *The Biblical Canon Lists from Early Christianity*; C. A. Evans and Tov, *Exploring the Origins of the Bible*; Collins et al., *Ancient Jewish and Christian Scriptures*.

11. On the kind of distinction I am making in terms of modern scholarship on canon, see Chapman, "What Are We Reading?," esp. 335–42; Chapman, "The Old Testament Canon and Its Authority for the Christian Church."

12. Hermeneutics itself is not even properly basic, as it is both theologically and philosophically grounded in a priori commitments. See Bartholomew, "Uncharted Waters"; Bartholomew, *Introducing Biblical Hermeneutics*, 281–334, 431–62.

13. In some ways this is a result of the prioritization of the "order of knowing" over the "order of being" in modern hermeneutical discourse, including discourse about the canon. On this distinction as it relates to hermeneutical issues, including issues of canon, see Collett, "Reading Forward," esp. 180.

14. Kruger makes a similar distinction between "functional" definitions of canon and "ontological" definitions (*The Question of Canon*, 34–45). He offers an expanded version of this argument, with slightly different terminology (canon as "community determined," "historically determined," or "self-authenticating"), in *Canon Revisited*, 27–124.

Related Projects

Here it is worth taking a moment to distinguish this project from other, related ones: the Theological Interpretation of Scripture (TIS), biblical theology, and the canonical approach. This book does not address directly the movement called Theological Interpretation of Scripture, although there are certain points of commonality. Most notably, both TIS and the canonical approach, as well as this book, attempt to deal seriously with *what the Bible is* from an ontological perspective. Nevertheless, I do not consider this book a work of TIS, nor do I agree with all that TIS has to offer (even though TIS is not a uniform movement to begin with).[15]

To attempt to distinguish between biblical theology, the canonical approach, TIS, and this book, we could say the following:

- Biblical theology attempts to trace patterns of thought throughout individual books, distinct corpora, each testament, and the whole Bible, by means of close attention both to literary features (e.g., intertextuality, genre-specific devices) and to historical context.
- The canonical approach[16] attempts to read along the grain of the final form of the text, whether individual book, distinct corpora, each testament, or the whole Bible, giving adequate attention to the text's literary features, to its historical context in light of the culmination of its final form, and to its theological context as God's Word received by God's people.
- TIS seeks to read the Bible as God's Word in light of Christian theology and with the aim of making theological claims from the text, giving attention to premodern modes of reading and preserving the unity of exegesis and theology.

15. For introductions to and examples of TIS, see Bartholomew and Thomas, *A Manifesto for Theological Interpretation*; Fowl, *Engaging Scripture*; Fowl, *The Theological Interpretation of Scripture*.

16. For an overview of the canonical approach, see Thiselton, "Introduction: Canon, Community, and Theological Construction"; Childs, "The Canon in Recent Biblical Studies." See also Driver, *Brevard Childs, Biblical Theologian*, for a thorough study and analysis of Childs's work. With respect to the contours of the canonical approach and its relation to TIS, see Seitz, "The Canonical Approach and Theological Interpretation."

- This book attempts to apply the loci of systematic theology to the doctrine of Scripture, and specifically to the major issues of canon, giving adequate attention most especially to the unity of the Bible as the triune God's revelation of himself in the person of Jesus Christ by the inspiration of his Holy Spirit.

Thus, while there is commonality between each of these, those first three categories should not be conflated with one another, and I am attempting to do something different from all of them—that is, to address the topic of canon from a distinctly dogmatic, or theological, perspective.

Still, it remains the case that, within each of these other approaches, certain scholars have emphasized repeatedly the theological nature of canon and therefore the theological context of addressing questions of canonical phenomena. For instance, Craig Bartholomew notes that "the limits of the canon and its authority can never be proved [i.e., by purely empirical methods]. . . . There are good reasons for resisting the radical approaches to canon being promoted nowadays. The theological dimension of this debate is *unavoidable*, and in our case everything hinges ultimately on what we make of Jesus and his authority."[17]

The Necessity of a Theological Approach

How, then, are questions about and studies of canonical phenomena ultimately theological?[18] First, the study of canonical phenomena is necessarily theological because of the nature of its subject matter—namely, what the canon *is*. If the Bible is God's revelation of himself to his people, we are engaging not merely in exercises of history, literature, and the like but in the reading and understanding of God's Word to us. And, if the Bible is God's Word, rather than

17. Bartholomew, *Introducing Biblical Hermeneutics*, 277.

18. This question, and this entire project, is thus an attempt to carry on the point made by John Webster: "[Topics] such as canonicity or the nature of reading in the community of the church are to be approached as extensions of a Christian theological treatment of the saving self-communication of the triune God, in particular of the theology of Word and Spirit" (Webster, *Word and Church*, 2).

just a collection of human words, and if its meaning is grounded in the reality of that same God, this has implications for how we understand the issues at stake in the canon conversation, including shape, order, intertextuality, and the like. Related empirical issues—such as differing manuscripts and lists, figural writing, canonical composition, and canonical shape—all have a broader theological context. While they are historical and literary matters, they are not *merely* historical and literary. These points of empirical data and the debates about how to interpret them are to be understood within the more fundamental theological framework of the doctrine of revelation.[19]

Second, the issue of canon is necessarily theological because at issue is what constitutes meaning. This is broadly acknowledged as a philosophical question, but it is also a theological one, and for the same reasons. Identifying meaning is an epistemological question: How can we know what we know, and how can we know what is meant in a particular text (or statement, or other type of locution)? Once again, we are led back to the more fundamental theological context of the doctrine of revelation. If, as Christians claim, and as the canon claims for itself, the Bible is divine speech from God to his people, this necessarily impacts not only what we understand to be canon but also how we articulate the source, locus, and intent of "meaning" with respect to the content of the canon.

Before we move on to the next section, it is important to state that, while the question of canon must consider its theological context, so theology must give attention to the empirical questions related to canon.[20] Theology as a discipline is not divorced from material questions about history or from empirical realities. The point here is not that canon conversations should move on from empirical questions and consider only the theological context. Perhaps another book could

19. Kevin Vanhoozer is another theologian who has regularly attended to the theological nature of the question of canon. See, most recently, Vanhoozer, *Mere Christian Hermeneutics*.

20. For an attempt to relate theological commitments about the biblical text, canonical approaches to reading, and the critical tools of modern exegesis, see Levering, *Participatory Biblical Exegesis*, esp. 1–62. While I differ with Levering's Roman Catholic perspective at points, he exhibits the kind of theological awareness about exegetical approaches that I am describing here.

consider what theological exploration would look like with empirical questions about canon at the forefront.[21] But this book is intended to bring the theological dimension to the forefront and consider the empirical questions about canon within certain theological contexts.

Canon and Dogmatics: Canon as Theological Rule

As we saw earlier, modern canon studies ask, "What *is* the canon?," with a focus on lists and manuscripts, and sometimes moves on to the hermeneutical question "What does the canon *mean*?," paying attention to intertextuality, figuration, and the order or shape of the canon. But, as we've seen thus far, these questions are not *merely* empirical. Questions about the canon's existence and meaning are ontological questions and therefore ultimately are theological.[22]

Early Christian writers recognized this reality. For them, broadly speaking, *canon* meant "rule" or "standard" not only in a material sense, as in a list of authoritative books, but in a theological sense as well.[23] Accordingly, there are those in modern canon studies who attend not only to historical and empirical data related to the canon but also to the theological context for those questions and, ultimately, the theological nature of the canon. As Christopher Seitz notes about the early use of the term,

> When the term canon appears in early Christian commentary . . . it has a more hermeneutical and explicitly theological purpose. The second century church father Irenaeus provides a classic example. He speaks of the "canon of faith"—*kanon* or *regula* as "the foundation and support of our conduct." He is not using the word canon here to refer to lists of biblical books or institutional councils within which decisions might be rendered about books being sacred and set apart or not. The

21. In fact, I think that this is much of what Christopher Seitz and Mark Gignilliat are doing. See especially Seitz, *The Elder Testament*; Gignilliat, *Reading Scripture Canonically*.

22. Rowan Williams's critique of empirical approaches to Christology applies also to issues of canon: "The notion of evidence does not fit well with the question" (*Christ the Heart of Creation*, 46; see 43–46 for a sustained critique of problems with a *strictly* empirical approach to metaphysical questions, of which canon is one).

23. See Bruce, *The Canon of Scripture*, 17–18.

> rule or canon in fact consists of articles concerning God's character as God. Canon functions in an explicitly theological context.[24]

Applied materially (that is, to empirical data such as manuscripts and lists), then, "the word canon can and does have a role to play in evaluating—not just the final stages of a collection's stabilization but also the early and medial episodes of canonical shaping."[25]

Accordingly, *canon* can and does refer to lists of authoritative books. But this list is authoritative, we should hasten to add, *precisely because* of the nature of the books listed: They are individual and collective instances of divine revelation.[26] The early church was not ignorant of the need to match this theological claim about what the canon is with the attendant canonical phenomena. This is how we should understand three of the four ancient criteria for canonicity:[27] Apostolicity, use in worship, and widespread acceptance were, in modern parlance, empirical data that could be studied and used as phenomenological evidence for canonicity. The fourth criterion, accordance with the rule of faith, is more explicitly theological and related to the argument of this book.[28] Canonicity, according to this criterion, is ultimately a matter of a document's divine source and as such is reflected in its (orthodox, christological) content.[29]

24. Seitz, *The Elder Testament*, 25–26.

25. Seitz, *The Elder Testament*, 28.

26. Again, Seitz reminds us: "But if this [material question regarding authoritative lists of books and the like] comes at the cost of misunderstanding the theological and hermeneutical dimensions that stand at the center of the term's historical use, the term will have become dislocated and distorted. The materialist question is simply too narrow a conceptual field on which to force the term to play its proper role" (*The Elder Testament*, 28). Cf. Kruger, *The Question of Canon*, 40: "Books do not *become* canonical—they are canonical because they are the books God has given as a permanent guide for his church."

27. See Metzger, *The Canon of the New Testament*, 251–54.

28. Of course, all four of these criteria are interrelated; see Laird, *Creating the Canon*, 183.

29. On the interrelation of *canon* as theological rule, in relation to the rule of faith, and "apostolicity" as an external marker of canonicity in the early church, see Bell, *Ruled Reading and Biblical Criticism*, 31–93. For a philosophical and theological exploration of the connection between the two, see C. S. Evans, "Canonicity, Apostolicity, and Biblical Authority," although I do not agree with his (theoretical) approach to the issue of pseudonymity. See also Kruger, *Canon Revisited*, 138–41.

To be clear, there are a number of modern biblical scholars who focus on canon and do so with these theological questions in mind.[30] I do not want to convey the idea that no one in modern canonical conversations pays attention to theology or to the theological context of canon. This is not true.

Here, I want to provide a few examples of how certain scholars think about canon theologically. These categories are not intended to be rigid; many of the scholars mentioned would fit in more than one category in some way or another. Nevertheless, I have attempted to identify the primary point of theological emphasis with respect to each scholar's work and the category in which I have placed them as a way to survey the field in relation to the focus of this book.

We begin with *ecclesial reception*.[31] In this category we include canonical approaches that emphasize the church's acceptance and arrangement of the biblical books in understanding the meaning of the text and of the canon's shape. At the forefront of this type of approach in New Testament (NT) scholarship are Robert Wall, Eugene Lemcio, and David Nienhuis. According to this approach, to understand canonical phenomena requires the interpreter to understand the ecclesial setting and rationale that prompted the text's "final form." So, for instance, the shape of the Catholic, or General, Epistles is to be interpreted according to a historically informed and empirically driven reconstruction of the church's final shaping of that corpus, a shaping that is imbued with the theological significance given to it by that final act of ecclesial reception.[32]

30. For a heuristic overview of the different ways that canon and theology intersect in relation to modern ecclesiastical movements (e.g., versions of Protestantism, Roman Catholicism), see J. Wilson, "Canon and Theology."

31. This category matches certain versions of Kruger's "functional" approach (*The Question of Canon*, 34–40). I have chosen to demarcate approaches slightly differently, but want to acknowledge commonalities with Kruger's heuristic categories.

32. See especially Nienhuis, *Not By Paul Alone*. Nienhuis's work should also be considered under the next category, composition, as he argues that the Catholic Epistles collection was deliberately composed, with attendant intertextual links and other compositional features, in order to provide an "anti-Marcionite reconciliation of Paul and the Jerusalem apostolate through the figure of Peter," with James being

While understanding the original composition of an individual biblical book in terms of its setting, author, audience, and so on remains important in this approach, the canonical final form of the corpus in which it is included, understood according to its ecclesially dictated final moment of reception, is the focal point of interpretation. Those who take this approach do not come to one uniform conclusion as to the theological significance of the text's final form, although Wall, Lemcio, and Nienhuis tend to emphasize that the unified canon puts Paul and the Jerusalem apostles on the same level in order to unify disparate parties within early Christianity.

A second theologically oriented category in canon studies is *composition*. This is a text-oriented approach that focuses on the shape of the canon as an organically formed reality accomplished via the process of biblical writing and editing. Evidence for composition mainly consists of instances of intertextuality at key intersections with the canonical material, although attention is also given to paratextual phenomena such as scribal notations.

Some scholars focus on composition within certain canonical corpora, such as Darian Lockett in his study of the Catholic Epistles[33] and James Nogalski on the Book of the Twelve.[34] Others, such as Stephen Chapman[35] and Ched Spellman,[36] take a more holistic approach, identifying ways in which an entire testament, or even the

composed pseudepigraphically as an introduction to the corpus. See also his essay on the subject, "The Letter of James as a Canon-Conscious Pseudepigraph."

My aim is not to address debates within canonical criticism, but I will say briefly here that I do not find Nienhuis's understanding of canon compelling, as it (1) places canonical authority ultimately in the hands of the church (or, really, the disparate churches that collectively operated to dictate canonicity), a model I will address in chap. 6; and (2) relies on what largely amount to arguments from silence to reconstruct an historical moment in which the Catholic Epistles collection was finalized by a compositional redactor. See also Nienhuis and Wall, *Reading the Epistles of James, Peter, John and Jude as Scripture*, as well as Emerson, "Review"; and Wall, *Studies in Canonical Criticism*, 44, as well as 24n1, 25n3.

33. Lockett, *Letters from the Pillar Apostles*.

34. Nogalski, *Redactional Processes in the Book of the Twelve*.

35. Chapman, *The Law and the Prophets*.

36. Spellman, *Toward a Canon-Conscious Reading of the Bible*.

entire Bible, exhibits evidence of composition. Casey Croy's[37] and Michael Shepherd's[38] recent works on this phenomenon examine both individual corpora and macro-level compositional shaping.

As with the first category, the goal of identifying and examining these evidences of composition is to understand the theological import of the text's "final form." And, as with the first category, there are a variety of conclusions as to what that theological import is. Nevertheless, canon and canonicity in this approach are not merely empirical phenomena but have theological significance and meaning.

Finally, there are canonical approaches that focus on the canon as the locus of *divine revelation*. Michael Kruger,[39] Mark Gignilliat,[40] and Christopher Seitz[41] fit in this category. Canon is to be understood as the textual artifact of God's revelation of himself in the person and work of Jesus Christ through the inspiration of the Spirit. Canonical phenomena, such as intertextuality, shaping, and lists, are to be understood in light of the fundamental fact of what the canon is.

Moving Forward: Canon as Theological Rule with Material Phenomena

My aim in the remainder of this book is not to refute directly or in a sustained fashion any of those surveyed above. In fact, while I have certain disagreements with Kruger, Spellman, Seitz, and Gignilliat, or at least alternative ways of making particular points, I find much in common with their theological commitments. I disagree more fundamentally with Lemcio, Wall, and Nienhuis regarding how the canon becomes the canon and therefore with how it functions and is to be read in the life of the church, but I also appreciate that they are attempting to approach the questions of canon in an explicitly theological fashion.

37. Croy, *Sequencing the Hebrew Bible*.
38. Shepherd, *An Introduction to the Making and Meaning of the Bible*.
39. Kruger, *Canon Revisited* and *The Question of Canon*.
40. Gignilliat, *Reading Scripture Canonically*.
41. Seitz, *The Elder Testament*.

But while John Webster has made serious arguments in relation to this question,[42] and while there are many excellent doctrinal treatments of Scripture on hand, the topic of canon, as the material artifact of God's revelation to his people, has not been explored systematically—that is, in relation to dogmatics and in a systematized fashion. That is the aim of this book: to consider canon via the doctrine of revelation, broadly speaking, and then in relation systematically to other Christian doctrines.

As Seitz argues consistently, the fundamental question of canon as a material artifact is its two-testament structure. What is this book, that it contains both Israel's prophets and the church's apostles? Chapters 2, 3, and 4 answer this question from the perspective of the canon's ontology—what the canon *is*—and from the vantage point of the doctrines of revelation, Christology, and pneumatology. The question of *why* the canon is one book is at the forefront in these chapters. Chapters 5, 6, and 7 answer this question from the perspective of the canon's phenomenology and its material composition, and from the vantage point of the doctrines of creation, ecclesiology, and eschatology. The question of *how* the canon is one book is at the forefront of this second section.

Throughout, I will argue that the biblical canon's phenomenological features, theologically understood, are material means of identifying and understanding the canon's more fundamental ontological unity. Another way to put this is that, in chapters 2, 3, and 4, we will see that the canon is one book because it is the Lord's revelation of himself through the person and work of Jesus Christ. It is one book

42. See especially Webster, "The Dogmatic Location of the Canon." I should also mention two other important works that motivated and, in many ways, shaped this book. First, Scott R. Swain's *Trinity, Revelation, and Reading* is a dogmatic treatment of the doctrine of Scripture and of attendant hermeneutical commitments. In many ways, therefore, much of what I say about the doctrine of Scripture is dependent on and follows Swain's (and Webster's) earlier work. Like Webster, though, his focus is broader than just the issue of canon. Second, part 2 of Vanhoozer's *The Drama of Doctrine*, "The Script" (115–242), is in many ways a theology of Scripture applied to the topic of canon. I find much in common with Vanhoozer's approach, but (1) my main aim, unlike Vanhoozer's, is not to articulate a comprehensive theological method; and (2) my main aim is to approach canon from a systematic perspective, which is included in but secondary to Vanhoozer's main aim.

with one witness, a unified witness to Christ. In chapters 5, 6, and 7, we will see that this unified testimony is communicated in material ways. In other words, the canon's unified testimony is materially mirrored in its unified and unifying phenomena. The canon's unified testimony to Christ occurs through a unified text. Finally, in chapter 8, we will consider the right reading practices for this one book, with respect to both its ontology and phenomenology.

TWO

The Ruled Canonical Location: Trinity and Canon

As a function of revelation, the canon is not merely list or code; it is a specification of those instruments where the church may reliably expect to encounter God's communicative presence, God's self-attestation.

—John Webster[1]

The Bible is the medium of divine address. To read the Bible as God's word is therefore to encounter something living and active (Heb. 4:12): the voice of God, God personally speaking, the triune God in communicative action, doing things with, in, and through human words.

—Kevin Vanhoozer[2]

As we saw in chapter 1, attending to theological considerations is essential in properly assessing canonical realities. For the Christian, the study of canon is situated theologically in the doctrine of revelation, and as such has its ultimate dogmatic location

1. Webster, "The Dogmatic Location of the Canon," 29.
2. Vanhoozer, *Mere Christian Hermeneutics*, 9.

in the doctrine of God. Scripture is divine revelation, and the canon is the boundary marker for what serves as divine revelation and what does not. A Christian understanding of canon will see it first and foremost as the rule for divine revelation, a rule governed and given by the triune God.

Scripture as Trinitarian Revelation

The first and fundamental theological context for canon is the doctrine of revelation, and more specifically the doctrine of Scripture. The word *canon* was used in antiquity to indicate a rule or standard, and the church adopted it to refer to the boundaries of the divinely inspired text. Because, therefore, canon is both a material phenomenon, assessed according to historical and literary criteria, as well as a theological judgment, rendered according to the rule (*kanōn*) of faith, we will first assess it theologically according to the doctrine of Holy Scripture. We thus need to take a step back for a moment to articulate the basic contours of the doctrine of Scripture in order to understand how canon fits within it.

Holy Scripture, as the triune God's address to humanity, is a covenantal and revelatory document. And, because it is spoken by the Trinity, it has a trinitarian source and shape. These features—covenantal, revelatory, trinitarian source, trinitarian shape—are fundamental to understanding the doctrine of Scripture and thus also to understanding the theological context of canon. We will examine them below as they relate to the doctrine of Scripture, and then will return to the questions of canon at the end of the chapter, and particularly to canon as boundary marker. Other aspects of canon will also be explicitly related to these fundamental features in the remaining chapters of the book.

Scripture's Trinitarian Source—Divine Revelation

The triune God exists on his own and without need of creation. In theological language, God is *a se*, existing eternally and apart from anything or anyone else. Nevertheless, even given God's aseity, he chooses to create. As with all of God's acts, internal and external, he acts in creation as the one God who exists in three persons, Father, Son, and Holy Spirit.[3] This first of God's external acts culminates with the creation of human beings, image bearers of the triune God who made them. We could talk at length about the trinitarian shape of creation, or what it means to bear the image of the triune God, or a whole host of other important theological aspects of the creation event. Here, however, we want to highlight one particular reality of creation, and especially of the creation of human beings—namely, the triune God's revelation of himself to his image bearers in the context of covenant.

When the triune God makes human beings, he first speaks in intratrinitarian fashion, as he does throughout the creation event: "Let us make man in our image, after our likeness. And let them have dominion over the fish of the sea and over the birds of the heavens and over the livestock and over all the earth and over every creeping thing that creeps on the earth" (Gen. 1:26). Just as on the other days of creation, and earlier on the sixth day, the triune God speaks things into existence, here too the triune God's speech precedes his creation of human beings. And just as on the fourth and fifth days God speaks about ruling and multiplying (the sun and moon ruling over the day and the night, Gen. 1:17–18; the birds and fish multiplying, 1:22–23), so also when God creates human beings, he speaks about ruling and multiplying.

One of the distinctive features of this last act in the triune God's whole act of creation is that, after speaking human beings into existence, he then speaks *to them*. Even though, on the fifth day, God blesses the birds and fish by saying, "Be fruitful and multiply" (Gen. 1:22), the verbal construction in 1:28 is slightly different, making it clear that God's address to Adam and Eve is personal and direct rather than merely categorical and general as it is on day five. We should not pass over this feature: God's revelation of himself in his word, in the context of creation and covenant, is uniquely given to human beings and is in some ways surprising in the unfolding context of Genesis 1.

3. For an introductory elaboration on this point, see Emerson and Smith, *Beholding the Triune God*.

To say it slightly differently, God's revelation of himself to his people is just as unnecessary and therefore gracious as the act of creation itself. God has no obligation to reveal himself to his people, and yet he does so immediately upon creation of his image bearers. Of course, this is related to the purpose of creation, including the creation of human beings: God wants his glory to fill the earth, promulgated by those who bear his image as they are fruitful and multiply and exercise dominion over all the earth.[4]

Scripture's Covenantal Context

The triune God's purpose for creating human beings—to fill his place with his people for the promulgation of his glory—is declared to them in covenantal expectation in Genesis 1 and 2. In Genesis 1:26–2:4, God's gifts of life and sustenance are coupled with his declared expectations of his image bearers: that they will be fruitful and multiply and fill the earth, having dominion over it and subduing it. Likewise, in Genesis 2:15–17, God declares his covenantal expectations related both to cultivation of his place and to obedience of his word. The triune God's image bearers, his people, are made in relation to him, located in his place, and given purpose directed and guarded by relationally bounded instructions. In other words, God's people in his place are in covenant with him, and this covenant includes verbally declared expectations. To put it as succinctly as possible, God's presence with and word to his people are given in a covenantal context.

And this covenantal context for revelation remains even after the fall. The triune God's revelation of himself to his people throughout the events of Israel's history, as well as the divine inspiration of the biblical text that inerrantly records, interprets, and communicates those events, happen within the context of covenant. Whether this revelation is given to Noah or Abraham or David or any other figure, God's speech is always related to his promises to his people and ultimately to his promise to Adam to restore what was lost in the fall.

4. Swain, *Trinity, Revelation, and Reading*, 35–60; see also East, *The Church's Book*, 3–38.

Ultimately and climactically, God reveals himself in the person and work of Jesus Christ. God the Son incarnate, in his life, death, descent, resurrection, ascension, and promised return, is the final and full revelation of the triune God to his people. And Jesus's revelatory incarnation and saving work happen in the context of covenant: He is the fulfillment of God's covenant with Abraham, and so in turn he is the fulfillment of God's covenant with Adam,[5] both with respect to crushing the serpent's head and defeating death and with respect to God's original purpose of creation, in which Adam and Eve were supposed to be fruitful and multiply and rule over God's place, filling the earth with worshipers of YHWH who would exercise his rule, cultivate his creation, and obey his word.

Jesus in his life and work thus reverses the curse of Adam's sin and also fulfills God's original intent for Adam and his progeny. Jesus, God the Son in the flesh, fulfills God's covenant of works with Adam and his covenant of grace given to Adam after the fall and passed on through Abraham, Isaac, Jacob, Israel, and David. And, in fulfilling these covenants, he finally and fully reveals who he is, as the Second Person of the Trinity enfleshed.[6]

Scripture's Trinitarian Shape

The NT is God's own testimony, written inerrantly[7] by Spirit-inspired human authors, to the person and work of Jesus Christ and the application of that work to Christ's church, the new humanity

5. On Scripture's covenantal context and in relation to Jesus's own understanding of his mission and of the nature of Scripture, see Barrett, *Canon, Covenant, and Christology*, esp. 41–96.

6. On the interrelation of God's covenant of salvation, his revelation of himself in Scripture, and the incarnation of God the Word in the person of Jesus Christ, see Work, *Living and Active*, esp. 36–66, 125–211.

7. Swain puts the claim that Scripture is without error this way: "As the Word of God written, the Bible speaks truth and only truth when it speaks (cf. Jn 16.13) and . . . the Bible is therefore completely without error (or 'inerrant') with respect to everything it speaks. *God's word is wholly true.* In his Word, God does not hide anything from us that would cause us to be misled. Moreover, *God's word is only true.* In his Word, God does not include anything that would lead us astray. His words are perfectly pure words, 'like silver refined in a furnace on the ground, purified seven times' (Ps. 12.6)" (*Trinity, Revelation, and Reading*, 78–79).

and the New Israel. The church does not replace Israel, but, by virtue of Jesus being True Israel, all who are engrafted into Christ by faith are now part of Israel, Jew and gentile alike. This new covenant people of God is constituted by the Spirit of God, and that same Spirit who brings them into covenant relationship to God through union with Christ also testifies to Christ in their midst by inspiring human authors in their witness to Christ. This is exactly what Jesus promised to the disciples in the Farewell Discourse when he tells them that the Helper will come and testify to Jesus and help them recall all they have seen and heard (John 14:26; 15:26).

These NT documents are not different in kind or status from the OT covenant documents, but together with them are the "sacred writings" (2 Tim. 3:15; 2 Pet. 3:16) that God inspired to reveal to us who he is—and ultimately in the person and work of Jesus Christ. Those documents written prior to Christ's coming testified to God's work in the people of Israel and looked forward to his coming, while the documents written after Christ's first advent testify to his arrival, apply his work to his people, and look forward to his return.

The Bible is, from beginning to end, then, the revelation of the triune God to his people, a revelation that centers on the person and work of Jesus Christ, God the Son in the flesh. To speak of Holy Scripture is to speak of divine revelation, a revelation that climaxes in the incarnation and that, textually speaking, testifies to the Christ event both by looking forward to it and by reflecting backward on it.

Further, this divine revelation is trinitarian in shape, not merely in its focus on God the Son incarnate but in its source and mode of delivery. Divine revelation, like all other works of God, is the inseparable work of the one triune God. Divine revelation is from the Father, through the Son, by the Spirit, because the one God exists in three persons: God the Father, who is eternally unbegotten; God the Son, who is eternally begotten from the Father; and God the Holy Spirit, who eternally proceeds from the Father and the Son. Scripture's revelatory nature and covenantal context are ultimately rooted in the divine mission of God's work of redemption, a mission that is a reflection of God's own inner life, the eternal relations of origin that constitute the persons of the Father, Son, and Spirit.

We find this kind of theology of revelation in the early church. As Matthew Crawford notes, Cyril of Alexandria "consciously shaped his theology of revelation in light of his Trinitarian theology. . . . The adjective 'Trinitarian' . . . describes not simply the content of divine revelation, but also the manner in which revelation occurs."[8] What Crawford means by this is that, for Cyril, God's revelation of himself is trinitarian in shape: from the Father, through the Son, and by the Spirit. This is because the order (or shape, or *taxis*) of God's economic mission, which includes his revelation of himself, is a reflection of his eternal processions.[9] An example of this kind of language comes in Cyril's gloss of Jesus's words in John 14:10:

> If the Father had spoken anything to you, he would have used these very same words that I am speaking to you now and no others. For I have such a great substantial likeness with him that my sayings are his, and whatever things I should do are believed to be his accomplishments. For by "dwelling in me" on account of the exact identity of substance, "he performs the deeds" (John 14:10). And since the Godhead is one and is understood to be in the Father and Son and Spirit, absolutely every word that comes from the Father is through the Son in the Spirit, and every deed or miracle is through the Son in the Spirit, and yet is accomplished as though from the Father. For the Son is not external to the substance of the one who begot him, nor is the Holy Spirit. Rather, the Only-Begotten exists in him, and again has his begetter in himself, and thus he says that the Father works. For the nature of the Father is effective and shines forth beautifully in the Son.[10]

Crawford summarizes Cyril's position:

> To say that the Son reveals the Father through the Spirit is nothing less than to say that divine revelation comes from the Father, through the Son, in the Spirit. In Cyril's view, the Father begets a Word who expresses what resides in him, and the Son reveals the Father's will through his incarnation and through his indwelling of the saints by

8. Crawford, *Cyril of Alexandria's Trinitarian Theology of Scripture*, 12.

9. Crawford, *Cyril of Alexandria's Trinitarian Theology of Scripture*, 23, 38, 42–55.

10. Cyril of Alexandria, *In Joannem* 14.10. This is Crawford's translation in *Cyril of Alexandria's Trinitarian Theology of Revelation*, 64.

> the Spirit who is consubstantial with him. The Son is thus the primary agent of divine revelation, although the Father is the object of revelation and the Spirit is the necessary means by which the Son operates.[11]

We will return to the trinitarian shape of revelation in the next two chapters. For now, the point is simply this: Scripture is the triune God's Spirit-inspired, textual revelation of himself to his creatures, and as such centers on the person and work of God the Son incarnate, Jesus Christ.

Canon as Boundary Marker for Trinitarian Revelation

This definition of Scripture informs how we think about canon. The word *canon* has come to mean almost exclusively today something like *list*. In this sense, *canon* is a rule in a material and empirical sense; a certain set of books is acknowledged as Scripture, while another set of books is rejected. This use of the word *canon* is not illegitimate, nor is it without warrant from the perspective of its use in the early church. We will return in a later chapter to the question of canonical lists, and there we will see that the early church did, in fact, use the term, in part, to refer to lists of books. But for the early church, and for the purpose of this book, *canon* has a more fundamental meaning: "rule" in the theological, and not merely empirical, sense. These meanings are not mutually exclusive, either in the early church or in this book, but the theological rule of canon grounds the empirical rule.

As Tomas Bokedal has recently demonstrated, the word *canon* in the early church was fundamentally related to the theological criterion by which canonicity was externally judged—namely, the rule of faith.[12] For some Protestants, the latter term brings with it (mis-

11. Crawford, *Cyril of Alexandria's Trinitarian Theology of Revelation*, 61.

12. For instance, Origen, early in the use of this language, coordinates the authoritative writings (i.e., the canon) and an accurate summary of the teachings of those writings (i.e., sound doctrine) as the "rule." His approach was hugely influential on the generations that followed him. See Martens, *Origen and Scripture*, 209–12, for an entryway to Origen's thought on the *regula*. On the *regula fidei* in the early church and particularly its relation to the question of canon, as well as how it is synonymous in the early church with both *canon* and the Bible's own statements about itself, see Bokedal, *Christ the Center*, 283–316; see also 83–86 for an overview of this notion of

guided) connotations of extrabiblical, second-order doctrinal standards that somehow gained authority over the Bible.[13] But, as Bokedal argues, in the early church the rule was not some kind of external authority but instead was a theological criterion that arose from the text itself, the criterion of Jesus Christ as the fulfillment of Israel's Scriptures. On the interrelation between exegesis and theology, and therefore between affirmation of canonical books and rejection of others, Bokedal notes,

> Together various such rules [as found in, e.g., Tertullian and Irenaeus] can be said to constitute an early "canonical approach" with emphasis given to the order (τάξις) and connection/sequence (εἱρμός) of the Scriptures, the hermeneutical play between textual parts and textual whole, the grasp of the *scopus* (the central point of view when seeking to understand a work appropriately), the "apostolic" and ecumenical Rule-of-Faith pattern of scriptural interpretation (*Haer.*, I, 8.1–10.2; III, 1.2), the cross of Christ as key to reading prophecies (*Haer.*, V, 26.1) and Scripture's self-sufficiency (Clem. *Strom.* VII, 16.96; Iren. *Haer.* II, 28.2). The scriptural organization and scope—here referred to as the entire, or complete, number of Scriptures in their regulative function vis-à-vis the church (*Haer.* II, 27.2), i.e., the scriptural canon—has a direct impact on these second-century interpretive patterns, and *vice versa.*[14]

In other words, the Bible's own content taught the early church this "proto-canonical approach" with respect to its interpretive practices,

rule in the work of Irenaeus. Finally, see Young, *Scripture, the Genesis of Doctrine*, for the relation between sound teaching, canon, and (later) creed in the early church, and in particular in Irenaeus (pp. 90–109) and Origen (pp. 136–55). At times, Young seems to maintain a tight connection between all three, but at other times she seems to prioritize sound teaching, or an "apostolic deposit" of doctrine, that guides canonical and (later) credal formulation. For that reason I find Seitz's approach (*The Character of Christian Scripture*, 192–99) clearer and more compelling.

13. Peckham, *Canonical Theology*, 130–36, for instance, seems to view the rule as an external, extracanonical measure of canonicity. Ironically, I agree with Peckham that the canon is the rule (e.g., 130–31), but I think he misunderstands the early church's reference to the rule and takes it as being somehow detached from or external to the canon itself. See Seitz, *The Character of Christian Scripture*, 192–99; see also Behr, "Scripture, the Gospel, and Orthodoxy," for examples from the early church.

14. Bokedal, *Christ the Center*, 86–87.

and these interpretive practices led the early church to receive some books as canonical and to reject others. If a book did not accord with the Bible's own rule of faith, it was not canonical, as is evidenced by Irenaeus's critique of, for instance, Ebionite attempts to "exclusively [hold] on to the Gospel of Matthew" and to dismiss "the Pauline epistles."[15] Bokedal goes on to argue that certain transmission practices related to the biblical text, such as the *nomina sacra* and numerical patterns, are evidence of the canon (particularly the NT canon) being received both in light of and with material markers of the theological unity of the biblical canon, a theological unity oriented around God's revelation of himself in the person and work of Jesus Christ.[16]

In addition to Bokedal's arguments in this regard, we could also point to both Deuteronomy and Revelation as evidences of Scripture's nature as covenantal communication and, therefore, as the theological grounding for canonical boundaries. In Deuteronomy, God tells Israel twice that they should not add to or take away from his words. In Deuteronomy 4:2, he says, "You shall not add to the word that I command you, nor take from it, that you may keep the commandments of the Lord your God that I command you." And, similarly, in Deuteronomy 12:32, he says, "Everything that I command you, you shall be careful to do. You shall not add to it or take from it."

In both instances, the command takes place in the context of YHWH's communication of his covenant with the second generation of Israelites. In other words, both the words themselves and the command to refrain from adding to or taking away from those words are inherently covenantal in nature. God's speech is given to his covenant people, and *only* what God speaks to his covenant people is to be considered as divine speech by his people. Further, *all* that God speaks to his covenant people is to be considered as divine speech—and thus obeyed—by his people. There is both a negative and a positive aspect to understanding canon theologically as the boundary of covenantal divine speech: Negatively, it sets the boundaries for what should be

15. Bokedal, *Christ the Center*, 86.

16. This is the focus of the whole book, but see particularly Bokedal, *Christ the Center*, 363–90, for concluding summaries and reflections.

and should not be included; positively, it means that *everything* within the boundary ought to be regarded as covenantal divine speech and therefore as life-giving (cf. John 6:68; 1 John 1:1) and authoritative. An example of this comes at the end of the biblical canon, in the final chapter of John's Apocalypse: "I warn everyone who hears the words of the prophecy of this book: if anyone adds to them, God will add to him the plagues described in this book, and if anyone takes away from the words of the book of this prophecy, God will take away his share in the tree of life and in the holy city, which are described in this book" (Rev. 22:18–19).[17]

In this sense, then, canon as rule is primarily theological, even while it entails empirical and material claims. Canon as *theological* rule means that canon serves as the boundary marker for divine revelation. Of course, this is an implication of canon even merely as a material marker, but it is important to get the order correct. Logically speaking, before canon is an empirical list, it is a theological rule. Historically, these two realities were always at play at the same time, but in terms of a logical or conceptual priority, the theological takes precedence. This theological rule itself rules the empirical lists. The danger of reversing the order is this: If the list comes first, then, at least theoretically, list determines theology. Instead, when theological ontology precedes list, what is determinative is who God is and his revelation of himself in the (rightly recorded and interpreted) person and work of Jesus Christ.

Canon as a theologically oriented term thus encompasses all Spirit-inspired texts, on the one hand, and thus, on the other hand, rejects any texts that are not inspired by the Holy Spirit. In the latter case, rejection does not necessarily indicate a lack of usefulness for particular noncanonical books—far from it. In the early church, there were a number of books that ultimately were judged noncanonical but were still used for devotional and formative purposes, such as the Didache or The Shepherd of Hermas. But the church also made it clear that these noncanonical books were not inspired by God and thus not finally authoritative for matters of doctrine or practice.

17. On the compositional function of Rev. 22:18–19, see Spellman, *Toward a Canon-Conscious Reading of the Bible*, esp. pp. 172–83.

In a later chapter, I will more fully develop the theological significance of canonical lists, especially as it pertains to the doctrine of ecclesiology. For now, it is important simply to state that canon as theological rule is an acknowledgment by the church that here and only here, in this particular location (that is, in these particular books), do we possess the divinely inspired Word of God. The church does not *decide* what has that status, but instead *acknowledges* what God has given to us in the context of his covenants with us. This is the most fundamental meaning of *canon*, and the one that will drive the remainder of what I say about canon in the rest of the book. Before turning to lists and other matters, though, it is important to say more about this central theological criterion for canonicity: the Trinity's self-revelation through the person and work of Jesus Christ.

Canonical Decisions and Trinitarian Revelation

The theological reality of canon is intrinsically connected to empirical judgments about canonical material. This was true for the early church and remains true today. Ultimately, the external criteria for canonicity, or internal textual and theological coherence, are simply empirical judgments in service of intrinsic realities—namely, the reality of the canon's coherence as trinitarian revelation. Or, to gloss on Webster's phrasing about Scripture, external judgments about canonicity are rooted in a recognition of and assumption about the Bible's ontology.[18]

Empirical criteria serve a purpose, but they are ultimately subservient to the ultimate criterion: the Spirit's inspiration of Scripture.[19] In other words, empirical criteria serve to demonstrate canonicity rather

18. See Webster, *Holy Scripture*, 42–67; Webster, "The Dogmatic Location of the Canon."

19. In this sense I disagree with John Peckham's articulation of canonicity when he says that "inspiration is, then, a necessary but not sufficient characteristic of canonicity" (*Canonical Theology*, 39). What Peckham is attempting to acknowledge is that, in certain times and places in the early church, other books, such as The Shepherd of Hermas, were considered to be inspired. Peckham therefore says that to be inspired is insufficient; a book must also be apostolic. What I prefer to say is that apostolicity was one of the external criteria by which the early church measured whether or not a supposedly inspired book *actually was inspired*. In other words, inspiration is the

than to act as its ground. We can provide reasonable and empirically demonstrable arguments for the canonicity of a particular book, but its status as canon is rooted fundamentally in its inspiration by the Holy Spirit. This is why discussion of empirical data *must* be connected to the *regula fidei*. The latter serves as a rule for our creaturely rules.

Mention of a standardized and standardizing *rule* may bring consternation to some readers. The reaction we have been trained to have about that term is that the rule itself is infamously nebulous, without explicit definition in the early church, and an imposition on Scripture's own diverse witness.[20] But that reaction is a mistake. The rule is not something that stands outside of Scripture, but instead is given from the Father through the Son by the Spirit in Scripture.

We see this first in the texts we have already explored above, Deuteronomy 4:2; 12:2; and Revelation 22:9–10. Scripture accords with Scripture. The *analogia fidei*, or analogy of faith, is an important internal criterion by which we adjudicate questions of canonicity.[21] There are several ways in which this is measured, and we will continue to explore some of them in the remaining chapters. Here, we want to focus our attention on the primary internal criterion given by the Lord Jesus during his earthly ministry.

As Kevin Vanhoozer notes (in contrast to Peckham; see n. 19 above), affirmation of *sola scriptura* does not preclude acknowledging either the *analogia fidei* or the *regula fidei*. Indeed,

> *sola scriptura* is shorthand for "Scripture interprets Scripture"—and for one's apprenticeship to this canonical practice. Canon is the crucial concept, for it refers to the means by which God rules his people. . . .

---

sine qua non of canonicity, but external phenomena can help us recognize it as such. For more on this, see chap. 6.

20. This seems to be what Peckham is saying, at least in my reading of him.

21. For representative examples of the analogy of faith in practice in the early church, see Athanasius, *Letters to Serapion on the Holy Spirit* 1.2.2 (p. 54); 1.3.2 (p. 56); 1.7.2 (p. 64); and 1.20.4 (p. 84); see also Athanasius, *On the Incarnation* 33–40 (pp. 121–39); 56 (p. 171); Cyril of Alexandria, *On the Unity of Christ*, pp. 51–52, and cf. pp. 53, 57; John of Damascus, *Three Treatises on Divine Images*, pp. 63, 84; Emerson, "The Role of Proverbs 8"; Provan, *The Reformation and the Right Reading of Scripture*, 37–53. On Luther's use of the analogy of faith in particular, see Hains, *Martin Luther and the Rule of Faith*, 12–32.

> Philip [in Acts 8] personifies canon consciousness and exemplifies "ruled reading" of Scripture when, in imitation of his master, Philip starts with Isaiah and proclaims to the Ethiopian eunuch "the good news about Jesus" (Acts 8:35). Philip enacts the rule for right reading, identifying Jesus as the ultimate reference of the Scriptures, and he does so as an apprentice to his master: "And beginning with Moses and all the Prophets, he [Jesus] interpreted to them [the disciples on the road to Emmaus] in all the Scriptures the things concerning himself" (Luke 24:27).
>
> This is also the purpose of the ancient Rule of Faith (*regula fidei*): to encourage canon-conscious and Christ-centered reading. Like Philip, the Rule of Faith summarizes the basic biblical story line and shows how the story is fulfilled in the death and resurrection of Jesus. Irenaeus believed the *regula fidei* to be necessary for the correct interpretation of Scripture . . . , *but only because it states succinctly and summarizes what Scripture is about.*[22]

In other words, both the *analogia fidei* and the *regula fidei* are drawn from the Bible's own statements about itself, and especially from Jesus's statements about how to interpret Scripture.[23]

In the fourfold Gospel corpus, the Evangelists provide Spirit-inspired interpretations of the life, death, and resurrection of Jesus.[24] Included in the Gospels are Jesus's own teaching and conflicts about how to read Scripture. In these passages, Jesus, the Word made flesh, teaches us how to read the Word. I will say more about this in the last chapter. For now, what is crucial to understand is that Jesus himself repeatedly gives us the rule for right reading.

Two examples will suffice. First, in Luke 24 (as noted above), Jesus spends an entire afternoon on the road to Emmaus teaching two

22. Vanhoozer, *Biblical Authority After Babel*, 127–28 (emphasis added).

23. On this synonymity between *Scripture*, *canon*, *analogy of faith*, and *rule of faith* in the early church, and for a definition of the "rule" that identifies it simply as a summary of the Bible's own teaching, see Provan, *The Reformation and the Right Reading of Scripture*, 44–53.

24. "Interpretations" does not mean "opinions," "perspectives," or any other purely subjective, creaturely mode of record. All events must be interpreted, and some interpretations are more correct than others. The interpretations given by the Evangelists are entirely correct because they are inspired by the Holy Spirit and therefore the only truly accurate, and indeed inerrant, interpretations of the life and work of Jesus.

disciples how to read Scripture (i.e., the OT). The risen Lord, "beginning with Moses and all the Prophets," interpreted to them "in all the Scriptures the things concerning himself" (v. 27). This hermeneutics lesson is repeated later that evening when he appears to the eleven and tells them, "These are my words that I spoke to you while I was still with you, that everything written about me in the Law of Moses and the Prophets and the Psalms must be fulfilled" (v. 44). Jesus is clear in both cases that the Scriptures speak about him and that they teach the story of his life, death, and resurrection (vv. 25–26, 45–47). The problem with the disciples' surprise at Jesus's death and, subsequently, his resurrection is that they should have seen these events in Scripture because Scripture testifies to Jesus and to his work.

The other example is John 5:46. This text is more adversarial; here Jesus confronts the Jewish leaders over their rejection of his message. They do not listen to Jesus, and instead charge him with blasphemy and seek to kill him (5:18), all while claiming to "search the Scriptures, because in them [they] think that [they] have eternal life" (v. 39). But, Jesus says, if they listened to the Scriptures, then they would not reject him, because the Scriptures testify to him. Jesus sharpens this point in verse 46, when he tells them, "If you believed Moses, you would believe me; for he wrote of me." It is Moses particularly, not just "the Scriptures" generically, that Jesus mentions here, and Moses "wrote of" Jesus. This is important for at least two reasons.

First, for Moses to have written "of Jesus" indicates that Moses wrote the Torah with the expectation of the coming of Israel's Messiah. While Peter makes it clear that Israel's prophets inquired "what person or time the Spirit of Christ in them was indicating when he predicted the sufferings of Christ and the subsequent glories" (1 Pet. 1:11), both Jesus and Peter teach us that the OT prophets, including Moses, expected the Christ to come and wrote their texts accordingly.

Second, and most important for our purposes, Jesus here gives us a "double rule," so to speak. He teaches us how to read Scripture by indicating to us that Scripture is about him. But he also reveals to us that from the beginning of God's revelation to us in his Word through Moses, the biblical authors wrote their texts in expectation of Israel's Messiah. This connects back to our earlier point about Deuteronomy 4 and 12, that nothing could be added to or taken away from the Torah, Moses's book, that did not accord with it. And to accord with Moses meant to write in expectation of Israel's Messiah. In other words, if the Torah can be described as "Moses wrote of [Jesus]," then everything else that accords with it has be able to be described as "they wrote of Jesus."

The Word tells us how to read the Word in his Word. This is the rule of faith. It is not an external, ecclesiastically invented, nebulous imposition on Scripture. Instead, it is given by the author of Scripture in his own Scriptures to help us understand those same Scriptures. Whatever accords with Moses is revelation from God, and to accord with Moses means to speak in Spirit-inspired fashion of the Spirit-anointed Messiah, Jesus of Nazareth.[25]

This should not surprise us. The canon of Scripture is God's revelation of himself.[26] God reveals himself to us in the context of the covenants he has made with his people, first with Israel in the OT and then, in fulfillment of his promises to Israel, with the church in the NT. The old covenant's stipulations, rooted in the covenant of works stretching back to God's instructions to Adam in the garden, are fulfilled in Jesus. The new covenant promises, rooted in the covenant of grace first promised to Adam and Eve after the fall in the *protoevangelium* ("first gospel"), are fulfilled in Jesus. To say that God reveals himself in the context of covenant, then, is to say that the culmination of God's revelation of himself is in the fulfillment of those covenants in the person and work of Jesus Christ.

But even this covenantal reality is rooted more fundamentally in who God is. God reveals himself to us in Christ because of who he is as the triune God—Father, Son, and Holy Spirit. God the Son is the image of the Father, the exact representation of his being. This is true in eternity through God's eternal relations of origin, but it is also true analogously in a creaturely mode through the incarnation. In other

25. Our insistence on the trinitarian source and shape of christological reading guards against a shallow or theologically deficient Christ-centered reading. This is, for instance, Brent Strawn's concern, but as he himself notes, a trinitarian doctrine of revelation that gives adequate attention to the divine missions and inseparable operations provides appropriate guardrails. See Strawn, "And These Three Are One."

26. For an entryway into relating a canonical approach to acknowledgment of the Bible as divine revelation, see Childs, *Old Testament Theology in a Canonical Context*, 25–29.

words, Jesus is the revelation of God to us both according to his divinity and according to his humanity. Further, the Spirit, both in eternity and in the economic missions of creation and redemption, testifies to the Father's love of the Son and the Son's love for and reflection of the Father. In the Spirit's work of inspiration, then, he testifies to the Son, the image of the Father, and so we should expect God's written revelation to us, Scripture, to testify to the Son. We should, then, accept the rule that Jesus gives us, for both covenantal and trinitarian reasons.[27]

To make canonical decisions requires us to attend to this intrinsic reality of canon. The rule by which canonical decisions are made is imposed on us not by other creatures but by God himself in the person of Jesus, God the Son in the flesh. It is a rule given to us in accordance with God's covenants with us, covenants fulfilled by Jesus, and in accordance with God's own essence and with his revelation to us in the economy of salvation.

Again, this does not negate the importance of empirical data or rational argument when considering issues of canon. But it does put them in their place. They are creaturely modes of thinking that are subservient to and servants of divine revelation. We do not, using these human-crafted tools, decide what is Scripture and what is not. Instead, using these tools, we recognize the reality of revelation and distinguish what accords with Moses—with the rule of faith—and what does not. This is a fine line, but one we must grasp if we are to talk about canon faithfully. Scripture is already Scripture whether I or any ecclesiastical body recognizes it as such. My role is not to determine, codify, approve, decide, or otherwise make a final judgment about what counts as Scripture. Instead, my role—indeed, the church's role—is to recognize, understand, and demonstrate what God has given us as Scripture.

As John Behr argues regarding the interrelation of the rule of faith and canonical decisions, and how the early church thought about this issue,

> The canon of truth, then, is not so much a list of obligatory beliefs, but a hypothesis or presupposition for reading Scripture *as Scripture*—to

27. On the interrelation of canon and covenant, see Vanhoozer, *The Drama of Doctrine*, 115–50.

> see in it the image of the King, rather than simply a curious collection of ancient texts which might be interesting for what they say, but do not have much to do about our relationship with God. The canon, in this sense, and this is its primary sense, is equivalent to the Christocentric reading of Scripture, seeing the whole of Scripture in the light of Christ and as speaking of Christ, the Old Testament invisibly in types and enigmas, the New Testament visibly in a clear epitome. This is, in fact, how Clement of Alexandria defines the canon: "The ecclesiastical rule is the concord of harmony of the law and the prophets in the covenant delivered at the coming of the Lord." This is the primary meaning of the term canon—the interrelationship between Scripture and Gospel, proclaiming Christ. *In light of this, certain apostolic works come to be called canonical, meaning that they are of the canon.*[28]

Canon, in its most fundamental sense, is the demarcation of God's inspired, textual revelation of himself, centering on the person and work of Jesus Christ. Canonical decisions, as Behr notes, are ultimately speaking to this reality. What we are doing when we talk about canon is recognizing and demonstrating, according to the rule of faith, what God has given to us in the text of Scripture to reveal himself through the person of his Son and by the inspiration of his Spirit.

28. Behr, "Scripture, the Gospel, and Orthodoxy," 225 (emphasis added).

THREE

The Ruled Canonical Story: Christology and Canon

Scripture, and therefore the canon, are a function of *Deus dixit*, trinitarianly construed as that complex economy of salvation which originates in God's self-knowledge and has its *telos* in the reconciliation of all things. Scripture and therefore the canon are ordered towards this economy; they are elements in a dynamic and purposive field of relations between the triune God and his creatures. This means, accordingly, that Scripture and its properties, including canonicity, can only be rightly apprehended as an item in this economy.

—John Webster[1]

The subject matter of Sacred Scripture is the incarnate Word with all its mysteries (*sacramentis*), both those that preceded Him from the beginning of the world and those that are still to come until the end of the world. And we must know that this whole order and extent of time can be divided into two states [old and new], three times [natural law, written law, grace], and six ages [Adam to Noah, Noah

1. Webster, "The Dogmatic Location of the Canon," 28.

> to Abraham, Abraham to David, David to exile, exile to Christ's first advent, Christ's first advent to his return].
>
> —Hugh of St. Victor[2]

One of the implications of dogmatically locating the canon in the doctrine of revelation is that the canon, like all of God's revelation of himself, is ultimately christological. This chapter argues that the canon's unity is grounded first in this Christocentric nature of revelation, and especially in the Christ-centered story of Scripture. Extracanonical books are so precisely because they do not fit into the larger Christocentric character and story of the canon. Special attention will be given both to Irenaeus's concept of recapitulation and to typology as canonical rules, with respect both to reading and to boundaries.[3] Portions of this chapter also address canonical books that are frequently charged with not fitting into the "metanarrative" of the Protestant Bible.

The Problem and Fact of Canon: The Two-Testament Bible

Canon finds its theological home in the doctrine of Scripture, but the reality is that the topic of canon today centers on concrete empirical data and claims. The most fundamental of these is that, in the Christian Bible, we have two testaments. The first, commonly called the Old Testament, consists of books originally written to the nation of Israel prior to Christ's first advent. The second, commonly called the New Testament, consists of books claiming that Jesus of Nazareth is Israel's Messiah, that salvation for Israel and the nations comes through his person and work, and that the covenant people of God therefore now consists of both Jews and gentiles united in Christ by his Spirit.

2. Hugh of St. Victor, "On Sacred Scripture and Its Authors," 229.

3. *Typology* is defined and engaged with in chap. 5, and *recapitulation* in chap. 8. For our purposes here, I mean by *recapitulation*, generally speaking, that all events, people, places, and so on find their fulfillment in Christ. By *typology* I mean heightened patterns of events, people, places, and so on that find their climactic summary in the person and work of Christ. The former can happen without a pattern in place, while the latter is an explicit acknowledgment of patterns throughout Scripture.

The two-testament Bible is the fundamental issue of canon.[4] Christians have placed these two testaments in apposition to each other throughout their history. Even so, ancient opponents of Christianity and modern scholars alike have asked, "Do these two testaments fit together, and, if so, how?" At Christianity's inception, both Jewish and gentile opponents argued against this new religion through appeal to the *disjunction* between the Hebrew Bible and the New Testament. More recently, certain facets of modern biblical scholarship have often appealed to various critical methods to demonstrate this alleged disjunction. In the face of both ancient and modern questions about canon, how can systematic theology help provide answers?

The most fundamental answer is that Christology grounds canon. While this book is organized by different systematic loci, each one is connected to—and we will continue to circle back to—Christology. Of course, as we saw in chapter 2 (and, as we will see again from yet another angle in chap. 4), this christological ground for the canon is ultimately and simply an acknowledgment that the Bible is the triune God's revelation of himself to his people in the person and work of Jesus Christ. In that chapter we focused on the fact that Scripture is from the one true God, who is Father, Son, and Holy Spirit. In the following chapter, I will articulate how this is related in particular to the mission of the Holy Spirit. In this chapter, though, we want to focus on the unity of God's revelation as expressed in the unity of the economy of salvation, God's work of redemption that centers on the person and work of Jesus. This economic mission is the story of God's actions to save his creation from the effects of sin, and it is a coherent story that is unified around Jesus. This is yet another facet of the theological ground for the unity of the biblical canon: the unity of the Godhead and his work in creation and redemption.

The Divine Missions and Divine Action in Christ

The claim that Scripture is a coherent, unified narrative is not new. The "grand narrative of Scripture" is a popular tool used in much contemporary biblical and theological scholarship (see footnote

4. See Childs, *Biblical Theology of the Old and New Testaments*, 91–94.

13 below). And, as we will see in the next section of this chapter, there is much to commend in this approach, both with respect to its phenomenological observations about the biblical text and with respect to many of its proponents' explicit affirmations of the unity of Scripture.

What is sometimes lacking in this approach is a sense of the ontological grounds for the Bible's narrative coherence. In other words, the Bible's narrative is unified not simply or only because the human authors achieved such a literary unity on their own. Nor is it unified simply or only because (as we will explore in the next chapter) the Holy Spirit chose to inspire them to write in such a narratively unified way. Rather than being mutually exclusive options, the reality is that both of these things are true. But this unity that is both inspired by the Spirit and conceptually and literarily achieved by the human authors is rooted in a more fundamental unity: the unity of the Godhead both in his inner life and in his works of creation and redemption. In this section, we will focus on the unity of the divine missions—that is, the unity of God's actions in creation and redemption. This unity of external action is rooted ultimately in the unity of the divine processions—that is, God's own self-existence as Father, Son, and Holy Spirit.[5]

Because God is one God who exists in three persons—Father, Son, and Holy Spirit—completely and utterly one in all of his perfections and distinct only in the relations of origin between the three persons of the one God, his actions are one. This affirmation, known as the doctrine of inseparable operations, means that God's acts in creation and redemption are unified in their origin (God's one will), purpose (God's singular glory), and end (the ordering of the cosmos toward the worship of the one God). To state it slightly differently, God's unity of being grounds his unity of action.

God is utterly and truly one. He does not consist of parts that can be separated from one another, either in theory or in reality. Nor, therefore, does there exist some kind of hierarchy among his perfections (or among the three persons). The only distinction to be made in God is between the three persons of God, Father, Son, and

5. On the relation between the divine missions and the Trinity's revelation of himself in Scripture, see Gordon, *Divine Scripture in Human Understanding*, 69–112.

Holy Spirit. Further, these distinctions are not differences in their essence; they each equally possess the one divine essence. To say it slightly differently, each of the divine persons possesses equally and truly each of the divine perfections (or attributes), including the one divine will. Any distinction otherwise, in attributes, actions, appellations (names), or adoration, would be an indication that they are not the three persons of the one God but instead three different gods. Instead, the only distinction between the three divine persons is their eternal relations of origin: The Father is eternally unbegotten, the Son is eternally begotten from the Father, and the Spirit eternally proceeds from the Father and the Son. These eternal relations of origin are indications of how each person subsists in the one divine essence and is therefore distinct from the other persons. There is no hierarchy, no differentiation of essence or glory, in the Godhead.[6] Father, Son, and Spirit are the one God, distinct from one another via their eternal relations of origin and yet also utterly one in terms of their shared and singular essence or being.

Because God is one, his acts—creation and redemption—are one. The three divine persons each equally and fully possess the one divine will, and so they each, together as the one God, are fully active in each of God's actions. According to the doctrine of inseparable operations, God's actions are not divided among the three persons. The Father does not create alone; the Son and Spirit are equally active in creation. The Son does not save alone; the Father and Spirit are equally active in redemption. The Spirit does not sanctify or glorify alone; the Father and the Son are equally active in sanctification and glorification. The Bible does appropriate to specific persons certain acts, but this is not an indication that *only* that divine person is responsible. Rather, this is a reflection of the corollary doctrine to inseparable operations: the doctrine of appropriations. God's external acts are undivided among the persons but nevertheless can be appropriately appropriated to a particular person. So, the Father does not create alone, but we can appropriate that action to the Father, and

6. While the Christian tradition acknowledges that there is a certain order, or *taxis*, to these relations, an order in which the Father can be said to have a certain priority or monarchy as the "fount of divinity," historically speaking this *taxis* was not understood to mean a hierarchy of authority (or essence or glory or power).

so on. The point here is that God's acts are one because his essence, including his will, is one. And because God's will, the source of all of his acts, is one, the purpose (his glory) and end (the eschaton) of his acts are also one.

This fundamental unity of God's acts, despite the proliferation of activities of his creatures both in creation and redemption, also means that there is a fundamental unity in *how* he accomplishes these acts. Specifically, the one God accomplishes his unified purpose and end in his unified acts of creation and redemption through the person and work of Jesus. The one God redeems his one creation through his one incarnate Son, God the Son in the flesh, by his one Spirit. This singular means is both a result of and a necessary consequence of the triune God's singular will, a singular will that is identical to the one God's essence or being. In other words, the triune God, the one God who exists in three persons, via his one will, accomplishes his purpose in creation and redemption through his one incarnate Son, Jesus Christ.

The Divine Missions, Divine Action, and Canon

Only after we have appropriately and thoroughly articulated the fundamental unity of the Godhead and, consequently, both his external mission and his means of accomplishing that mission can we speak of the *singularity* and *unity* of the canon. God's singular essence (and, therefore, will) demands unity in the three persons' missions, their means of accomplishing those missions, and, therefore, his revelation of himself and his work—that is, the canon.

The Singular Canon

As we saw in the last chapter, the triune God chooses to reveal himself to his creatures, ultimately through his incarnate Son, Jesus Christ, but also through his inspired Word. This gives unity to the definition of canon: It is God's inspired revelation of himself. In the next chapter, we will see how that word *inspired* ensures canonical unity at a textual and a conceptual level. Here in this chapter, our attention is on the singularity or uniqueness of the canon as the exclusive revelatory document in God's mission of redemption, and on its attendant unity.

The canon is unique as a revelatory document. It is the exclusive covenantal record; there is no other. This claim is grounded in the unity of God's actions in redemption: his acts of salvation through the person and work of his incarnate Son, Jesus Christ, and by the power of his Holy Spirit. This unity of action in accomplishing salvation is in turn a corollary of the unity of the divine missions and, ultimately, of the divine persons in terms of their shared essence (and, therefore, will). Because the one God accomplishes his one purpose through his one incarnate Son, there is one and only one revelatory record of his actions in creation and redemption: the Spirit-inspired biblical canon. Because God is one and because his actions are one, his revelation of himself in the inspiration of the text of Scripture—the canon—is one. To say it yet another way, the utter uniqueness of God is reflected in the utter uniqueness of God's singular work of salvation in Jesus Christ, which in turn is reflected in the utter uniqueness of God's inspired, textual revelation of himself in the singular covenantal document, the canon of Scripture.

Just as this is not a claim divorced from theological realities, so it is not a theological claim divorced from biblical realities. Over and over throughout Scripture, the unique status of God's Word is highlighted over and against any other word. We see this, for instance, in the commands related to discerning between true and false prophets (e.g., Deut. 13:1–10; 18:21–22; Jer. 23:9–40).

Additionally, this unique status of God's Word is *directly tied to a specific document*. We see this most clearly in three passages already mentioned: Deuteronomy 4:2; 12:32; and Revelation 22:18–19. Paul's exhortation to the Galatians to reject any other gospel that comes to them, even from an angel (Gal. 1:8), is probably also related not just to the conceptual unity of God's Word ("another gospel") but also to the singular unity of the documented reality of the canon. To put it slightly differently, just as the gospel message is singular, so is the divinely inspired written revelation of it. It is not merely that God's Word, wherever it may be heard or found, is the only truly revelatory word, but that *this written Word can be found only in one place*, the biblical canon.

To make the christological analogy explicit: Just as God's final, ultimate, incarnational revelation of himself to humanity can be found only in one place, the person and work of Jesus Christ, so his textual, covenantal revelation of himself can be found only in one place, the biblical canon. There is no other canon, just as there is no other Christ. There is one incarnate Son who testifies to the Father, and there is one Spirit-inspired canon that testifies to the incarnate Son. This relates to the original meaning of *kanōn* in the ancient church: It is not just the rule or standard by which other material was judged; it is that rule or standard *precisely because* it is the unique, exclusive Word of the Lord.[7]

The Unified Canon

The relation between canon and Christology does not end with the uniqueness of the canon, however. These two topics also relate with respect to the issue of story or narrative. In recent years, the "story of Scripture" has been a popular mode of discourse, both in terms of whole-Bible biblical theology and in terms of explaining the unity of the canon. This approach in many ways has its roots in the modern Biblical Theology Movement inaugurated by Johann Gabler and self-consciously distinguished from systematic theology.

In Gabler's version of the discipline, biblical theology asks what theological teaching and themes emerge from the biblical text itself, whereas systematic theology asks theological questions of the text that arise from the church (and, presumably, philosophy). There is a sharp dichotomy between the two and therefore between the tools and methods used to pursue answers to their distinct questions. Biblical theology is, in essence, a historical discipline. While it moves beyond exegesis of particular passages to consideration of themes, Gabler and those who have followed him limit the discipline's consideration

7. This, by the way, is also the impetus for the Reformation's emphasis on *sola scriptura*. The Bible is the *norma normans non normata*, the norming norm that is not normed. In that respect, the first Protestant theologians were not saying something novel but were returning to the ancient church's original insistence that Scripture alone is the exclusive and therefore norming normative Word of the Lord by which all other words should be judged.

to what the human author would have intended to convey to his original audience in his particular book (or, at most, his particular corpus, as in the case of, e.g., Paul's letters).[8]

Brevard Childs, and later his student Christopher Seitz, have (along with others) moved the Biblical Theology Movement beyond this severely limited vision of Gabler through what has been called the "canonical approach." In some ways, their work retains Gabler's, and, more broadly, modern biblical studies' emphasis on the original intent of the human author. But, instead of limiting authorial intent to each separate book, Childs and Seitz point to evidences of redaction to argue for a canonical approach, one that considers not just the historical setting of individual books but also the final form of the entire canon, a form in which these disparate books are placed alongside one another and thereby made into one book, the "final form."[9] This approach has gained wide traction among biblical theologians, even if they continue to disagree with Childs, Seitz, and one another about exactly what constitutes a canonical approach or about how to read canonically.

Childs and Seitz have more fundamentally theological reasons for reading the Bible as one book, reasons that are in many ways similar to the concerns of this book. My point here is simply that the Biblical Theology Movement, insofar as it follows Gabler's original vision, and despite the influence of more theologically robust versions of the canonical approach (e.g., Seitz), has largely followed the historical-empirical model for demonstrating canonical unity and form.[10] In this mode of biblical theology, the canon is unified because we can

8. In this version of the discipline, one even finds biblical theologies of Paul's undisputed letters as opposed to the entire corpus.

9. For an overview of the canonical approach, see chap. 1. Here I will simply point to Seitz's "The Canonical Approach and Theological Interpretation," a version of which also appears in Seitz, *The Character of Christian Scripture*, 27–92.

10. Again, Childs and especially Seitz, as well as Gignilliat, ultimately ground the unity of the biblical canon in the unity of God himself and his work of redemption. I am not saying that they and others have not raised the theological points I am making. Rather, I am saying that the Biblical Theology Movement *as a whole*, even while taking into account the canonical approach, by and large operates under the historical-empirical model described. For robust statements that Scripture's unity is grounded in the unity of the triune God and his mission, see Seitz, *Figured Out*, 64–66, 108–10.

demonstrate it to be so, both literarily (e.g., intertextuality) and materially (e.g., manuscripts and lists).

Within the discipline of biblical theology, though, there is disagreement about whether there really is either literary or material unity.[11] Much ado has been made, by both Old and New Testament theologians, about alleged disunity between particular voices within those respective corpora or at least disparate voices that are not easily unified, especially by something like a "grand narrative."[12] In response to these claims, other biblical theologians have sought to prove the opposite, that the Bible *is* a unified narrative, and we can demonstrate it textually and literarily.[13]

Before responding to this approach, we also need to note that the Biblical Theology Movement has had attendant effects on systematic theology (despite Gabler's attempt to keep the two disciplines separate). In a "Bible as story" approach to biblical theology and its subsequent incorporation into systematic theology, what often happens is that the doctrine of God is oriented toward the narrative. That is, God becomes another character in the narrative, rather than the external and totally, ontologically distinct source of the narrative and its documentation. When this happens, it is easier to adopt views about God that are outside the bounds of the classical understanding of the Trinity. For example, in a classical understanding, God is immutable and impassible, but in a narratival emphasis, God is sometimes reduced to merely another character in the story who responds, adapts, and changes as the story proceeds.[14]

11. For a dated yet still helpful overview of these issues, see Hasel, *Old Testament Theology*; Hasel, *New Testament Theology*.

12. Perhaps the most strident example is James D. G. Dunn, and in particular his *Unity and Diversity in the New Testament*.

13. See, e.g., Alexander, *From Eden to the New Jerusalem*; Bartholomew and Goheen, *The Drama of Scripture*; Beale, *A New Testament Biblical Theology*; Emerson, *The Story of Scripture*; Gentry and Wellum, *Kingdom Through Covenant*; Hamilton, *God's Glory in Salvation Through Judgment*; Scobie, *The Ways of Our God*; M. Williams, *Far as the Curse Is Found*; Wright, *The New Testament and the People of God*. In many ways, these approaches are the conceptual descendants of Vos's *Biblical Theology*.

14. One wonders how far back this sentiment actually goes. We can trace it to the modern Biblical Theology Movement, but something much deeper may be at work. One thinks of nominalist articulations of divine voluntarism in the

This is a rather extreme example. Perhaps less extreme, but just as important, a narratival approach to biblical theology can limit what we can say about God to what is stated within the narrative. Note that I did not say "what is stated within the Bible"; everyone who shares basic commitments to biblical authority would agree with that statement. I said, "within the narrative." Some would caution against speaking of who God is apart from creation and redemption, or attempting to postulate about his life *ad intra*. In other words, what we can say about God is primarily what we see of him within the frame of the biblical narrative.[15] In this approach, God's life *ad extra* and *ad intra* are virtually synonymous, so that, for instance, to speak of the eternal begottenness of the Son from the Father apart from his incarnation is, at best, a speculative distraction from the witness of the Bible's main emphasis.[16]

---

late Middle Ages, in which what can be known and said about God's providential ordering of the world is only what is said in the biblical text. See Oberman, *The Dawn of the Reformation*, 25–29, 52–56, 90–93. Perhaps this nominalist instinct is related to what I am describing here in terms of a narratival approach to divine ontology and action?

15. For an attempt to identify and address the problems with this approach, and from the vantage point of systematic theology, see Dolezal, *All That Is in God*. Dolezal identifies historical and contemporary examples of this approach in the field of systematics (see esp. pp. 1–8 for examples of what Dolezal calls "theistic mutualism"). While I do not agree with all of Dolezal's assessments about his interlocutors, I do agree with his assessment of the challenges of a "narratival approach" to God's identity.

While I hesitate to bring other specific examples to the fore, given the lack of space to summarize or address them carefully, perhaps a relatively uncontroversial example is found in Robert Jenson's work. Jenson famously insisted on the importance of the biblical narrative in articulating God's identity (see, for an entry point, Jenson, *A Theology in Outline*, 48–51). Even more caution is required to mention Karl Barth, but it may be sufficient simply to note that Barth is often *accused* of such a conflation between the temporal events of creation and redemption and the identity of the eternal triune God. As an entry to the discussion, see Torrance, "The Trinity." And now that I'm already in trouble, I might as well end by bringing up the (in)famous Rahner's Rule: "The economic Trinity is the immanent Trinity, and the immanent Trinity is the economic Trinity." Whether Barth or Rahner actually affirmed the "narratival approach" I'm describing, I will not attempt to adjudicate. I will say, however, that these appear to have been cited as warrant for such an approach by others since.

16. Seitz notes similar concerns about the limits of narratival approaches to biblical theology and canonical reading in *The Elder Testament*, 71–84 (and throughout).

In response to both above cases, what I want to say instead is that the God of the Bible is the God who exists *a se*, apart from and outside of the biblical narrative. God encompasses—indeed, God is the ground and source of—the biblical narrative, not the other way around.[17] This is a subtle but important difference in how we speak about God and about what the Bible tells us about him. The Bible itself is a creature, even if the only divinely inspired textual creature, and as such it sits within the created order. Further, its purpose is covenantal, and so it sits within not only God's created order but also God's covenant of redemption. Indeed, it is God's revelation of himself to his creatures, and in particular to those with whom he covenants, and his work of redemption on their behalf.

We *must* attend to this reality when we speak of the biblical story and God's relation to it. While God is in one sense an actor alongside the other actors within the biblical story, he is not simply another character, even if the main character, within that story. He is the source and ground of the story and all its attendant realities. As an analogy, we might say that God is the author and narrator of the story who has also entered into his own story as the main character.

For our purposes, this means that the biblical story is unified precisely because its unity is grounded in something beyond itself: the one God.[18] The Bible isn't a story *merely* because we can empirically demonstrate it to be so (and I believe this can be demonstrated, as I note below). Instead, we can empirically demonstrate the Bible's unity *precisely because of* the fundamental unity of the Godhead and his work in creation and redemption accomplished in Christ Jesus by his Spirit. The unity of the divine missions, grounded in the unity of the divine processions, is what grounds the unity of God's work of redemption and therefore the conceptual and textual unity of the covenantal book that reveals to his people God's nature and his work on their behalf.

17. See Dolezal, *All That Is in God*, 1–8, 19–21.

18. On the unity of the biblical story and issues with a predominantly "storied" approach to biblical theology and the nature of the Bible, see Seitz, *The Elder Testament*, 51–62, 71–84. See also Collett, "Reading Forward," esp. 187–89.

The Story of Scripture and the Singular, Unified Canon

That the canon is singular and unified addresses a number of challenges, and has done so since the first centuries of Christianity. Irenaeus, for instance, combats the arch-heretic Marcion by articulating Scripture's inherent conceptual and narratival unity. Regarding its conceptual unity, Irenaeus postulates the *hypothesis* of Scripture, by which he means the underlying thesis, which is that the Bible's content is ordered toward the person and work of Jesus Christ. When understood rightly—by which Irenaeus means when the distinct parts of the Bible are read together in the way that God intended—the Bible is God's revelation of himself in the person and work of Jesus Christ. This is along the lines of what I have been saying in this chapter and the previous one.

But it is another of the terms Irenaeus uses, *oikonomia*, that highlights the Bible's structural unity.[19] By this term, Irenaeus means that the Bible has an intended and inherent structure or order, a narratival structure that centers on the person and work of Jesus Christ. This narratival unity is derivative of the conceptual unity provided by Scripture's *hypothesis*, but it is also mutually reinforcing of that unity.[20] In other words, the Bible is a narratival unity precisely because of its conceptual unity rooted in its nature as God's revelation of himself,[21] but this conceptual unity is demonstrated in its narratival unity.[22]

This is in contrast to Marcion's and other Gnostic teachers' attempt to disjoint the biblical data, and especially its unified story

19. On Irenaeus's reliance on the structural unity of the Bible to combat Marcion and other theological opponents, see Young, "Divine Discourse," esp. 71–79.

20. A recent attempt to demonstrate the interrelation between the Bible's overall message, its main storyline, and canonical shape can be found in Spellman, "Two Testaments to Tell."

21. "We must read the Bible canonically, as one book. Each part has meaning in light of the whole (and in light of its center, Jesus Christ)" (Vanhoozer, *The Drama of Doctrine*, 178).

22. We should note that there are those who affirm, even if in attenuated fashion, the narratival connection between canonical books even while setting to the side the question of inspiration and articulating the canonical process in terms more or less in line with what I've called the "ecclesial reception" model. See, for instance, Timothy H. Lim's "indicative definition" of canon, which relies on a "family resemblance" model grounded in association with the story of Israel (Lim, "An Indicative Definition of Canon").

of creation, fall, redemption, and new creation. These teachers (although not in exactly the same way) superimposed a metaphysical breach onto the biblical story, with all of the OT and much of the NT narrating not the one true God's work in the world but an evil Demiurge's creation of the material realm. The real God, the God who sent Jesus, is the true God of the spiritual realm. Jesus's work isn't to redeem creation from sin's curse but instead to free us from the sinful reality of the physical creation.

Obviously, this is a very different story from the one Irenaeus tells in, for instance, the *Demonstration of the Apostolic Preaching*, and that is precisely the point. Irenaeus argues rightly that the biblical story is not a disjointed clash between the evil god of the material realm and the one true God of the spiritual realm, but instead is a unified story of the one and only true God's redemption of his good creation through the person and work of Jesus Christ and by his one Holy Spirit. Irenaeus grounds the unity of the story of the Bible in the unity of the Godhead and, derivatively, the unity of his work. He also demonstrates the Bible's unity through what we might call a sustained exegetical and narratival survey of the Bible, showing how each of its distinct parts points toward and is fulfilled in the Bible's center, the person and work of Jesus Christ.[23]

Irenaeus affirms the four canonical Gospels, for instance, precisely because they are situated within, and provide the culmination for, this singular, unified story of the one God's work of creation and redemption. In his famous statement on the fourfold Gospel corpus, Irenaeus argues for the unique and unified message of Matthew, Mark, Luke, and John in contrast to Gnostic material. Irenaeus's discussion is worth quoting at length:

> It is not possible that the Gospels can be either more or fewer in number than they are. For, since there are four zones of the world in which we live, and four principal winds, while the Church is scattered throughout all the world, and the "pillar and ground" of the Church is the Gospel and the spirit of life; it is fitting that she should have four pillars, breathing out immortality on every side, and vivifying men

23. See Irenaeus, *On the Apostolic Preaching*. (This is the title of the Popular Patristics volume containing *Demonstration of the Apostolic Preaching*.)

afresh. From which fact, it is evident that the Word, the Artificer of all, He that sitteth upon the cherubim, and contains all things, He who was manifested to men, has given us the Gospel under four aspects, but bound together by one Spirit. As also David says, when entreating His manifestation, "Thou that sittest between the cherubim, shine forth." For the cherubim, too, were four-faced, and their faces were images of the dispensation of the Son of God. For, [as the Scripture] says, "The first living creature was like a lion," symbolizing His effectual working, His leadership, and royal power; the second [living creature] was like a calf, signifying [His] sacrificial and sacerdotal order; but "the third had, as it were, the face as of a man,"—an evident description of His advent as a human being; "the fourth was like a flying eagle," pointing out the gift of the Spirit hovering with His wings over the Church. And therefore the Gospels are in accord with these things, among which Christ Jesus is seated. For that according to John relates His original, effectual, and glorious generation from the Father, thus declaring, "In the beginning was the Word, and the Word was with God, and the Word was God." Also, "all things were made by Him, and without Him was nothing made." For this reason, too, is that Gospel full of all confidence, for such is His person. But that according to Luke, taking up [His] priestly character, commenced with Zacharias the priest offering sacrifice to God. For now was made ready the fatted calf, about to be immolated for the finding again of the younger son. Matthew, again, relates His generation as a man, saying, "The book of the generation of Jesus Christ, the son of David, the son of Abraham"; and also, "The birth of Jesus Christ was on this wise." This, then, is the Gospel of His humanity; for which reason it is, too, that [the character of] a humble and meek man is kept up through the whole Gospel. Mark, on the other hand, commences with [a reference to] the prophetical spirit coming down from on high to men, saying, "The beginning of the Gospel of Jesus Christ, as it is written in Esaias the prophet,"—pointing to the winged aspect of the Gospel; and on this account he made a compendious and cursory narrative, for such is the prophetical character. And the Word of God Himself used to converse with the ante-Mosaic patriarchs, in accordance with His divinity and glory; but for those under the law he instituted a sacerdotal and liturgical service. Afterwards, being made man for us, He sent the gift of the celestial Spirit over all the earth, protecting us with His wings. Such, then, as was the course followed by the Son of God, so was also the form of the living creatures; and such as was the form of

> the living creatures, so was also the character of the Gospel. For the living creatures are quadriform, and the Gospel is quadriform, as is also the course followed by the Lord. For this reason were four principal (καθολικαί) covenants given to the human race: one, prior to the deluge, under Adam; the second, that after the deluge, under Noah; the third, the giving of the law, under Moses; the fourth, that which renovates man, and sums up all things in itself by means of the Gospel, raising and bearing men upon its wings into the heavenly kingdom.[24]

Irenaeus argues here that these four and only these four Gospels rely textually on God's unified revelation of himself in the OT to teach about who Jesus is and what he has done, and in such a way that they are theologically aligned with and dependent on the OT as well. While his references to the four corners of the earth and four winds might strike us as strange today, he is making a fairly simple point about the Gospels' unity: It is a unity that is due to their reliance on the OT both textually and conceptually, and so in some sense is analogous to the unity of God's creation.[25] To say this slightly differently, just as God's creation is a unity because of its divine source, so Scripture is a unity because of its divine source. And, more granularly and to the focal point of Irenaeus's argument here, just as creation's unity is seen through its various interconnected material (physical) features, so Scripture's unity is seen in its various interconnected material (textual and literary) features.

Notice also that Irenaeus makes sure to note the connection of each Gospel to the OT and to its theological message about the Godhead. Additionally, he notes that both the gospel message and the number of Gospels culminate the covenants given by God in the OT. A positive way of stating this is that the fourfold Gospel corpus is canonical, and each book in the corpus is canonical, because this corpus as it stands culminates the story of the Bible in the person and work of Jesus Christ.[26]

24. Irenaeus, *Against Heresies* 3.11.8 (pp. 428–29).

25. We will return to this connection between Scripture's unity and creation's unity in chap. 5.

26. A modern example of this type of argument can be found in Burridge, *Four Gospels, One Jesus?*, 174–78, which draws out the explicitly doctrinal implications of

A more negative, but conceptually identical, way to put this is that other gospels—that is, so-called apocryphal gospels, from the early centuries of the church's life—are not included in the canon precisely because they are not intricately connected to Israel's story and therefore to the story of the whole Bible. Simon Gathercole has recently argued this point, noting the stark theological, conceptual, and exhortatory differences between the four canonical Gospels, on the one hand, and the apocryphal gospels, on the other. According to Gathercole,

> the four New Testament Gospels share key elements of theological content that mark them out from most of the noncanonical Gospels. . . . This becomes evident when the various Gospels are examined for what they say about the "kerygmatic" themes of Jesus' messiahship, his saving death and resurrection, and his fulfillment of scripture. In these respects, it is the four New Testament Gospels—including John—that are far closer to one another theologically than most of the noncanonical Gospels are to them.[27]

The rest of Gathercole's book details the ways in which the four NT Gospels are intricately connected to both the message and the text of the OT, while noncanonical gospels are not.[28]

Ultimately, then, the canonical status of a particular book is related first to its nature as God's revelation of himself and (necessarily therefore) second to its fit within the economic structure of that same revelation. Noncanonical status is not necessarily a judgment on a

---

recognizing these four Gospels, as opposed to other heretical gospels written during the early period of the church's life.

27. Gathercole, *The Gospel and the Gospels*, 12.

28. Gathercole, *The Gospel and the Gospels*, 294–460, examines the Gospel of Peter, Marcion's Gospel, the Gospel of Thomas, the Gospel of Truth, the Gospel of Philip, the Gospel of Judas, and the Coptic Gospel of the Egyptians. Craig A. Evans comments, "The Jesus we find in the writings that the church selected—over the course of centuries, in ad hoc settings and in formal councils—seems to be a Jesus that is deeply rooted in his Jewish first-century setting, a setting that ongoing historical and archaeological work continues to confirm and clarify. . . . The Jesuses found in the apocryphal writings, including those included in the proposed expanded New Testament [Gospel of Peter and Gospel of Thomas], tend to be far removed from the early Jewish Jesus" (Evans, "The Gospels of Peter and Thomas," 192–93; see also C. A. Evans, "The Christian Apocrypha").

particular book's historical veracity or spiritual benefit for readers. Joseph and Aseneth, for example, can be read for encouragement regarding God's faithfulness to his people during difficult times and also, perhaps, for historical purposes. But in terms of its furtherance of or fit within the main story of the Bible, its story is tangential rather than central. The biblical narrative focuses its attention on the search for the Seed of Woman, the son of Abraham and David, YHWH in the flesh, who will crush the serpent's head and restore what Adam lost. Noncanonical books focus their attention elsewhere.

One might ask, What about Esther or Daniel? Aren't these books also about God's faithfulness in exile, and don't they refrain from mentioning the line of the Seed and so on? This apparent lack of relation to the "main" biblical story is perhaps most acute with Esther. But in both of these books, one of the central figures—Mordecai and Daniel, respectively—is portrayed as a new Joseph, a faithful vicegerent given authority over a prosperous land. The Joseph story, in turn, is supposed to remind us of Adam as he was prior to the fall. But with all three postlapsarian figures, Israel is still in exile and the serpent's head has not been crushed. They look like new Adams but are not the Last Adam. They are therefore continuing to point their readers forward (as Daniel does most explicitly, but as Gen. 38 and 49 also do in the midst of the Joseph narrative) toward the hope of the Seed of Woman, Israel's Messiah. Biblical stories of postlapsarian figures resemble the story of Joseph and Aseneth as examples of God's faithfulness to his people in exile, but the latter lacks the explicit messianic typology of the canonical books mentioned.[29]

Much has also been made of the "story" approach to the Bible in relation to supposedly nonnarrative texts, like the so-called wisdom literature of the OT[30] or the epistles of the NT. What we can and need to say about both of these corpora, as well as about all other biblical books, though, is that they are situated within the larger narrative of Adam, Israel, and Israel's Messiah, and they often either

29. "Joseph and Aseneth was read as a source of inspiration and moral strength, at times for historical information, and indubitably often just for fun" (Charlesworth, *The Old Testament Pseudepigrapha*, 2:196).

30. But see Kynes, *An Obituary for "Wisdom Literature,"* on the problems with this genre classification.

implicitly or explicitly relate their own material to that overarching story. First, by virtue of the two-testament canon that is bookended by God's works of creation and new creation, the intervening material is necessarily couched within that narrative frame. The main story of the Bible is the context for every biblical book, regardless of whether or not that book actually tells a story within that main story. Second, even the books that are not narrative in genre still often (maybe even always?) make reference to this larger story. For instance, it is now commonly agreed that there is a "narrative substructure" to the NT epistles,[31] one that relies on the story of Jesus as the fulfillment of Israel's story, God's mission to redeem his people and place through the work of Israel's Messiah. Further, the NT epistles often make reference to that story; for instance, Paul's introduction to his letter to the Romans makes explicit reference to the story of Israel vis-à-vis Jesus's fulfillment of the OT (1:2) and his Davidic lineage (1:3).[32]

The same can be said of the OT wisdom literature. Psalms 1–2, the introduction to the Psalter, allude to the lives of Moses, Joshua, and David.[33] Proverbs begins with both a reference to "the king's son" (Prov. 1:1–19) as well as a covenantal promise and warning related to the Spirit's presence in Israel's life (1:20–33), and the contrast between Lady Wisdom and Lady Folly in chapters 1–9 is filled with allusions to the tree of life and the garden. Ecclesiastes, by being commonly attributed to Solomon, is connected to the (continued, not yet fulfilled) expectation for the heir of the Davidic promises to rule forever. Song of Solomon, likewise, looks for the son of David to come out of the wilderness (Song 3:6–11) and marry his garden/temple-like bride (4:1–16).[34] Job looks like a new Adam in his initial wealth and like a better Adam in his refusal to rebel against the Lord

31. This language is typically traced to Hays, *The Faith of Jesus Christ*.

32. See also Wright, *The Climax of the Covenant*, for a variety of ways in which Jesus fulfills Israel's expectations and, as Wright puts it, "stands in Israel's place" as Israel's Messiah and Adam's recapitulation (18–40). (This is not intended as an endorsement of Wright's view of the law, but merely a reference to his careful work in demonstrating Christ's place as fulfillment of Israel's Adamic vocation and Messianic expectations.)

33. On these psalms and their connection to one another and the rest of the OT, see Cole, *Psalms 1–2*.

34. See Emerson, "Land, Burial, and Temple," esp. 190–94.

(Job 1–2). For each of these books, we could multiply exponentially the intertextual allusions it makes to other OT material. That would be too long of an excursus. For our purposes here, the point is that each of these books is clearly connected to the story of Israel.

Still, we need to attend to Seitz's caution about narratival approaches to biblical theology and to canonical criticism. While the Bible can be said to tell an overarching story, we cannot and should not limit the Bible's revelation of the triune God to narratival categories. God often reveals himself in Scripture in ways that are more ontologically basic than simply acting within the story at hand (e.g., Exod. 3; Isa. 6), because in fact God *is* more ontologically basic than the story at hand. To say this slightly differently, God is not just another actor in the story; he is the ground of the story, of all reality. He is life and only in him does life exist. The canon is a creaturely reality given by the Creator, and, though it is used by God to rule his revelation of himself, it does not rule or bound God. God stands outside of the canon and is not merely another character within it. Thus, when we talk about the canon as a ruled story about God's work of creation and redemption, we must be careful to state at the same time that God stands outside of and grounds that same story.[35]

Conclusion

God's revelation of himself in the covenant document that is Holy Scripture centers on the person and work of Jesus Christ, the culmination of the story of creation and redemption that begins in Genesis 1–3. This is the story of the triune God's economic mission to redeem the good world that he created and to restore it and his image bearers to their purpose, which is to bring glory to him throughout the earth and dwell with him in his creation.[36]

The "rule" of canon is thus an economic rule, a rule that, in a positive sense, gives the inspired, inerrant record and interpretation of God's economic mission that is accomplished in the person and

35. Seitz, *The Elder Testament*, 71–84.

36. On this understanding of Scripture's unity from an historical perspective in relation to the beginning of the Reformation, see M. Thompson, *A Sure Ground on Which to Stand*, 152–77.

work of Jesus Christ, God the Son incarnate, Israel's Messiah and the world's Savior.[37] The canon rules our understanding of who God is and what he has done through this biblical metanarrative. This rule also rules what is included in the canon. Those books that center on and contribute to this story of God's work of redemption are included, while those books that are tangential to or not related to the "grand narrative" of God's salvation are not included.

37. On the conceptual unity of the Bible in connection to the unity of Christ's person as the incarnate Son, fully God and fully man, see Collett, *Figural Reading and the Old Testament*, 45.

FOUR

The Ruled Canonical Text: Pneumatology and Canon

The Scriptures, although they too are written by men, are neither of men nor from men but from God.

—Martin Luther[1]

What is θεόπνευστος is "God-breathed," produced by the creative breath of the Almighty. And Scripture is called θεόπνευστος in order to designate it as "God-breathed," the product of Divine spiration. . . . What it affirms is that the Holy Scriptures owe their origin to an activity of God the Holy Ghost and are in the highest and truest sense His creation.

—B. B. Warfield[2]

God was not waiting till Matt. 1:1 to make himself triune.

—Mark S. Gignilliat[3]

1. Luther, "Avoiding the Doctrines of Men," 153, quoted in M. Thompson, *A Sure Ground on Which to Stand*, 68.
2. Warfield, *The Inspiration and Authority of the Bible*, 296.
3. Gignilliat, *Reading Scripture Canonically*, 92.

This chapter builds on chapters 2 and 3 and argues that the canon is Christocentric due to its inspiration by the Spirit. The Spirit's economic mission of testifying to the Son entails that his work of inspiration is centered on the Son. Once again this theological insight will be applied to our understanding of the canon, specifically with respect to canonical boundaries and intertextuality. Regarding the former, much the same point as chapter 2 will be made, but with reference to the Spirit's inspiration of Scripture. With respect to intertextuality, this chapter argues that the inner-biblical allusions in Scripture are (1) a function of divine authorship; (2) a primary means by which the Christocentric nature of the canon can be discerned; and (3) the product of authorial intent, both human and, ultimately, divine. The nature of authorship and its relation to canon will be discussed here as well, and particularly the notion of "final form."

The Spirit's Testimony to the Son

In the economy of redemption, the divine processions are expressed in the economic missions of the divine persons. With respect to the Father and the Son, we see this, for instance, in the "sending" language of John's Gospel; the Father, who is eternally unbegotten, sends his only eternally begotten Son, and so Jesus can speak of "being sent" from the Father. With respect to the Spirit, who, according to the Western tradition, eternally proceeds from the Father and the Son, we can speak of the mission of agency. The Spirit is the agent of the Father's sending of the Son, in the sense that it is the Spirit who, for instance, brings about the incarnation of the Son ("the Holy Spirit will come upon you [Mary]," Luke 1:35) and through whom Christ "offered himself without blemish to God" (Heb. 9:14). This agency of the Spirit as one of his personal economic missions is directly correlated to his eternal procession from the Father and the Son; as the divine person whose eternal existence can be accurately described (even if analogically) as the gift of love between the Father and the Son, it is fitting that he binds together in the economy the will of the Father and the willingness of the Son.

The Spirit's Economic Mission and Scripture's Inspiration

Another of the Spirit's economic missions is that he testifies to the Son. In one sense, this is the obverse of his mission as the divine agent of the Father's sending and the Son's sent-ness. In the act of sending, the Son is sent from the Father by the Spirit. In the act of testimony, the Son is seen by humanity through the testimony of the Spirit so that they can see the Father. What is from the Father through the Son by the Spirit in the incarnation is seen by the Spirit testifying to the Son who shows us the Father.

Jesus mentions this mission of the Spirit a number of times in the Farewell Discourse, and in the context of the disciples' anxiety over seeing the Father and following Jesus to the place where he is going (John 14:5–14). Although he does not yet speak of the Spirit's testimony to the Son, Jesus makes the connection apparent in John 14:16–17, when, after allaying their fears about him leaving, Jesus gives them this promise: "I will ask the Father, and he will give you another Helper, to be with you forever, even the Spirit of truth, whom the world cannot receive, because it neither sees him nor knows him. You know him, for he dwells with you and will be in you."

Later in the same chapter, as Jesus is teaching his disciples that he will remain present with those who obey his commandments, he tells them, "These things I have spoken to you while I am still with you. But the Helper, the Holy Spirit, whom the Father will send in my name, he will teach you all things and bring to your remembrance all that I have said to you" (John 14:25–26). In other words, this same Spirit of truth is the only one who will bring to remembrance what Jesus has taught and done in their presence. Or, to say it slightly differently, the truth to which this Spirit testifies is Jesus, who is the Truth (14:6), and in both his sayings and his deeds.

Jesus heightens his discourse about the Spirit in John 15:26–27, where he teaches not only that the Spirit testifies to him but also that the Spirit's economic mission is rooted in his eternal procession: "But when the Helper comes, whom I will send to you from the Father, the Spirit of truth, who proceeds from the Father, he will bear witness about me. And you also will bear witness, because you have been with me from the beginning."

The Holy Spirit, "the Spirit of truth," testifies to the Son because he is sent by the Son from the Father, and his sent-ness is an economic reflection of his eternal procession from the Father. Further, the fact that the Spirit is sent not only from the Father but also by the Son in the economy of redemption suggests that the Spirit also proceeds from the Son eternally. In other words, the Spirit's economic mission to testify to the Son, the one who makes known to us the Father, is a reflection in the economy of redemption of the Spirit's eternal relation to both the Father and the Son in the inner life of God as the Spirit who proceeds eternally from the Father and the Son.

The Spirit's mission to testify to the Son is mentioned a third and final time by Jesus in John 16:12–15. Here, the emphasis is on Jesus's authoritative teaching of the disciples, a teaching that will continue through the ministry of the Holy Spirit. Even though Jesus is "going away," he insists,

> I still have many things to say to you, but you cannot bear them now. When the Spirit of truth comes, he will guide you into all the truth, for he will not speak on his own authority, but whatever he hears he will speak, and he will declare to you the things that are to come. He will glorify me, for he will take what is mine and declare it to you. All that the Father has is mine; therefore I said that he will take what is mine and declare it to you.

Here again we see the connection between what the Spirit does (his economic mission) and who he is (his eternal procession), this time in reference to the Spirit's authority to speak. The Spirit hears what the risen and ascended Son says and speaks it, and the Son hears, speaks, and receives what he has from the Father. The Spirit's authoritative testimony is given to him by the Son who receives it from the Father, and the Spirit is sent by the Son who receives him from the Father. This is because the Son is eternally begotten from the Father, and the Spirit eternally proceeds from the Father and the Son. To say it as succinctly as possible, *the Spirit testifies to the Son in his economic mission, a mission that includes the inspiration of Scripture, for two reasons: first, because it is through seeing the Son that we see the Father in the economy, and second, because the Spirit proceeds from the Son and the Father in eternity*. The Spirit's economic mission to testify to the Son is both an economic necessity and a reflection of the immanent life of God in eternity.[4]

It is crucial to understand this trinitarian shape of revelation as we reflect on what exactly we mean by *canon*. Ultimately, canon as boundary marker is a matter not only of extrinsic criteria but also of intrinsic criteria, and in that regard there is only one criterion: the Spirit's inspiration of a given text. If the Spirit inspired the text, it is canonical; if he did not, it is not. Canon is dictated not by the church but by the Spirit who inspires Scripture. The Holy Spirit both sets and gives shape to the boundaries of Scripture, because Scripture is God's own revelation of himself in the person and work of Jesus Christ given through the inspiration of his Holy Spirit.

To say this slightly differently, Scripture is not first an anthropological or ecclesiological reality, even though we cannot speak of Scripture without accounting for anthropological and ecclesiological factors.[5] What this means is that Scripture is not just any testimony about Jesus, but *divinely inspired* (i.e., the Spirit's own) testimony to Jesus.[6] Canon is in this sense a boundary, but one that is not merely ecclesial but fundamentally pneumatological and regulated by the incarnate Son's own teaching.

The Spirit and the Rule of Faith

This last sentence bears further explanation. The Spirit testifies to the Son according to his own economic mission, which is a reflection of his eternal procession, but he also testifies to the Son because, as Jesus puts it, "he will not speak on his own authority, but whatever he hears he will speak" (John 16:13). To state this positively, the Spirit's testimony to the Son is entirely aligned with the Son's testimony about himself. And we have already seen that Jesus testifies to himself

4. On the trinitarian shape of divine revelation, see Crawford, *Cyril of Alexandria's Trinitarian Theology of Scripture*, 10–66, esp. 20–21. See also pp. 67–114 for specific attention to the mission of the Spirit in the inspiration of Scripture.

5. On anthropological concerns, see below ("The Dual Authorship of Scripture"); on ecclesiological concerns, see chap. 6.

6. See Swain, *Trinity, Revelation, and Reading*, 138–39.

by demonstrating Scripture's own testimony to him. Or, to say it yet another way, (1) Jesus interprets Scripture about himself because the Spirit who inspires Scripture has an economic mission to testify to him, and (2) the Spirit has an economic mission to testify to the Son because he speaks in accordance with the incarnate Son's authority. This is the same Son from whom he proceeds, along with the Father, in eternity. To understand what the Spirit speaks, then, we should look at Jesus's own understanding of the Scriptures.

In this respect, we can return to Jesus's comments about what the Bible means, both in John and elsewhere. In John 5:46, for example, Jesus tells his opponents, "If you believed Moses, you would believe me; for he wrote of me." Similarly, in the Gospel of Luke, Jesus in at least two places indicates that a right reading of Scripture (specifically, the Jewish Scriptures, or what we would call the Old Testament) must be a reading that centers on him. First, in Luke 16:31, at the end of the parable of Lazarus and the rich man, Abraham tells the rich man, "If they do not hear Moses and the Prophets, neither will they be convinced if someone should rise from the dead." In other words, if they do not read Scripture rightly—and, more specifically, as testifying to Jesus of Nazareth as Israel's Messiah—then they won't even believe him when he rises from the dead. Later, in the final chapter of Luke's Gospel, Jesus teaches both the disciples on the road to Emmaus and then those in the upper room that the entire OT ("Moses and all the Prophets," 24:27; "the Law of Moses and the Prophets and the Psalms," 24:44) points to him.

In terms of the narrative of the Gospels, the reason why the Jewish leaders reject Jesus in the end is that, according to Jesus, they do not read the Scriptures correctly; that is, they do not read them as pointing to him, Israel's Messiah. Drawing on Jesus's other teaching elsewhere throughout the Gospels, we could say that they do not read the Scriptures in such a way that they recognize who Jesus is: YHWH in the flesh (e.g., Luke 22:70–71; cf. also, e.g., Matt. 26:62–67; John 8:58). And the reason the disciples can recognize him, finally, is because they are taught liturgically (Luke 24:30–31, and esp. v. 35) and communally (24:45) by Christ their Head how to read the Scriptures properly.

We have to emphasize that this christological hermeneutical rule—the rule of faith—is *given to us by Jesus in the Spirit-inspired text of*

Scripture. The Spirit's economic authority, an economic authority that is used to inspire Scripture and that is concordant with Jesus's own economic authority, is exercised here by giving us Jesus's own rule for interpreting the text, the same text that the Spirit inspires. This chain of relation between Jesus's authority as Israel's Messiah, the Spirit's concordant economic authority to testify to Jesus, and the authority of the text as Spirit-inspired is crucial in understanding what Scripture is and, therefore, what we must say about canon.

While there is an ontological difference between, on the one hand, the Son and the Spirit as two of the three divine persons of the triune God and, on the other hand, Scripture as the text inspired by the Spirit to testify to the Son, we also need to insist that this text exercises authority derived from the Holy Trinity because it is given to us by that same Holy Trinity. And the authority it exercises includes *interpretive* authority; that is, it demands we recognize that the whole of history, both creation and redemption, is summed up in the person of Jesus Christ, Israel's Messiah, God the Son incarnate. In this one man, who is both God and human being in one person, the triune God is revealed, because he is the Son of the Father and the one to whom the Spirit testifies.

All this is to say, again, that pneumatology intersects with bibliology in the mission of the Spirit to testify to the Son. As a divine work carried out inseparably by the triune God but most often in Scripture appropriated specifically to the Holy Spirit (e.g., 2 Tim. 3:16; 2 Pet. 1:21), the Bible's ultimate author is the Third Person of the Trinity. This person, the Holy Spirit, testifies to the Son in his work of inspiration, and so the Bible is a book that intends to testify to the Son, and specifically to the Son in his incarnation, life, death, resurrection, ascension, and imminent return as the fulfillment of God's promises to Adam, Abraham, and David. The Bible is all about Jesus because it is written by the Spirit whose economic mission is to testify to Jesus.

The Dual Authorship of Scripture

Saying that the Bible is written by the Spirit requires us to address the dual authorship of Scripture. That is, because the Holy Spirit did not simply drop the text from heaven but rather used human beings to write down his inspired words, we must account for both the human and the divine aspects of the authorship of Scripture.

In certain approaches to modern biblical scholarship, these two different modes of authorship, and thus of authorial intent, are pitted against each other, as if authorship is a zero-sum game. Most often, both in evangelical articulations of authorship and in broader academic discussions, the human author's intent wins. This kind of approach is exemplified in aphorisms like "What it means is what it meant" (i.e., to the human author according to his sociohistorical context) and "The text cannot mean what it never meant" (i.e., again, that it cannot mean what it did not mean to the human author according to his sociohistorical context). In this kind of understanding, the human author's original sociohistorical context dictates what the text could have meant, both to the human author and to the original audience. Divine authorship, when it is affirmed, is reducible to that same historically situated intent of the human author.

But this approach does not acknowledge the theological reality that is the Creator-creature distinction, or the subsequent affirmations of God's own life that follow such an acknowledgment. Instead, this is a kind of pneumatological kenoticism, an assumption that the Spirit empties himself of his divine attributes in the process of inspiring human authors. In Christology, *kenoticism* refers to a particular understanding of the Son's incarnation: that in the hypostatic union, God the Son emptied himself of his divine attributes. The miracles performed and the supernatural statements made by Jesus of Nazareth were thus entirely a function of the Holy Spirit's anointing empowerment, not of Jesus's divine nature. Further, God the Son becoming incarnate, according to kenotic Christology, means that he no longer accesses his divine attributes in any sense; in other words, it is not just in reference to the miracles and supernatural statements of Jesus, but in reference to the entire life of the Son, that this emptying occurs. It is as though God the Son incarnate entirely limits himself to the abilities, attributes, and conception of his human nature.[7]

7. For a wide-ranging treatment of the subject of kenotic Christology and from a variety of scholars, disciplines, and perspectives, see C. S. Evans, *Exploring Kenotic Christology*. For a sympathetic treatment of the position, in relation to current Barth scholarship, see McCormack, *The Humility of the Eternal Son*.

This kenotic approach to Christology is analogous to the way in which many modern biblical interpretive methods relate the intention of the divine and the human authors of Scripture (if the divine author is acknowledged at all). That is, much of modern biblical interpretation assumes a kind of pneumatological kenoticism,[8] in which the divine author of Scripture, God the Holy Spirit, limits himself to the abilities, attributes, and conception of the human author(s) and editors of a particular biblical book, corpus, and/or testament.

In some ways, contemporary versions of this model can be traced to reliance on a theory of meaning promulgated by E. D. Hirsch Jr. In his *Validity in Interpretation*, Hirsch says that "verbal meaning is whatever someone has willed to convey by a particular sequence of linguistic signs and which can be conveyed (shared) by means of those linguistic signs."[9] While I do not disagree with Hirsch here, many modern hermeneutics texts make a twofold move that goes perhaps further than Hirsch intended.[10] First, meaning is defined as Hirsch describes here,[11] and then second, and crucially for our purposes, meaning is limited to what the human author could have consciously meant at the time of writing.

8. Note that this is not intended as a critique of Telford Work's different use of the term *kenosis* in his correction of Barth; his is the more biblical (and therefore) Chalcedonian use of the term, and thus not to be identified with the nineteenth- and twentieth-century kenotic movements to which I am referring. See Work, *Living and Active*, 97–100.

9. Hirsch, *Validity in Interpretation*, 31; see also 133.

10. In fact, Hirsch was not addressing authorship or meaning in relation to the Bible as a specific kind of book, but was simply setting forth definitions of such within a general philosophy of language and therefore a general hermeneutic. He even says at one point, "Yet certain texts such as the Constitution of the United States and the Bible do seem to require that meaning go beyond anything that a human and historical author could possibly have willed" (Hirsch, *Validity in Interpretation*, 121–22; thanks to Brandon Smith for pointing out this quote). To apply Hirsch's definitions wholesale to the Bible, without attending to its unique features (namely, divine authorship), is to use Hirsch's conclusions for unintended purposes. The irony of "unintended" is thick.

11. Perhaps most influential is Osborne, *The Hermeneutical Spiral*, who notes his broad agreement with Hirsch's theory of meaning on pp. 23–24. Even while stating his reliance on him, Osborne registers criticism of Hirsch as well (495–97), although this critique does not fall along the same lines of the argument being presented here. For a similar, if truncated, treatment of Hirsch, see Newport, "Contemporary Philosophical, Literary, and Sociological Hermeneutics," 142.

Again, while I do not disagree with Hirsch's notion of "verbal meaning," or with his wider concern to defend the notion that meaning is objective and can be rightly discovered in a given text, it is an inadequate account of the unique mode of the authorship of Scripture: Scripture has both a human author *and* a divine author for every text. When we follow Hirsch too narrowly—in other words, when we do not give adequate attention to the *divine* authorial intent of Scripture along with the human authorial intent—we end up with pneumatological kenoticism.

One can find evidence of this kind of approach in various statements that reduce the perceived intention of a given biblical text to some aspect of the text's historical setting. Most often, this reduction occurs through equating the divine author's intention with what the human author could have consciously or subconsciously meant given his historical milieu. But there is similar emphasis in contemporary hermeneutics texts on what the original audience could have understood the text to mean, again given their historical milieu. The meaning of a particular text, so this approach says, is limited to the conscious or subconscious intention of a particular human author and to what the original audience could plausibly have understood the text's meaning to be.

One influential example of what I am describing can be found in two of Walt Kaiser's essays on hermeneutics.[12] Less obvious examples might be found in other evangelical hermeneutics texts[13] wherein the author(s), like Kaiser, clearly acknowledge the Spirit's inspiration of the text[14] and therefore his status as divine author, but then limit the text's meaning to what the human author could have consciously intended given their contextually located cognitive finitude.[15] In other

12. See, e.g., Kaiser, "Single Meaning, Unified Referents," esp. 52–54; Kaiser, "The Single Intent of Scripture."

13. For instance, Corley et al., *Biblical Hermeneutics*.

14. See, e.g., the survey and summary of Lemke, "The Inspiration and Truthfulness of Scripture," 148–54, 160–62. At one point Lemke cites Paige Patterson and says that the latter, "while warning against undiscerning use of historical criticism, has stated that 'the reverential use of historical-critical method should not be rejected' (Patterson, 57)." This occurs in the context of Lemke emphasizing human authorial intent and "good hermeneutics."

15. Corley, "A Student's Primer for Exegesis," 6–8, for instance, and especially p. 6: "Exegesis has and should approach the biblical text as a window to see into the

words, there is no explicitly stated consideration of how the Spirit's own omniscience relates to the human author's finitude with respect to the meaning of a given biblical text, even while there is acknowledgment elsewhere of the Spirit's superintending, unifying work of inspiration for the whole biblical text.

Another representative, clear example comes from Robert H. Stein's *A Basic Guide to Interpreting the Bible*:

> At this point someone might raise the following objection: But isn't God the author of Scripture? This sounds devout and pious, but Scripture does not claim God as its immediate author. Paul's letters do not begin, "God, the Father, Son, and Holy Spirit, to the church at Rome, Galatia, and so on." No book of the Bible claims God as its immediate author. Christians believe that behind the books of the Bible stands the living God, who inspired his servants in the writing of these works. But the Scriptures were physically written by men, not God. As a result, to understand the meaning of the biblical texts we must understand what their human authors consciously willed to convey by their texts. *The divine meaning of the biblical texts is the conscious, willed meaning of God's inspired prophets and apostles. . . . To understand the divine meaning of Scripture, then, is to understand the conscious meaning of God's inspired servants who wrote it. It is in, not behind or beyond, the meaning the biblical author wished to share that we find the divine voice of God in the Scriptures.*[16]

To state the obvious, this limits the meaning of the text to what is cognitively available to the human author with respect to their unique sociocultural and historical settings. Stein labors elsewhere to clearly acknowledge the inspiration of all of Scripture by the Spirit and the attendant affirmations regarding inerrancy and infallibility.[17] But, according to his view, the Spirit's verbal plenary inspiration of the whole Bible does not translate to a theory of meaning for any given biblical text that accounts for his divine omniscience in relation to the human author's creaturely finitude.

---

world of the author." The context makes it obvious that "author" at the end of the sentence is a reference to the human author specifically.

16. Stein, *A Basic Guide to Interpreting the Bible*, 21 (emphasis added).

17. Stein, *A Basic Guide to Interpreting the Bible*, 56–67.

An even more recent iteration can be found in John Walton's "Lost World" books. For instance, in his introduction to *The Lost World of the Prophets*, and in summarizing his purpose and approach for the entire series, he writes, "The details of interpretation[18] are worked out in accordance with a consistently applied methodology that finds God's authoritative message in the text as being contained in the communication as it was understood by the human instruments (speakers or writers) and their audience(s). In this way these books are working out the principle that the Bible is written for us but not to us."[19] What Walton appears to be doing is delimiting the meaning of a given text in its entirety to the conscious frame of the human author and his original audience. There is some aspect of the biblical text, rooted in its purpose as God's address to us, that "transcends" this original context and allows us to apply it to our day, but we have to "translate" that original meaning to modern application.[20] Another way to press the point is to ask how Paul finds warrant in saying that "these things were written for our instruction" in 1 Corinthians 10 or Romans 15 if the OT authors could not possibly have had the cultural context of Paul and his readers in mind.

We can acknowledge that there are laudable commitments in each of the works cited above, as well as in others that follow similar paths regarding authorial intent. For instance, each of the works cited emphasizes the need to exegete individual texts carefully, including in ways that give adequate attention to the human author's and original audience's historical setting. I agree with this emphasis. We can also

18. By "details of interpretation" he means, in the context of the two immediately preceding sentences, a "close reading of the Old Testament" both in terms of "textual work" and "informed knowledge of the cultural context of the ancient Near Eastern world" (Walton, *The Lost World of the Prophets*, 1).

19. Walton, *The Lost World of the Prophets*, 1–2. There are attempts later in the book to address the issue of God's divine knowledge (e.g., pp. 86, 111, 123), and Walton does acknowledge God's omniscience (esp. p. 86). But, in so doing, he also explicitly redirects the reader to what he considers to be the interpretive locus (i.e., where to identify the meaning of the text): in the conscious intention, and therefore the limited creaturely cognition, of the human author(s) of a given passage (again, p. 86).

20. Walton, *The Lost World of the Israelite Conquest*, 10. I take it that Walton's method is similar in many ways to what Klink and Lockett identify as "biblical theology as historical description." On that approach as well as attendant examples, see Klink and Lockett, *Understanding Biblical Theology*, 29–58.

commend these works' commitment to a high view of the Bible's inspiration by the Holy Spirit and its attendant perfections, both conceptual (the unity and infallibility of Scripture) and textual (the inerrancy of Scripture). This commitment is incredibly important and fundamental to an adequately Christian account of Scripture's nature, purpose, and production, and therefore also to a theory of meaning. But, in failing to account adequately for the Spirit's omniscience, and in relation to his inspiration of the biblical authors, these works have unwittingly passed over a foundational tenet of the biblical doctrine of God: the ontological distinction between Creator and creature.

In failing to adequately account for this Creator-creature distinction, the foregoing approaches and those like them also fail to acknowledge the reality of the Holy Spirit's divine attributes, attributes he shares fully and equally with the Father and the Son. We need to account for both God's aseity and freedom in what we say about the relation of divine action and creaturely action, especially as that relation pertains to divine inspiration and authorial intent. Regarding both aseity and freedom, we need to say first that God is not just another "thing" in the world. He does not exist or operate in the same ways that creatures do. In particular, he alone possesses "life in himself" (cf. John 5:26). That is, only the triune God exists on his own, independently from everything else, without need for anything else. He is, in systematic terms, *a se* (Latin: "from himself"). This confession of aseity means not only that God exists independently, unlike his creatures (i.e., everything else that exists), but also that he operates freely, unlike his creatures. This is not a denial of creaturely free will; human beings can and do make decisions for themselves. But they are not "free" in the same sense that God is free—human beings are finite, for one thing, and fallen, for another.

Both of these realities—God's aseity and his freedom—impinge upon what it means for him to act in the world and in relation to his creatures. Unlike his creatures, God is neither finite nor fallen, and so his action in relation to ours is not a zero-sum game. To spell this out a bit further, and first in terms of creaturely finitude: If we were considering the distinct but hypothetically opposed wills of two finite creatures, they would be operating in the same field of play, so to speak, and so only one of those wills could "win" when they are opposed. But God's infinite and eternal will is *not* on the same playing field as a finite, temporal will. These are two distinct metaphysical realities. They are, therefore, not in competition with each other, but rather operate via different modes of existence and thus in a noncompetitive fashion. (The same is true, mutatis mutandis and supremely so, of the human and divine wills in the one person of Christ.) Second, God is not fallen, either. And while his perfect, holy will *is* in opposition to unrepentant, rebellious, fallen wills, he can and does redeem his creatures and thus align their wills with his. To put it as succinctly as possible, because of the Creator-creature distinction, and specifically as it applies to the act of inspiration, God's operation in his world is not in competition with human free will, either with respect to the creature's finitude or with respect to fallenness.[21]

Third, and again with respect to the Creator-creature distinction, it is important to recognize that, while creatures change, God does not.[22] God—the triune God, Father, Son, and Holy Spirit—is who he is eternally. This is, in large part, what it *means* to be God. God exists on his own (aseity), always (eternality), perfectly and without limit or boundary (plenitude and infinitude), and without changing (immutability). God does not acquire, lose, or change his attributes—ever. He is always perfectly good, just, and holy, and he is always omnipotent, omniscient, and omnipresent (among other divine perfections). He cannot "turn off" his divine attributes. This faulty assumption that he can do any such thing leads to christological kenoticism and to its equivalent with respect to pneumatology.

21. See Webster, *The Domain of the Word*, 7–17, 38–41, on the relation of the human author to the divine author, especially in connection with the Creator-creature distinction and the nature of the text as a *signum*. See also R. Williams, *Christ the Heart of Creation*, for a thorough historical, philosophical, and theological analysis of the Chalcedonian question—that is, how to describe the relation of Christ's two natures. As Williams notes in the preface, attending to Christology "clarifies other areas of what Christians say" (xi). In this case, clarifying how the Creator-creature distinction helps us speak accurately of the hypostatic union—that is, that his natures are not in competition with each other—also helps us speak accurately, by way of analogy, of the dual authorship of Scripture.

22. On the exegetical warrant for and interrelation of divine aseity, simplicity, and immutability, see Duby, *Divine Simplicity*, 91–150.

When we consider the biblical material, then, we cannot articulate an understanding of meaning or authorial intent that requires the Holy Spirit to change or modify his own nature by "turning off" his divine attributes. He, along with the Father and the Son, has always been and always will be all-knowing, and that includes while he (the Spirit) inspires Holy Scripture. To put the point very finely, the Holy Spirit doesn't pretend to be ignorant that the promise of Genesis 3:15 will find its fulfillment in the culmination of history in the life and atoning work of God the Son incarnate. We should not read the OT, or theorize about its human authorship, in ways that undermine the eternal existence of God as Father, Son, and Holy Spirit or that suggest that the Holy Spirit limits his divine knowledge to the finite confines of the human author's consciousness.

To again quote Mark Gignilliat, "God was not waiting till Matt. 1:1 to make himself triune." In fact, the context for this quotation makes explicit the connection between God's unchanging nature and the process by which the Bible was written, transmitted, and codified in canonical form:

> The verbal character of the Old Testament, a verbal character worthy of respect in the idiom of the Old Testament's material form, is in associative relationship with the whole of the Christian Bible, Old and New Testaments. Its sentences mean more—if by "meaning more" we mean *go beyond the epistemic horizons of the authors and editors*—because of the associative-field mapping of a two-Testament witness *centered on a single subject matter and single authorial voice.* Put in pedestrian terms, God was not waiting till Matt. 1:1 to make himself triune.
>
> The triune identity of God emerging from Scripture's total witness pressures Christian readers to yield to the hermeneutical significance of Paul's claim in Colossians: "And he [Jesus Christ] is before all things" (Col. 1:17). *"Before all things" certainly includes the Old Testament canon.* Such a claim about God's being as triune, self-communicative, and self-revealing resists the reduction of Holy Scripture's semantic reach to the epistemic horizons of those involved in the compositional and textual history of the Old Testament canon—whether with abstract categories or descriptors, like "God" apart from triune identification of that God, or in seemingly faithful approaches

like "Christotelism" (Christ as the telos/goal of the Old Testament promises). Christotelic readings run into the danger of fusing the ontological character of Israel's Scripture with the epistemic horizon of those who wrote, edited, and compiled them. Even though Moses might not have been a self-conscious trinitarian, we can be assured that God was.[23]

To bring this back to the focal point of this section: Even when we acknowledge the human authorship of Scripture and all of its attendant historical features, we cannot pretend that the Holy Spirit divested himself of his divine attributes—and particularly, his divine omniscience—in inspiring those varied human authors in their varied historical circumstances. Again, to put this concretely, and with respect to the central subject of Scripture (Christ and his work), we cannot posit a theory of meaning that suggests the Holy Spirit (1) somehow willfully "turned off" or changed or modified his divine attributes as the Third Person of the Trinity, or, therefore, (2) somehow made himself willfully ignorant of who Israel's Messiah would be. Nor, therefore, can we posit a theory of meaning suggesting that any given OT text is devoid of the intention to reveal the triune God in the face of Israel's Messiah, Jesus Christ. Doing so would require a pneumatological kenoticism that does not adequately account for the Holy Spirit's nature as the Third Person of the triune God or for the Creature-creature distinction.[24]

23. Gignilliat, *Reading Scripture Canonically*, 92–93 (emphasis added). See also pp. 111–14.

24. Another issue with this kind of approach—one that limits meaning to what the original audience might have understood a text to mean—is that it ignores the intentions of the human author to speak beyond their own historical horizon. There are many indications that the human authors of the Bible intended their work to be read and understood by those who came after them. Note, for instance, Childs's comment: "The religious function of the biblical material was communicated in numerous ways on all the various levels of composition, but with a view to continuing to address the future generations with the reality of God—his presence, his saving activity, his will. . . . Even the superscriptions point to a theological rendering of narrative which moved it beyond its original limited function (cf. Gen. 18.1; Ex. 3.2)" (Childs, *Old Testament Theology in a Canonical Context*, 23). Note also Childs, speaking of Joel's place among the Minor Prophets and the varied historical contexts of those books, and of the effect of canonical shaping that places them together without clearly historically related ordering: "It is characteristic of the canonical process that original

When we give adequate attention to the Creator-creature distinction, then, neither of these kenotic approaches is needed to affirm the full humanity of a given reality, whether it be the human nature of the person of Jesus Christ or the human authorship of Holy Scripture. God's omniscience and omnipotence are not in competition with the human authors' limited knowledge or with their own free will (in this case, their literary intention). Therefore, God does not need to—and, indeed, cannot—empty himself of his divine attributes of omniscience and omnipotence in order to accommodate or allow for human authorial intent. Instead, the divine author providentially inspires the human author, via the human author's own human means and intent, to accurately convey the divine author's intent in the text.

The Spirit's Inspiration of Scripture and Chalcedonian Analogies

In order to accurately reflect the theological claims made above, I suggest that those who affirm the dual authorship of Scripture should do so not under the rubric of kenoticism but with Chalcedon in mind. Here, I do not wish to imply that the Bible has two distinct but hypostatically united natures in one person—the Bible is not a person, human, divine, or both at once, and texts do not have natures in the same sense that persons do.[25] But Chalcedon provides an appropriate analogy to the kind of theological judgments we must make when addressing the nature of Scripture, and specifically its authorship and our understanding of it.

According to the Chalcedonian Definition, Jesus Christ is "one person with two natures, hypostatically united without mixture, change, division, or separation." That is, he is fully divine and fully human, without either nature changing into or mixing with the other, and without separating the two natures to the extent that there are essentially two different persons rather than one. I believe we can

sociological groupings have been subordinated to a theological definition of what constitutes the people of God" (*Introduction to the Old Testament as Scripture*, 393).

25. On the limits of this analogy, see Prothro, "The Christological Analogy and Theological Interpretation." While I affirm that there are limits to this analogy, I am also not the first one to use it in a Protestant sense. See Mark Thompson's discussion of Martin Luther's use of this analogy in *A Sure Ground on Which to Stand*, 105–7.

state the dual authorship, and thus intention, of Scripture similarly: Scripture is one book with two authors, human and divine, written with the intention of both authors without mixture, change, division, or separation.

First, there is, for any passage of Scripture, both a fully human author and a fully divine author, the Holy Spirit. This means that, in a way analogous to the incarnation, every passage has two authors, much as Christ always has two natures. Further, each author, like each of Christ's natures, is not lacking any aspect of their nature with respect to their authorial intent. For the human authors of Scripture, this means that their human faculties and capacities were fully engaged in the writing process. For the divine author of Scripture, this means that his divine attributes remain unchanged in the authorship process, even while inspiring a human author who remains fully human in the process.

Second, neither the human author nor the divine author mixed or changed their humanity or divinity to accommodate the other. The human author's faculties and capacities were not overridden in the writing process. And God did not have to "turn off" his divine attributes in order to accommodate the fully human authorship of any given passage of Scripture. This is in accordance with what I said above regarding pneumatological kenoticism and the Creator-creature distinction.

All of this means that Scripture's meaning in any given passage is, at the same time, not reducible to the human author's finitude but also not disconnected from the human author's intent. To state it positively, the Holy Spirit's intent in any given passage is always intimately connected to the human author's intent but also not limited by the latter's finitude.[26]

It is in this way that the church could articulate a "spiritual sense" of Scripture, one that was tied to the details of the text and its historical setting but also that pointed through those historical realities to the reality of Jesus Christ, God the Son in the flesh. It is because the Holy Spirit, along with the Father and the Son, is omniscient that a

26. See Swain, *Trinity, Revelation, and Reading*, 65–71; Billings, *The Word of God for the People of God*, 31–70; Collett, *Figural Reading and the Old Testament*, 28–47.

particular text can be understood both in terms of its original intent for its original audience and also in terms of the Spirit's use of that historical reality to refer to something cosmic in scope: the economy of redemption. Both typology and intertextuality, in which interpreters note repetitive patterns between events and words, respectively, in particular texts, are rooted ultimately not only in literary repetition by human authors noting real patterns in history but ultimately in the omniscient providence of the triune God, who, through the economic mission of God the Holy Spirit, has ordered history and inspired the biblical text that records that history as repeating itself in a pattern that culminates in the person and work of Jesus Christ.

What I am saying about the relation between the divine author's intent and the human author's intent, then, is that they are the same, conveyed by the same words and yet distinguished by the kind of knowledge possessed by each: infinite and eternal according to the divine author, finite and temporal according to the human author. This does not pit them against each other, but rather allows them to work together in a non-zero-sum game (what is often called a "concursive" model of inspiration). On the divine side, if the (divine) author knows the ultimate referent of a particular text (and he does), then that is part of the intent of the text.

This is why the "what it means is what it meant" dictum is many times problematic, even if, on the face of it, we are simply attempting to convey commitment to understanding carefully the human author's intention. The problem arises not when we attempt to discern carefully what the human author meant according to his own time and context. Rather, the problem is that if "what it means is what it meant" limits the text's intentions *at the time of writing* to the finite consciousness of the human author, the text *cannot* have supervening divine intention *at the same time of writing*. That model requires an interpretive leap to bridge the gap between OT promise and NT fulfillment, and one that moves from "meaning" to something else (fulfillment, significance, etc.). Instead of arguing that one author, either human or divine, "wins" in the act of writing biblical texts and thus imbues the text with meaning that accords with the nature of the "winner," we should once again state clearly that the dual authorship of Scripture is not a zero-sum game. Instead, in ways that are analogous but not identical to the incarnation and Christ's two natures, the Spirit's intent and the human author's intent are one, but according to the distinct natures of each. To recall one of the main points of this chapter, this is why we can affirm the entire OT as "christological" in intent even while attending to the unique sociohistorical and redemptive-historical contexts of each of its human authors.

Excursus: Incarnational Analogies, Inspiration, and Inerrancy

This rather circumspect analogy to the incarnation in relation to the dual authorship of Scripture should be immediately distinguishable from other, more robust (but by no means more theologically accurate) "incarnational" models for Scripture. Saying that Scripture is fully human does not necessitate that it includes error. Alexander Pope observed that "to err is human," but that does not mean that to be human is inherently to err. Rather, it is to be finite. This is true both for the incarnation (thus allowing for Christ's impeccability) and for inscripturation (thus allowing for infallibility and, I would argue, inerrancy). To assume that "fully human" means "errant" is a category mistake, and one made frequently in this discussion. Perhaps most famously and influentially, this is how Karl Barth differentiates between "revelation" and "the Bible as witness to revelation."[27]

More recently, Peter Enns has made an analogy to the incarnation in his work on the nature of Scripture. For Enns, to acknowledge the human nature of Scripture's authorship is to attend to its historical particularities, including sociocultural analysis and the inherent linguistic and epistemic limitations of human (that is creaturely) authorship.[28] Perhaps on the surface

27. Barth, *Church Dogmatics* I/1, 111–20: "The unity of revelation guarantees the unity of the biblical witness in spite of all its multiplicity and even contradictoriness" (117). See, perhaps even more acutely, Barth, *Church Dogmatics* I/2, 506–14. Barth says, for instance, "We know what we say when we call the Bible the Word of God only when we recognize its human imperfection in [the] face of its divine perfection, and its divine perfection in spite of its human imperfection" (508). And: "The vulnerability of the Bible, i.e. its capacity for error, also extends to its religious or theological content" (509).

28. See Enns, *Inspiration and Incarnation*. Though not in exactly the same way, Kenton Sparks attempts to make a similar argument, describing his approach as one that "allows for accommodation of error in Scripture," based on theological and

this sounds rather innocuous, since many evangelicals are (and should be) interested in the historical particularities of the biblical text. The problem is that Enns makes at least two category errors in this analogy.

First, as I have already mentioned above, to be fully human is not to err; it is to be finite. In his initial foray into the subject, Enns stopped short of affirming the possibility of human error in the biblical material, but in later writings he has become increasingly clear that this is indeed entailed. For instance, in *The Bible Tells Me So*, Enns comments that "at times these stories of Jesus and Israel contradict each other." He says this without any qualms about positing both divine inspiration of the Bible and its inclusion of contradictions.[29]

Even more explicit is his essay in *Five Views on Biblical Inerrancy*, where he says,

> I do not think inerrancy can be effectively nuanced to account for the Bible's own behavior as a text produced in ancient cultures. . . . Indeed, despite its apparent interest in seeing God as so powerful that he can overrule ancient human error and ignorance, inerrancy portrays a weak view of God. It fails to be constrained by the Bible's own witness of God's pattern of working—that God's power is made known in weakness, he reigns amidst human error and suffering, and he lovingly condescends to finite human culture.[30]

Perhaps as a summary of this position one might say, as Enns seems to suggest, that error is not the same as sin.

To some degree this is correct. Answering a math problem incorrectly on an exam is not a sin. Calling someone "Mark" rather than "Matt" is not a sin. But those are not equivalent kinds of communication to what is happening in Scripture. The biblical authors over and over again claim of their own accord, about their own writings and previous biblical material, that Scripture gives a fully truthful (including historically accurate) account. Indeed, unlike other kinds of speech, God's speech given through the prophets and

---

epistemological categories for understanding what Scripture is. See Sparks, *God's Word in Human Words*, 354–55.

29. Enns, *The Bible Tells Me So*, 76.

30. Enns, "Inerrancy, However Defined, Does Not Describe What the Bible Does," 91. While Enns does not say in this quotation or the previous one that the Bible or any particular biblical passage is in error, he is still attempting to make room, from theological reasoning, for that conclusion.

> apostles can be trusted precisely because of its truthfulness, not merely in its overall ideas but in relation to what has actually happened in history and especially in the economy of God's redemption through Israel's Messiah. Contrary to Barth, Enns, and others, human nature is defined not by the event of the fall but by the purposes of God's will. While the former certainly affects human nature after the fall, God's providential, sanctifying, and redeeming grace can and does overcome the effects of the fall, restoring us to what we were created to be. So, not only does Enns make a category error about what it means to be human and what it means to err in truth-telling, but he also minimizes the biblical authors' own claims in relation to their truth-telling function.
>
> The second category error is related to his christological analogy, and it is analogous to a christological heresy, Nestorianism. By reducing human authorship to what is merely human, Enns (and others) has so separated the kinds of authorship of the Bible that we can no longer meaningfully speak of dual authorship. If meaning and speech are not only reducible but in actual fact reduced to the limited, finite, and (in theory, in Enns's view) erroneous view of the human author, then the Spirit's authorship is ancillary and extraneous. It is another intention altogether. It is thus akin to Nestorianism in that the two natures of Christ are separated and divided to such an extent that we can longer meaningfully speak of one person.

We will return to this issue in chapter 8, but for now it is simply important to note the intricate interwovenness of divine and human intention in the text of Scripture.[31] The Spirit's intent is not divorced from the human author's intent, but neither is the Spirit's intent reducible to the human author's because intention in this dual authorship model is not a zero-sum game. The "spiritual sense," then, is not a wax nose either, because intention, akin to the hypostatic union (but not completely analogous to it), is not Nestorian. Just as

31. An issue we will not address here is whether or not the human authors of the biblical text were consciously aware of the Spirit's inspiration, or, in other words, aware that they were writing Scripture. For my part, I agree with Michael Kruger that the human authors of Scripture were consciously aware of their inspiration by the Spirit and thus of the authoritative—i.e., canonical—status of their writings. See Kruger, *Canon Revisited*, 184–94; Kruger, *The Question of Canon*, 119–54. Alternatively, see, for instance, Lee McDonald's interaction with Kruger in his *The Formation of the Biblical Canon*, 2:12–13.

the person of Jesus Christ cannot be split into two persons, one for each nature, so the text of Scripture cannot be separated or divided into "human intent versus divine intent." The human and divine intentions exist without separation or division but also without mixture or change. This is because, to use a christological analogy again, there is one intention with two authors, divine and human, at work in a compatible way and without competition with each other, much as in the one person of Christ there are two wills, one for each nature, at work in a compatible way and without competition with each other.

To bring this all together, we can happily affirm the christological intent of any given passage because we know that the Spirit intends to testify to the Son according to his (the Spirit's) divine mission. And we can do so without fretting over whether this subverts, contravenes, or ignores the human author's intent, because the divine and the human authors' modes of knowledge expressed in textual intention are not in competition or tension with each other.[32]

The same is true, mutatis mutandis, of literary phenomena such as typology and intertextuality. We can readily acknowledge these in Scripture because the divine author, who is omniscient and omnipotent, is always at work in the inspiration of the human author. Even if we cannot prove empirically that a human author had a particular intertextual referent in mind (and how would we verify an author's internal, conscious thoughts?), or a particular type, or a particular christological sense (and, often, all three of these amount to the same thing), we can have confidence that there is one divine author, the Holy Spirit, who has providentially ordered the text of Scripture to

32. While we have focused our attention thus far on acknowledging the Spirit's divine, and therefore omniscient, intention, it is important to maintain the equal acknowledgment of the human author's creaturely, and therefore cognitively finite, intention *in a way that does not pit them against each other*. So, for instance, while Bruce Waltke and Charles Yu admirably emphasize both the Spirit's divine attributes in the act of inspiration and the triune God's intent to reveal himself through Jesus Christ in the entire biblical text, they also seem to put these affirmations in tension, at least hypothetically, with the human author's limited cognitive capacity (Waltke and Yu, *An Old Testament Theology*, 46–48, and esp. p. 48: "Consequently, if there is any tension between Christ and his apostles versus the original author [of an OT text], Christ and his apostles have priority. Our task is to understand and to accept both as the Word of God, while giving the final word to Christ and his apostles").

be intricately connected both literarily, typologically, and christologically through his inspiration of the human authors. The Spirit's intent—in intertextuality, typology, and Christocentric reading, for example—is never divorced from the human author's, but neither is it reducible to what was in the human author's mind at the time (as if we could even know that).

The Spirit and the Canon

The Spirit's work in inspiration, including both the words and the intentions of the human author, applies to the question of canon in at least two ways.

The Spirit and Canonical Boundaries

First, the Spirit's inspiration, as the mode of God's inscripturated revelation of himself to his people, is the sine qua non criterion for canonicity. To declare that a book is canonical is, at root, to recognize it as inspired by the Holy Spirit. To declare that a book is not canonical is to say that it is not inspired by the Holy Spirit. Canonical boundaries are boundaries of inspiration.

This is why it is important to recognize, as we did in chapter 2, that the biblical text itself articulates this boundary in Deuteronomy 12 and Revelation 22. The command "Do not add to or take away" anything from this book is a command concerning canonical boundaries. And while there is a material reality to this—writings subsequent to Deuteronomy, including the NT, are literarily, historically, and theologically connected to Deuteronomy—that material reality is grounded in a more fundamental one: the reality of the triune God's revelation of himself in the Spirit-inspired text of Scripture.

Decisions about deuterocanonical, disputed, and apocryphal books are therefore not simply decisions made by sifting through empirical data. Rather, they are an attempt at spiritual discernment—namely, the discernment of the Spirit's voice in the text of what truly is Holy Scripture. There are material realities that help us adjudicate that question: literary phenomena such as intertextuality and historical phenomena such as lists, manuscripts, and so on. But, ultimately, the question is whether or not the Spirit testifies to the Son in a particular text. That is the primary, fundamental question.

As we've noted already in the previous two chapters, there are examples of such examinations and, ultimately, decisions regarding canonical boundaries readily available, such as the treatment of apocryphal gospels and apocalypses from the first few centuries of the church's life.[33] In this sense, this chapter on the Spirit's activity in inspiration is another angle from which to say what I've already said: Canonical boundaries are the limits set by God's own revelation of himself in Scripture. This is not to say that the Spirit is not at work in any other proclamation of God's word to his people, but it is to say that Scripture, as defined and delimited in the biblical canon, is unique in the kind of work the Spirit is doing in it.

The Spirit and Canonical Form

But there is a second way in which the focus of this chapter impinges upon our understanding of canonical decisions and phenomena. The Spirit's inspiration of the biblical text informs the issue of composition, and with respect to at least two compositional categories: intertextuality and the text's "final form."

The Spirit and (Inter)Textual Realities

The Spirit's inspiration of the text both constrains and releases the conversation about intertextuality. On the one hand, acknowledging the Spirit-inspired nature of the text means that we must give attention to "the way the words go."[34] The Spirit does not speak apart from the human authors, but rather speaks through them and their own individual creative literary endeavors and within their own sociohistorical

33. For treatment of these books from historical, literary, and/or theological perspectives, see Bovon, *New Testament and Christian Apocrypha*, esp. 161–288. See also, more recently and including treatment of both NT and OT apocrypha and pseudepigrapha, Collins et al., *Ancient Jewish and Christian Scriptures*.

34. This phrase is found in various synonyms among early church exegetes, and refers to examining the historical and literary details of the text; see, for instance, Cyril of Alexandria's reference to the importance of the "sequencing of ideas" in his preface to his commentary on Hosea (*Commentary on the Twelve Prophets*, 1:28).

context. The lexical, grammatical, genre-related literary details of the text remain important to understanding the author's intention, as does the author's sociocultural background, because the text's intention is conveyed through both the human author's mode of knowledge and the Spirit's. In this way, the Spirit's intention is not divorced from the human author's intention, but instead the two are one, distinguished by modes of knowledge, and this one intention is found in the details of the text.

This matters for our understanding of intertextuality. Intertextual phenomena can and should be traced to the intent of the human author as conveyed through textual details.[35] G. K. Beale, for instance, has labored for decades to demonstrate that the inner-biblical allusions we find in both the Old and New Testaments are intentional and appropriate given the intertextual referent's intent at the time of writing.[36] In other words, we can and should demonstrate that the human author's intent in making an intertextual allusion is both truly present and also in accordance with the previous human author's intent.

But acknowledging the Spirit's inspiration of the text releases us from constricting the conversation on intertextuality in at least two ways. First, we are not restricted only to reading backwards.[37] Another way to say this is that intertextuality is not merely a phenomenon of textual reception. Exploration of and discussions about intertextuality are often constricted to what the human authors could have consciously intended at the time, at the level both of the later author who quotes an earlier text and of the earlier author who wrote the text being quoted or alluded to by the later

35. For a recent treatment of intertextuality from the perspective of methodological approaches to identifying and understanding instances of it, see Schnittjer and Harmon, *How to Study the Bible's Use of the Bible*.

36. See, e.g., Beale and Carson, *Commentary on the New Testament Use of the Old Testament*; Beale et al., *Dictionary of the New Testament Use of the Old Testament*; Beale, *The Right Doctrine from the Wrong Texts?*; Beale, *Handbook on the New Testament Use of the Old Testament*; Beale, *A New Testament Biblical Theology*.

37. While the phrase "reading backwards" is commonly associated with Richard Hays (*Reading Backwards*), I use it here not as a reference to or critique of his work, but instead as a reference to the kind of reading and approach to intertextuality I am describing.

author.[38] This is true both for those who affirm Scripture's complete truthfulness and for those who do not. The former focus attention on showing how later intertextual referents to earlier biblical texts treat the earlier text in accordance with its human author's original intent, while the latter often want to show divergences between intents of the two (or more) human authors.

This conversation has become quite sophisticated over the last few decades or so, with a wide variety of scholars attempting to bring all available tools to the question, including newly popular canonical and literary ones. Two examples of this vast conversation—but ones that I hope represent, in different ways, approaches I have been describing in this chapter—are found in the works of G. K. Beale[39] and Robert Wall.[40] Each of them handles Matthew's quotation of Hosea 11:1 (Matt. 2:14–15) by bringing Hosea's own narrative and canonical context—including its own intertextual allusions—to the table. And each, in different ways, attempts to explain how Hosea's own context and intent can be said to preview the events of Matthew 2. Beale, in his careful attention to the details of Hosea 11 as well as its canonical context, provides a rationale to understand Matthew's quotation as exegetically warranted according to Hosea's own contextually situated (human) intention. (Wall is less concerned with this aim.) In both cases, however different their approaches, both Beale and Wall want to understand the intent of each text according to the human author's textually discerned conscious intent. For Beale, Matthew is exegetically warranted to do so, while for Wall, the exegetical warrant in Hosea 11:1 is suspect, even if he can still make sense of Matthew's citation from within the latter's own context. The point is, to state it once more but slightly differently, that both authors attempt to explain an instance of intertextuality with reference to the cognitive field of the human authors in question. And, to be clear, from our perspective, *attending carefully to human authorial intent in consideration of intertextuality is vitally important*. We should

38. See, e.g., parts 3–5 of Beale, *The Right Doctrine from the Wrong Texts?*, which are titled "Did the New Testament Authors Respect the Context of the Old Testament Text?" followed by a subtitle specific to each part (134–312).

39. Beale, "The Use of Hosea 11:1 in Matthew 2:15."

40. Wall, *Studies in Canonical Criticism*, 7–20.

never take our eyes off "the way the words go."[41] In the case of Beale's work and similar projects, attending to the *harmony* of the human authors' intentions in instances of intertextual resonances helps us both to engender confidence in the Bible's truthfulness and authority and also to understand the meaning of the biblical text.[42]

The challenge is with limiting the intentionality behind a particular intertextual reference *to the later human author's conscious (empirically demonstrable) use of an earlier text*. Intertextuality can only go one way—backward—in this view. To put this in terms of Matthew and Hosea, this approach would say that Matthew appropriately picks up Hosea's text by looking backward to it, but that there is no exegetical warrant for understanding Hosea 11:1 as pointing forward to the events of Matthew 2. Even if we agree with Beale and others (and I do) that Hosea is looking forward to Israel's salvation in Hosea 11:1, and therefore that Matthew is warranted in citing it in Matthew 2, many remain reluctant to say that *the intention in Hosea 11:1 includes its intertextual resonance with Matthew 2*. Intertextuality, in other words, is a backward-looking phenomenon, a benefit of hindsight, rather than something that works both backward and forward. But when we take into account the Spirit's intention in any given biblical text, intertextuality can *and must* be read forward as well. Earlier biblical texts are not merely used by later biblical authors; they intentionally point forward to that future use, by the Spirit and through the human author's intent. The Spirit *knows* that Hosea 11:1 points forward to Matthew 2, and it does so in accord with Hosea's own original forward-looking intent in that passage.

Hosea's original intent includes, ultimately, pointing forward to Israel's new exodus, realized in its coming Messiah, an intention that points beyond its own context and to its fulfillment in the person and work of Jesus Christ. Or, to say it slightly differently, Hosea knows

41. As mentioned in n. 34, this phrase was commonly used in the early church to acknowledge the literal sense's importance and role in interpretation. For examples of typological reading in the early church that give attention to the theological foundations we are covering in this chapter, see Boersma, *Scripture as Real Presence*, 81–104.

42. In this respect, Beale's *Handbook on the New Testament Use of the Old Testament* is among the most philosophically sophisticated, exegetically rigorous, and theologically sound works on the subject.

that, in Hosea 11:1, he is looking forward to Israel's Messiah, who brings the new exodus. He just doesn't know that the person he is looking for is Jesus of Nazareth, or that Jesus's coming up "out of Egypt" will be caused by Herod's persecution under the guise of Roman rule. Hosea is pointing forward to "the time and person" of the Messiah, even if he does not consciously know either detail. The Holy Spirit *also* intends for this passage to look forward to Israel's coming Messiah, who will bring the new exodus, and he *already knows* that that person is Jesus of Nazareth, who will be born of the virgin, Mary, and suffer under Pontius Pilate.

So, while the human author can only "look for the time and person in which the Messiah would come" (1 Pet. 1:10–12), the Holy Spirit knows it is Jesus of Nazareth—and knows that *at the time of the writing of Hosea* (cf. 2 Pet. 1:20–21).[43] We cannot and should not reduce the divine author's intent to the consciousness of the human author; that is pneumatological kenoticism. Instead, we should affirm that intertextual references are intended *both ways*—that is, *forward and backward*. The Holy Spirit, through the human author's intent, intends to point forward to a particular text's continuation and/or fulfillment in a later text. Likewise, the Holy Spirit intends the author of that later text to demonstrate the fulfillment of the earlier text.[44] Or, as Christopher Seitz poetically and forcefully puts

43. So Work, *Living and Active*, 58:

> Augustine's affirmation of divine authorial intent should be taken neither as a denial of human authorial intent in the Scriptures, nor as an equation of the human and divine intents. The two overlap but are not identical. . . . Scripture arises through human authorial intentions; yet God superintends those in such a way that neither "original" authorial intentions nor later reinterpretations ever limit its meaning. Augustine's proposal is a brilliant way to interpret 2 Peter 1:20–21, which has misled so many bibliologians into endorsing a kind of biblical monothelitism that denies all human intentionality in the inspiration of Scripture.

While Work emphasizes the denial of human intent as a kind of "biblical monothelitism," here I want to say that the opposite can be and is a problem in biblical studies: the overemphasis of the human author's intent to the point that divine intent is denied or at least negligible in the discussion of meaning. See also Carter, *Interpreting Scripture with the Great Tradition*, 40.

44. On the relation between human authorial intent and divine authorial intent, with attention given to figuration, canon consciousness, intertextuality, typology,

it, "The One who inspired Israel's Scriptures is the One who raised Jesus from the dead."[45]

Richard Lints, among others, has described such an acknowledgment of the Spirit's unified authorship of the whole canon in both its overall story and its intertextual interconnectivity as a "redemptive-historical, canonical" hermeneutic.[46] Whatever we wish to call it, we are simply acknowledging the divine author's superintending, inspiring intent throughout the canon of Scripture and in "the way the words go" of each human author. To attempt to separate the Scripture-inspiring Spirit's omniscient knowledge from the Israelite or early Christian human author's limited knowledge, and, further, to rule in favor of the latter as the only factor in authorial intent, is to put asunder what God has joined together in the authorship of Holy Scripture.

The Spirit, Intertextuality, and Scripture's Final Form

Once we establish this connection between the divine author's intent and the human author's use of intertextuality as an intentional literary device, we can talk about the canon's organic development and its final form. We need to acknowledge both the divine author's and the human author's intention to grow the canon textually through the means of intertextuality.

The canon's organic growth can be seen from multiple vantage points. One way this happens is through allusions and echoes within a particular book that advance that book's narrative or remind readers

---

and allegory—in other words, the relation between the literal sense and the figural sense—see Vanhoozer, *Mere Christian Hermeneutics*, 105–92. See also Collett, *Figural Reading and the Old Testament*, 25–60.

45. Seitz, *Word Without End*, 16.

46. See Lints, *The Fabric of Theology*, 294–95. See also the discussion of this approach, with implications for understanding intertextuality and typology, in Barrett, *Canon, Covenant, and Christology*, 24–37, with discussion of Lints's categories on p. 37. Note also Beale's comment that "if we assume the legitimacy of an inspired canon, then we should seek to interpret any part of the canon within its overall canonical context (given that one divine mind stands behind it all and expresses its thoughts in logical fashion)" (Beale, "Did Jesus and His Followers Preach the Right Doctrine from the Wrong Texts?," 401).

of previous material.[47] For instance, in Genesis, the narrative of Adam's creation and fall is echoed in the story of Abra(ha)m. God's promises to Abraham in Genesis 12, 15, 17, and 21 allude to God's intentions for Adam to be fruitful and multiply as God's image bearer, work and keep the land that God gave to him, subdue and have dominion over God's place, and obey God's word. Abraham's fall, when he "listened to the voice of Sarai" (Gen. 16:2), also echoes Adam's own fall, when he "listened to the voice of [his] wife" (Gen. 3:17). In this way (and others), Moses[48] portrays Abraham as a new Adam, both in terms of God's promises to him and in terms of Abraham's fall into sin.

This, along with the Noahic parallels to Adam, is thematic repetition that serves to heighten the anticipation for the expected "seed of woman" (Gen. 3:15), the one who will destroy the serpent and restore what Adam lost. This expectation, as well as the repeated theme of a "new Adam," runs like a thread through Genesis and thus serves to tie the various narratives together and give them a *telos* (final goal or purpose). We will return to this eschatological aspect of typology and its implication for canon in chapter 7. For now, it is important simply to say that the inner-biblical allusions between Genesis 1–3 and the rest of the book serve to bind it together as a whole.[49] And, for the purposes of this chapter, this organic, intertextual growth of

47. We should note that this literary growth is also oriented historically, i.e., throughout the history of Israel: "The discipline of Old Testament theology derives from theological reflection on a received body of scripture whose formation was the result of a lengthy history of development. The process began in the early pre-exilic period of Israel's history and extended through the final structuring by the Jewish synagogue during the Hellenistic era. Central to its history was a hermeneutical activity which continued to shape the material theologically in order to render it accessible to future generations of believers" (Childs, *Old Testament Theology in a Canonical Context*, 6).

48. I realize not every reader will take this attribution of Mosaic authorship as credible. While I affirm Mosaic authorship, the claims being made in this section do not stand or fall on the reader's agreement with that assessment. For a treatment of the authorship of the Pentateuch that is attendant to historical-critical arguments while still affirming Mosaic authorship, see Sailhamer, *The Meaning of the Pentateuch*, 48–56, 283–354.

49. On the relation between Adam, Abra(ha)m, and Israel, and the implications of that historical, literary, and theological relationship on the composition and shape of the Torah, see Postell, "Abram as Israel, Israel as Abram."

Genesis is attributable both to the intent of its human author, Moses, and to the Holy Spirit.

This organic growth continues with the other books in the Torah.[50] Moses's basket of reeds is made using the same stuff ("bitumen and pitch," Exod. 2:3) as Noah's ark (Gen. 6:14), for instance. Israel's story in Exodus and Numbers is the story of Adam, Abraham, and Israel. The laws of Exodus, Leviticus, and Deuteronomy are intended to prepare Israel to dwell with God as Adam did in the garden and to propel them toward success in their calling to have dominion, be fruitful and multiply, and cultivate and keep in the promised land.

Of course, both in the Torah (in Exod. 15–19 and 32–34, as well as in Num. 11 and following) and in its later story, Israel, like Adam and Abraham, fails at this task. But the point here is that the very language used to describe Adam in Genesis 1–3, for instance, is repeated in Noah's and Abraham's and Israel's life. In this way, the human author intends the Torah to grow organically—that is, textually, and in accordance with the intent of the omniscient divine author. As new events and places and people are described, they are described with language from earlier stories and material. And because the omniscient divine author knows the Torah's ultimate christological *telos*, he inspires the human author to write such organically interconnected and eschatologically oriented material from the latter's own sociohistorical context and with an intent that takes that context into account. The organic growth of the Torah, in other words, is intended by both the human and the divine author, and in ways that account for the mode of knowing of each.

Throughout the rest of the biblical canon, we see the same kind of organic growth, via continued intertextual allusions to previous material.[51] The so-called Deuteronomistic History, Joshua through Kings (and excluding Ruth), continually refers back to Deuteronomy,

50. On the organic growth of the Bible, including discussion of some of the OT examples used in this paragraph and the surrounding paragraphs, see Shepherd, *An Introduction to the Making and Meaning of the Bible*, 3–25, 70–133. On canon consciousness in the OT in relation to that organic growth, see Chapman, "'The Law and the Words.'"

51. On a "core canon," see Chapman, "Brevard Childs as Historical Critic"; Chapman, "The Canon Debate."

as well as to the rest of the Torah, to interpret the events of Israel's life between their entry into and exile from the promised land. And the Latter Prophets and the Writings also continually allude to and echo both the Torah and the Former Prophets.[52]

The NT's declaration that Jesus of Nazareth is the fulfillment of God's promises to Israel and to the world culminates the organic growth of the biblical canon. The same Spirit who spoke through Israel's prophets now declares through Christ's apostles that Jesus is Israel's Messiah, the world's Savior.[53] The narratives of the Gospels and Acts are intertextual tapestries that constantly allude to Israel's Scriptures in order to demonstrate who Jesus is.[54] The epistles repeatedly quote and allude to the OT in order to show how the church has been grafted into the people of God through the person and work of Jesus Christ by his Spirit. John's Revelation is an intricate web of textual and figural allusions to the OT prophets that paints a picture of the people of God in the last days, eagerly awaiting Christ's return in glory to judge and restore. The entire Bible is thus a textual tapestry of organic growth, intended by each human author from within their own individual contexts and also by the divine author, who superintends the whole book from his own divine omniscience. These are not mutually exclusive categories; rather, intertextuality is a particular canonical phenomenon that demonstrates the inherent unity of Scripture. The Bible's organically developed intertextual tapestry is intended by both the human authors and the divine author to convey the unity of Scripture at historical, literary, and conceptual

52. See Seitz, *The Goodly Fellowship of the Prophets*, 77–103; Seitz, "Scriptural Authority and Canonical Prophet"; Dempster, "Torah, Torah, Torah."

53. Didymus the Blind, *On the Holy Spirit*, sections 7 (p. 145), 197–98 (pp. 203–4), 203–5 (p. 206).

54. For an in-depth study of the organic growth of the NT, see Brodie, *The Birthing of the New Testament*. While I do not agree with Brodie on a host of historical and interpretive issues, his work still includes one of the most rigorous attempts to trace the intertextual tapestry that comprises the NT. See also, with respect to the Gospels in particular, Watson, *Gospel Writing*. Although I disagree with some of Watson's conclusions (e.g., regarding the motivation for certain Gospel writers), he carefully demonstrates the textual interdependence and individual uniqueness of the four canonical Gospels. See also Hengel, *The Four Gospels and the One Gospel of Jesus Christ*.

levels, a unity that centers on the person and work of Israel's Messiah, Jesus Christ.

Conclusion

In this way, intertextuality is both a sign of canonicity and canon's end. That is, a sign of a book's canonicity is whether or not it is intertextually connected with previous biblical material. To put it more positively, a book is canonical in part because its authors, human and divine, intended to connect textually to previous Scripture. This is, in turn, related to the second canonical purpose of intertextuality: It is a sign of the canon's end or *telos*. All the intertextual webs that I have described find their *telos* in the narratives of the Gospels and Acts, the climax and center of the biblical canon.[55] Intertextuality is thus a canonical phenomenon that is firmly and creatively centered on the person and work of Jesus Christ.

55. In this way, the Gospels can be said to be the "archway" of the canon; see Pennington, *Reading the Gospels Wisely*, 229–58.

FIVE

The Ruled Canon and the Cosmos: Creation and Canon

History consistently looks like Jesus.

—Ephraim Radner[1]

The Old Testament's figural witness to Christ depends on the doctrine of providence inherent to its self-witness. . . . The LORD's providential ordering of history is the authorizing context in which Old Testament prophecy speaks a word to the future generations, as well as to the people of its own day. Its christological efficacy depends not on human cognition but on the providential and figural links the LORD establishes between the Word of Old Testament promise and the Word made flesh in time.[2]

—Don Collett

1. Radner, *Time and the Word*, 34.

2. Collett, *Figural Reading and the Old Testament*, 3. Note that by the phrase "depends not on human cognition," Collett is not denying the human authors' ability to intend figuration, but rather fronting the theological truth claim that typology and figuration are ultimately grounded in God's providence.

As a revelatory document, the canon is both from God and not God. Canonicity is first a function of trinitarian mission (chaps. 2–4), but it is secondarily a function of the order of creation. The interpretive means by which we see the canon's Christocentrism—intertextuality, typology, and allegory—are possible because creation itself is Christocentric, or *Logos*-centric, as Maximus the Confessor would put it. All of creation derives its being and orderliness from the eternal Word, the Word that the Father speaks and breathes by his Spirit at creation. The canon exists as a unified textual document because it participates in the orderliness of creation and in the *Logos* who gives and maintains order.

Creation, Providence, and the Economy of the Triune God

In order to situate the text of Scripture within the order of creation, we first need to summarize the doctrines of creation and providence. We will do this by considering four elements of these theological loci. Attention to the trinitarian missions (subsection 1 below) and the economy of redemption (subsection 2 below) provides fundamental avenues for understanding God's creation and providence. After working through these two foundational contexts, we will then consider the *Logos*-centric nature of creation (subsection 3 below), as well as how to understand God's providence in relation to what's been said to that point about the trinitarian missions, the economy of redemption, and the *Logos*-centric nature of creation.

Economy as Trinitarian Mission

The economy of creation and redemption is the double act of the mission of the triune God. God's purpose in the economy is, ultimately, to bring glory to himself. But secondarily and in accordance with this primary goal, he also purposes to reveal himself to his creatures and bring them into relationship with him. In creation, this occurs as he dwells with his image bearers, human beings, Adam and Eve. He gives them a law to keep and tasks to perform. Those tasks include being fruitful and multiplying, cultivating and keeping the garden, and subduing God's creation under God's rule. He thus reveals himself and places himself in relation to his creatures through his presence with them and his proclamation of his word to them.

We need to be clear, before moving on to the rest of the biblical storyline, that the whole of creation is oriented toward these purposes. The shape of creation itself is oriented toward God dwelling with his people in his place. Genesis 1 makes this clear in the pattern of creation, in which God first makes what you might call the "containers" of creation—the sky, the sea, and the land—and then subsequently fills them with his creatures: birds, fish, animals and insects, and, ultimately, human beings, God's image bearers. The centerpieces of God's creation, then, are the land and the humans, his place and his people.

Everything else I will say below hinges on this point. God created the world with a particular purpose: to dwell with his people, his image bearers, in his place, the land. To what end is all of creation ordered? All creation is ordered toward God revealing himself to and living in relationship with his people in his place.

The Economy of Redemption and Centrality of Christ's Person and Work

Adam and Eve do not obey God's word, though, and they are thus exiled from God's presence in the garden. Although God revealed himself to them and placed himself in relationship with them, they choose created things over their Creator and thereby usher death—physical and spiritual—into the world. Physical death removes human beings from the place of God's dwelling, the land, and spiritual death removes them from dwelling in loving relationship with him. In response to their sin, God does not abandon his people, though. Instead, he covenants with them to redeem them through the "seed of woman" (Gen. 3:15). In this covenant of redemption, God promises to redeem all that Adam lost. We see this especially in the covenant he makes with Abraham, when he promises, in addition to bringing the seed through Abraham's line, to give Abraham a land, to give him many descendants, and to bring kings from his line. These promises are promises to do what Adam and Eve did not and to restore what they lost. Thus, like creation and in restoration of it, redemption is ordered toward God dwelling with his people in his place. This is accomplished through the first coming of Christ and consummated at his return.

The Logos*-centric Nature of Creation and Redemption*

This mention of Jesus's person and work brings us to God's crucial and central work of creation and redemption, and thus, derivatively, to the crucial point of this chapter. As we've noted above, everything in God's good creation testifies to and is ordered toward his revelation of himself to his people and his dwelling in relationship with them. But there is an even more succinct way to put this: Everything in creation testifies to and is ordered toward the *Logos*, God the Word, the Wisdom of God by whom and for whom and through whom all things were made.

Paul's hymnic description of Jesus in Colossians 1:15–20 gives us much of the biblical language we need to make this point:

> He [God's "beloved Son," v. 14] is the image of the invisible God, the firstborn of all creation. For by him all things were created, in heaven and on earth, visible and invisible, whether thrones or dominions or rulers or authorities—all things were created through him and for him. And he is before all things, and in him all things hold together. And he is the head of the body, the church. He is the beginning, the firstborn from the dead, that in everything he might be preeminent. For in him all the fullness of God was pleased to dwell, and through him to reconcile to himself all things, whether on earth or in heaven, making peace by the blood of his cross.

Notice the two halves of Paul's description: creation in verses 15–17 and redemption in verses 18–20. Jesus Christ, God the Son in the flesh, is at the center of both acts of the triune God's economic mission. Regarding creation, "all things" were made by him, and through him, and for him (v. 16). It is also he who holds all things together (v. 17). God the Son, along with the Father and Spirit, is creation's maker.

Here, though, Paul wants to appropriate creation and its providential care to God the Son particularly, as well as creation's *telos* or end. He does so because he is highlighting the Son's unique status as "the image of the invisible God," a phrase that applies in this case particularly to the incarnation but that also is reflective of the Son's eternal begottenness from the Father. (The divine missions reflect the divine processions.) It is this Image who is the center of God's work of creation, as the one by whom and through whom and for whom all things were made and in whom all things hold together, who is also the center of God's work of redemption, as the one who took on flesh, died on a cross, rose from the dead, and gifted his Spirit to his body, the church. Through this Image, creation is united in its purpose and new creation is united in its end. To say, then, that creation is *Logos*-centric is simply a way to summarize Paul's point in Colossians 1:15–20.

Other texts make this explicit as well. For instance, the writer of Hebrews opens his address with these words: "Long ago, at many times and in many ways, God spoke to our fathers by the prophets, but in these last days he has spoken to us by his Son, whom he appointed the heir of all things, through whom also he created the world. He is the radiance of the glory of God and the exact imprint of his nature, and he upholds the universe by the word of his power" (Heb. 1:1–3a). Much like Paul in Colossians, the writer to the Hebrews emphasizes God's creation of the world through his Son, as well as the Son's activity in creation's providential, sustaining care ("he upholds the universe by the word of his power"). And, like Paul, the author ties this explicitly to the Son's status as God's Image (v. 3a). Because God the Son is the Image ("he is the radiance of the glory of God and the exact imprint of his nature") of God the Father, it is through the Son that God the Father made the world. Because God the Son is the Image of God the Father, it is by the word of the Son's power that the world is upheld. His authority as Son, along with his other divine attributes, is inherently and eternally communicated to him from his Father, who, along with the Spirit of the Father and the Son, is the one God. But here the point is not merely to note this text's importance for trinitarian theology; instead, we want to draw out explicitly the connection between the Son's status as the Father's Image and his status as the centering point of God's economic works of creation and redemption.

Again, we see the same sort of thing in the Prologue to John's Gospel: "In the beginning was the Word, and the Word was with God, and the Word was God. He was in the beginning with God. All things were made through him, and without him was not any thing made that was made. In him was life, and the life was the light of men. The light shines in the darkness, and the darkness has not overcome it" (John 1:1–5). God the Son, this time named by John "the Word," is God with God and, along with the Father (and the Spirit), made "all things" at creation. John, like Paul and the writer to the Hebrews, uses the same prepositional phrase, "through him," to describe the Son's activity at creation. It is through the Son, the Word, that all things were made. This is, of course, reflective of the creation account of Genesis 1, in which God makes all things on each successive day *through* speaking his *Word*. He is both creation's mode and its end, as well as the center of its redemption, as the life and light of men.

Each of these NT texts, along with others I have not mentioned (e.g., 1 Cor. 8:6), indicates that creation happens *through* the Son and is therefore in one sense *Logos*-centric. They are each reflective of OT teaching, and in that respect there is perhaps no more important text to cite than Proverbs 8:22–31.

> The Lord possessed me at the beginning of his work,
> the first of his acts of old.
> Ages ago I was set up,
> at the first, before the beginning of the earth.
> When there were no depths I was brought forth,
> when there were no springs abounding with water.
> Before the mountains had been shaped,
> before the hills, I was brought forth,
> before he had made the earth with its fields,
> or the first of the dust of the world.
> When he established the heavens, I was there;
> when he drew a circle on the face of the deep,
> when he made firm the skies above,
> when he established the fountains of the deep,
> when he assigned to the sea its limit,
> so that the waters might not transgress his command,

> when he marked out the foundations of the earth,
> then I was beside him, like a master workman,
> and I was daily his delight,
> rejoicing before him always,
> rejoicing in his inhabited world
> and delighting in the children of man.

Once again, we see the same themes arise. Wisdom is the one we have been calling "the Son" and "the Word," for Jesus, the Word in the flesh, is "the power of God and the wisdom of God" (1 Cor. 1:24). And this Wisdom is with God before creation, because Wisdom is God with God (vv. 22, 25); Wisdom creates all things with God, because Wisdom is God with God (v. 30); and Wisdom is God's delight, the one through him he makes all things (vv. 30–31). Wisdom pervades creation in this text (and other texts about the orderliness of creation) because God creates all things through his Wisdom, the Word, God the Son. This is yet another way that creation is *Logos*-centric: It is centered on the Word because it was made by and through the Word, but it is also centered on the Word because the Word is Wisdom and Wisdom provides orderliness, *logic*, to creation.

Maximus the Confessor puts it this way:

> [The Logos of God the Father] is the beginning and cause of all things *in whom all things were created, in heaven and on earth, visible and invisible, whether thrones or dominions or principalities or authorities—all things were created from him and through him and for him* (Col. 1:15–17; Rom. 11:36). Because he held together in himself the *logoi* before they came to be, by his gracious will he created all things visible and invisible out of non-being. *By his Word and by his Wisdom he made all things* and is making all things, universals as well as particulars, at the proper time. . . . The Logos whose excellence is incomparable, ineffable and inconceivable in himself is exalted beyond all creation and even beyond the idea of difference and distinction. This same Logos, whose goodness is revealed and multiplied in all the things that have their origin in him, with the degree of beauty appropriate to each being, *recapitulates all things in himself* (Eph. 1:10). Through this Logos there came to be both being and continuing to be, for from him the things that were made came to be in a certain

> way and for a certain reason, and by continuing to be and by moving, they participate in God.[3]

In this section Maximus repeatedly refers to created things as *logoi* to communicate the idea that all of creation is centered on and grounded in the *Logos*, God the Son, God's Word and Wisdom. Creation receives its orderliness and orientation from the Word (order) and Wisdom (orientation) of God the Son, and so creation is ordered and oriented toward that same Son.

There are still a few other things to be said about creation, but here I should start to tie this theological point together with what I want to say about Scripture and its canonical phenomena. Scripture too is a created entity, and, as part of God's creation, it is fundamentally ordered toward and centered around the *Logos*.[4] This is true holistically and conceptually, but it is also true at the level of its creaturely features—that is, the text itself, the very words that compose it.

Before we explore this in further detail, though, we need to discuss one other aspect of the doctrine of creation, God's providence over it, and note its center in the person and work of Christ as well.

The Triune God's Providential Ordering of Creation's History

God's work in creation includes not only making all things but also providentially ordering them toward their end. As I've said above, the end of creation is God's revelation of himself to his people, with whom he dwells in the place he has made for them. This means that history itself—the sequence of events from creation to new creation—is ordered toward that same end.

Rather than being a series of random, chaotic, unrelated events, history has a particular goal or end point: the redemption of God's creation through the person and work of Christ. In this sense, history culminates in the events of God's work of salvation in Jesus, from his incarnation all the way to his return but particularly in his

3. Maximus the Confessor, "Ambiguum 7," 54–55.

4. For a recent exploration of this concept in light of philosophical and theological metaphysics, and from a Roman Catholic perspective, see Betz, *Christ, the Logos of Creation*, esp. 461–69 for a brief summary.

death and resurrection. In one sense, then, Jesus's life, death, and resurrection are the midpoint of history, the centrifugal force, so to speak, around which all other events—past, present, and future—are ordered.[5] In another sense, the entirety of the Son's mission—from incarnation all the way to his return—is the end of history. Both of these christological realities are the historical, providential, textual, and ultimately theological grounds for typology and figuration.[6]

We have already explored the christological nature of the biblical narrative in an earlier chapter, so we do not need to belabor this point. We do need to be clear, however, that the christological centrality of the biblical narrative is grounded fundamentally in the christological centrality of all of providentially ordered history. The person and work of Jesus Christ are the midpoint and endpoint of history, and therefore he and his work are also the midpoint and endpoint of Holy Scripture.[7] To put as fine a point on this as possible: Scripture, as a created thing, like all other created things, is oriented toward creation's center and its end, the person and work of Christ.

But Scripture is not just any created thing; it is the terminus of God's revelation of himself via created things. The ultimate revelation of the triune God is the person and work of Jesus, God the Son in the flesh, the Incarnate Lord, who is fully God and fully human. And, while Scripture's divine inspiration is in some ways analogous to the incarnation, these two divine actions are not univocal. Scripture does not have a divine nature, even if it has a divine author, the Holy Spirit. It is not *both* creature and Creator, two natures hypostatically united in one person, as Jesus is. It is instead the enduring, created, divinely

5. So Watson, *Text, Church and World*, 138: "In this canonical context, the particular story of Jesus functions as the mid-point between the universal horizons of creation and eschaton: against the background of the one it points toward the other." See also 152.

6. See Seitz, *Convergences*, 43–65. For a broadly literary and historical definition of figuration, we should turn to Auerbach's classic study, *Mimesis*: "An occurrence on earth signifies not only itself but at the same time another, which it predicts or confirms, without prejudice to the power of its concrete reality here and now. The connection between occurrences is not regarded as primarily a chronological or causal development but as a oneness with the divine plan, of which all occurrences are parts and reflections" (*Mimesis*, 555). See also Collett, "Reading Forward," esp. 179–80.

7. Billings, *The Word of God for the People of God*, 157.

inspired testimony to God's work in Christ, the created means by which we continue to have epistemological access to the triune God in the face of Jesus Christ. As this enduring, creaturely testimony that is ultimately a testimony written by God himself, it is uniquely positioned among created things to be centered on the person and work of Jesus. Of all things in existence, we should expect Scripture supremely to be oriented toward the triune God's revelation of himself in the person and work of the incarnate Son.

This point requires a further note about an approach to biblical theology sometimes referred to as "the story of Scripture." I have discussed both the promise of and the danger with such approaches to biblical theology in chapter 3. Here, I need to briefly articulate yet another methodological caution about narrative and revelation. Because all of Scripture is oriented toward the triune God's revelation of himself in the person and work of the incarnate Son, we should expect each part of Scripture to be oriented thus. That is, both the whole story and the individual stories (as well as individual passages from other genres) are oriented toward revealing the triune God in the person and work of Jesus Christ.

To state this in the obverse, and to get more directly to the point, it is *not* the case that the story of the Bible merely progresses toward Jesus, with individual parts of the story being individually more or less directly oriented toward Jesus himself. Every story, every passage, is a revelation of the triune God in the face of Jesus Christ. Further, it is not merely the case that individual stories point beyond themselves to the story of Jesus, at which point the triune God is fully revealed in the face of Christ. Rather, the triune God is always revealing himself in sacred Scripture, both the OT and the NT, in passages that are both "messianic" and whatever adjective we want to use for the others. As Christopher Seitz puts it, "Making the Old Testament function as chapters in a drama that heads to Jesus and us misunderstands how he is already at work within them and within the people of Israel, long before in the fullness of time he is born of a virgin and opens time onto a people far off but now brought near, who were once outside the covenants, without hope, and without God in the world."[8]

8. Seitz, *The Elder Testament*, 129.

Speaking of Irenaeus's approach to this question, Seitz says that he and his "contemporaries did not believe the scriptures just pointed beyond themselves to a moment in time freshly to be regarded as Incarnational Time. Rather, the scriptures spoke of God in his personal life with Israel in time in ways that bespoke his eternal character as triune."[9] In other words, the Trinity reveals himself to Israel in ways that fit with the latter's temporal and economic location and that prefigure the final revelation of himself to Israel and the world in the person and work of Jesus Christ.

To be clear, this is true of *Israel's Scriptures*—that is, the OT. The NT claim is that these scriptures are "a witness fulfillable," and that this fulfillment occurs in the person and work of Jesus. "But," as Seitz goes on to say, "before there was a New Testament, the single scriptures [of Israel] disclosed the life of God, God the Word, and God the Holy Spirit in a way that belonged to its character as rule or canon."[10]

In this "pre-formed form," as Seitz calls it, the OT, through "figures," "types," and even "*allegoria*,"[11] both reveals the triune God and points beyond the people, places, and events of its own time to the center of time, the person and work of Jesus Christ.[12] This is, according to Seitz, the way that Irenaeus "uses a term like 'preformed'" to speak about "a providential overseeing by God whereby the revelation given to Israel in concrete times and places says what it says meaningfully [that is, to reveal the triune God] but also bespeaks realities subsequently to be disclosed [that is, Jesus Christ's person and work]."[13]

All of this means very simply that the OT both reveals the triune God to Israel in its temporal and economic location and also points beyond itself to the person and work of Jesus. It does so because, as a created entity and as a book uniquely inspired by the Spirit of God, it is providentially ordered toward the person and work of Jesus Christ

9. Seitz, *The Elder Testament*, 30.

10. Seitz, *The Elder Testament*, 30.

11. Seitz uses this word because other ancient commentators use it to describe what the OT is doing (*The Elder Testament*, 30).

12. See Radner, *Time and the Word*, esp. 83–110.

13. Seitz, *The Elder Testament*, 31.

in order to reveal the triune God. This is the fundamental basis of typology and figural reading,[14] and indeed the "primary sense" of the ancient use of the word *canon*: "seeing the whole of Scripture in the light of Christ and as speaking of Christ, the Old Testament invisibly in types and enigmas, the New Testament in a clear epitome."[15] While it is not my goal in this book to wade into intramural debates within canonical approaches, it is worth mentioning here the emphasis on the "discrete witness" of the OT and how to understand it theologically. Seitz is once again helpful:

> It seems to me that the chief "theological move" in respect to the Old Testament as Christian testimony is theological and ontological. From this flows the economic conviction that *it is speaking of Jesus Christ in its own, pre-New Testament idiom*. That is, the God of the first witness is God alone, and Jesus Christ is one with the God there revealed. This is the rule of faith. . . . This is the warrant for allowing the Old Testament scope to do its work theologically without requiring it only to have voice in the form of the New Testament's reception of it, in order to function in its special testimony to God in Christ. . . . What guards the character of the Old Testament as a discrete theological witness is not merely that the use made of it in the New Testament is widely diverse and has nowhere been lifted into something like a coordinated level of interpretation, in the form of the New Testament canon. . . . Rather, what keeps the Old Testament from being heard chiefly as the New Testament makes use of it is that it bears testimony

14. As Mark Elliott puts it, "Allegory arises out of a sense that the Scriptural text must mean something" (*The Song of Songs and Christology in the Early Church*, 8). Indeed, the "something" at the end of Elliott's sentence is decidedly christological for the early church and according to the theological commitments I have laid out thus far in this book. In other words, allegory is a recognition that the details of the text are signs of the *Logos*, the Word, and his incarnation. Note also Michael Graves's comment that "allegorical interpretation was not primarily a tactic for resolving interpretive difficulties but was above all a means to find the theological unity of Scripture. The Christian Bible is the product of a historical process that created, in the midst of diversity, a host of recurring themes, images, and symbols. Through figurative interpretation the early Church was able to tie these recurring elements together into a unified theological narrative with Christ as the central figure" (Graves, *Biblical Interpretation in the Early Church*, xxvi).

15. Seitz, *The Elder Testament*, 33–34, quoting John Behr's explanation of Irenaeus.

> to God in its own idiom. . . . But one and the same Lord has given himself to be known truly and faithfully in them both.[16]

Reading typologically and figurally, then, does not erase the OT's character as God's divine revelation of himself to his covenant people, but instead helps us to read it as such.

Returning to our point about the story of the Bible, it is important that we insist that the canonical shape of the Christian Bible, the two-testament testimony to Jesus, is centered on the person and work of Jesus *both* at the level of the larger story *and* at the individual level of particular stories or passages. The OT does not merely progress toward revealing the triune God in the face of Jesus Christ; it is, from the beginning, the revelation of the triune God to his people, Israel. There is still a sense of progression, in that the OT prophets were "searching for the time or person" in which the Christ, about whose sufferings they prophesied, would be revealed (1 Pet. 1:12). In other words, the prophets knew they were looking for the Messiah, but did not know it would be Jesus of Nazareth during the reign of Caesar Augustus.

Nevertheless, this *epistemological* progression is decidedly not an indication of *ontological* progression in God's revelation of himself. He has always been triune, and to reveal himself means to reveal who he is—the triune God. But the order of our knowing grows as the canon grows and comes to full fruition in the incarnation of God the Son. Still, even with this epistemic progression, God has always, from Genesis 1:1 forward, been revealing himself to his creation, which necessarily means revealing himself as the triune God. That is who he is!

And so, with respect to the story of the Bible, we need to be careful to say that the whole story, including its individual parts, is a revelation of the triune God, not simply a progression toward that revelation. The doctrine of creation, both in terms of creation's *Logos*-centric character and in terms of God's Christ-centered providence, insists that both the parts and the whole of the Bible are oriented toward Christ Jesus. Thus, as Don Collett says, "The OT's

16. Seitz, *Convergences*, 80.

Christological sense is . . . [grounded] in an objectively real link between Christ and the OT's words established by God's providential ordering of things."[17]

We are close to drawing out the implications of the doctrine of creation for the issue of canon. For now, I will simply leave it at this: Scripture, as both created thing and God's enduring testimony to and revelation of himself in the person and work of the incarnate Son, is oriented toward Christ and his atoning work. This is true not simply of Scripture *in toto* but also in each of its parts, even to the level of the very words and letters themselves, for these also are created things; the parts, as well as the whole, are creaturely entities oriented toward the same christological end.

The Canon of Scripture and the Doctrine of Creation

As the enduring, Spirit-inspired testimony to the triune God, Scripture is the predominant creaturely mode of God's revelation of himself to us. Of course, we need to note again that the ultimate special revelation of the triune God to his people comes in the person and work of the incarnate Son, who is one person with two natures, divine and human. In that sense, Jesus according to his human nature is the predominant creaturely mode of God's special revelation. But Jesus is not merely fully human; he is also fully divine. Scripture, on the other hand, has no divine nature, even if it has a divine author. It is exclusively creaturely in terms of its nature. The Spirit is its divine author, the Spirit illuminates it for the sanctification of God's people, and the Spirit brings his people into the presence of Christ through its proclamation, but it is not God. The Bible is a creaturely thing.

Nevertheless, as I have said repeatedly, the Bible is inspired by the Holy Spirit of God. The Spirit's purpose is God's purpose—to reveal the triune God to his people and to dwell with them in the place that he has made for them. This purpose is culminated in Jesus Christ. So, the Spirit's inspiration of the text of Scripture is a special work of revelation in the midst of God's broader work of creation and redemption, but it is also a work that has the same purpose and end

17. Collett, "Reading Forward," 180.

as all other of God's works. We should not be surprised to find, then, that Scripture's very fabric is reflective of this purpose.

Again, though, the Bible is a creaturely thing. Its purpose, content, and details all center on and are oriented toward the end for which God made all things—namely, to reveal himself to and dwell in relationship with his people in the place that he made for them—an end that finds its terminus in the person and work of Christ. Therefore, much as I said in the previous chapter about the Spirit's mission related to his testimony to the Son, so now I say about Scripture as a creaturely thing: It is *necessarily* oriented toward the person and work of Christ, both conceptually as a whole and in all its various components.

This last phrase, "its various components," gets us to the main canonical point of this chapter. The canon is a unified whole first because of its source in God's revelation of himself in the person and work of his Son, Jesus Christ, and by the power of his Holy Spirit. But it is also unified in its creaturely components—its textual realities. Here we bring to bear all that has been said thus far in this chapter on the text itself. Scripture's fabric, the text—the very letters, lexemes, words, phrases, narratives, and so on—is an interwoven whole, an intertextual web, *precisely because it is inspired by the same Spirit* (chap. 4) and *because it is a specially directed creaturely thing that perfectly accomplishes what it was meant to do: reveal God in Christ* (chap. 5).

To say this a bit differently, intertextuality, the repetition of words, phrases, and so on throughout the text of Scripture, exists *first* because of the divine authorship of the Holy Spirit; *second*, because it is reflective of the *Logos*-centric character of the universe, and, as a divinely inspired but still creaturely thing, the text is constantly oriented toward the *Logos*, God the Son, who became incarnate; *third*, because it is reflective of the divine providence over history, in which all events, past, present, and future, but particularly those that compose the history of salvation, find their consummation and culmination in the person and work of Jesus Christ; and *fourth*, because the human authors consciously intended to connect their writings to other biblical books.

I do not place the human author's intention last in this sequence to denigrate it or deny it. Rather, I place it last in order to emphasize that the divine author works *through* the created realities of the human authors—their cultural contexts, literary techniques, and, for our purposes here, allusions to other biblical texts. I do believe we can demonstrate that the human authors of Scripture intended to connect their own writing intertextually and typologically to that of previous biblical authors. I put it last because this is the proper order of consideration. The Bible is not an intertextual tapestry that portrays Christ *only* or *first* because the human authors decided to write that way; the Bible is an intertextual tapestry *ultimately* because it is a reflection of the divine authorship of Scripture, its creaturely purpose to reveal God in Christ, and its creaturely situatedness in the divine ordering of history.[18] The human authors write this way because they, too, are creatures, oriented toward God's revelation of himself in Christ—creatures who in this instance perfectly and inerrantly achieve that purpose for which they have been made, not through some ingenuity or willpower but through the providential and superintending inspiration of God the Holy Spirit. The Bible's textual unity is first a product of its status as God's special, enduring, written (creaturely) revelation of himself to us, and secondarily a product of the human authors' use of literary devices to convey their intentions, not the other way around.

Canonical Connectivity: Intertextuality and Typology

This brings us, at last, to certain phenomenological issues of canon—namely, the material means of the canon's unity in source, purpose, and goal: intertextuality and typology.

Intertextuality

Intertextuality was discussed at length in the previous chapter. Here, I need to add two comments. First, intertextuality is, as we

18. So Levering, *Engaging the Doctrine of Revelation*, 221: "Scripture displays this providential and active involvement of God in history by drawing typological connections between events, connections of a kind that are hardly possible for secular historiography to admit. . . . The presence of typology in Scripture's historical narratives shows that Scripture's view of history is quite different from views that make human history autonomous from God."

saw in chapter 4, the result of the Spirit's superintending work in the inspiration of the human author. The Spirit inspires the human authors to testify to the Son in a textually connected manner. But intertextuality is also the result of creation's *Logos*-centric character. As a creaturely reality, the text of Scripture, the very words of which it is composed, are oriented toward the Son. Their collective interconnectivity is thus a result of their individual connection to the Son. Because each text is connected to the Son, each text is also connected to every other text.

The Spirit's inspiration, the creaturely (*Logos*-centric) reality of the canon, and the human author's intention are not at odds with one another. Rather, the Spirit's providential, Son-oriented inspiration of the human author ensures that the creaturely orientation of both the human author's faculties as well as the text itself communicates their *Logos*-centric intent without the effects of sin distorting that intent. That is, the Spirit's inspiration ensures that the human authors communicate, via the text, in an inerrant fashion, and in accordance with their creaturely orientation toward the Son. In ensuring such inerrant, Christocentric communication, the Spirit also ensures that the text is imbued with intertextual connections. This intertextual web is thus a result of the Spirit's inspiration (chap. 4) *and* of the creaturely orientation of the human author and the text itself toward the *Logos* (chap. 5).

A second comment about intertextuality is necessary, given the phenomenon of canonical "seams." This term refers to the instances in the biblical canon, and particularly in the Hebrew Bible, in which the beginnings and/or endings of particular books and/or corpora possess high degrees of textual similarity. So, for instance, the prophetic books in the Book of the Twelve (Hosea–Malachi) are often described as possessing catchwords at the beginning and end of individual books. These repeated words and phrases link those twelve books together and form a whole book out of twelve individual books.[19]

19. See Nogalski, *Redactional Processes in the Book of the Twelve*; Seitz, *The Goodly Fellowship of the Prophets*. This linking was also recognized in the early church; note, for example, Didymus the Blind, who says that Zechariah is "the Eleventh of the Twelve Minor Prophets" (*Commentary on Zechariah*, 27). Cyril

Another example of seams is found in the book of Ruth. In the Old Greek manuscripts, as in our English Bibles, Ruth is included in the Historical Books, after Judges and before 1 Samuel. In the Masoretic Text (what many refer to as the Hebrew Bible), Ruth is included in the Writings, after Proverbs and before Song of Solomon.

As Casey Croy has noted, Ruth is textually connected to both locations. With respect to the former, Ruth demonstrates textual similarity to Judges and Samuel, while, with respect to the latter, Ruth textually resonates with Proverbs and Song of Solomon (at least).[20] As Stephen Dempster has noted, there are reasonable arguments for placing Ruth at either of these positions, and each has a different, even if related and relatable, hermeneutical effect.[21] The point here is not to argue for one order over another but simply to note the intertextual resonances that exist within the Hebrew Bible and provide hermeneutical guidance for its readers.

At a wider canonical level, some canonical interpreters also posit that seams exist between various corpora. Stephen Chapman, for instance, argues for intertextual links between the Law (Genesis–Deuteronomy) and the Prophets (Joshua–Malachi).[22] Others, such as John Sailhamer,[23] Michael Shepherd,[24] and Casey Croy,[25] argue that such seams exist at the beginning and end of the three major sections of the Hebrew Bible: the Torah (Law), the Nevi'im (Prophets),

of Alexandria also expresses awareness (and preference) for the Hebrew order and connection between these books in his preface to his commentary on Joel (*Commentary on the Twelve Prophets*, 1:259–60; see also Robert Hill's comments in the introduction on p. 6).

20. Croy, *Sequencing the Hebrew Bible*, 106–31.

21. Dempster, "A Wandering Moabite." Dempster himself argues that Ruth fits at the head of the Writings, just ahead of Psalms, following the order in Baba Batra 14b. On the sequencing of Ruth, see also Stone, "The Search for Order." While Dempster and Stone (and Croy) do not see eye to eye on every detail of this conversation, their works (among others) give a good overview and analysis of the phenomena I am addressing in this chapter.

22. Chapman, *The Law and the Prophets*, esp. 160–240. Regarding seams in particular, see 111–49, as well as Chapman, "What Are We Reading?," esp. 342–44.

23. Sailhamer, *The Meaning of the Pentateuch*, 48–56; Sailhamer, *Introduction to Old Testament Theology*, 239–52.

24. Shepherd, *An Introduction to the Making and Meaning of the Bible*, 9–13, 24–25, 94–97, 107–17.

25. Croy, *Sequencing the Hebrew Bible*, 173–205.

and the Ketuvim (Writings). The textual and conceptual similarities between Deuteronomy 34, Joshua 1, Malachi 4, and Psalm 1 are, according to these scholars, evidence of intentional canonical redaction. Further, according to Sailhamer and Shepherd, these texts' focus on the coming prophet like Moses, the wise king who will rule the nations, provides the OT with a shape that focuses on "eschatological messianic hope."[26]

While discussion of seams typically is concentrated on OT canonical phenomena, some have posited seams in the NT as well. For instance, Robert Wall has noted the fittingness of Matthew 1 as a sequel to the entire OT,[27] but particularly to the Tanakh, which ends with Chronicles.[28] Matthew's genealogical focus on Abraham and David resonates with an OT order that starts with Genesis and its focus on Abraham and ends with Chronicles and its focus on David.

Regarding the NT epistolary corpus, Wall has explored the relation of the ending of Acts to the beginning of Romans,[29] and various others have noted the relation of Acts to the Catholic Epistles.[30] Brevard Childs's final published book concerns the textual shaping of the Pauline corpus.[31] Ched Spellman has also argued, as we saw in a previous chapter, that Revelation 22:18–19 provides a fitting conclusion not only to the entire NT but also to the entire biblical corpus. As an echo of Deuteronomy 4 and 12, it serves as the close

26. Sailhamer, *Introduction to Old Testament Theology*, 206; Shepherd, *An Introduction to the Making and Meaning of the Bible*, 71–79. We will explore this shape more in chap. 7.

27. Wall, *Studies in Canonical Criticism*, 8–9.

28. For an analysis of this placement, see Koorevaar, "Chronicles as the Intentional Conclusion to the Old Testament Canon"; Croy, *Sequencing the Hebrew Bible*, 132–72. For clarity regarding my claims in this paragraph, when I say "The Tanakh . . . ends with Chronicles," I am referring to the fact that the order in JPS Tanakh has Chronicles last, following Baba Batra 14b. But the Aleppo Codex and Codex Leningradensis have Chronicles as the first book of the Writings (and reference is made to that later on in this book).

29. Wall, "Romans 1.1–15."

30. On the relation of the Catholic Epistles collection to the book of Acts, and especially with respect to circulation patterns in the early church, see Nienhuis, *Not By Paul Alone*, 76–79; Trobisch, *The First Edition of the New Testament*, 22–44, esp. 25–29, 39. See also Wall, "Acts and James."

31. See Childs's suggestion that 2 Tim. 1:3–12 and Rom. 1:8–17 serve in such a shaping capacity in Childs, *The Church's Guide for Reading Paul*, 71–72.

of "the prophets," and as an end to the NT, it is the close of "the apostles."[32]

Typology

The other phenomenon related to canonical connectivity as a creaturely reality is typology. This term refers to instances of literary and/or historical similarity between persons, events, and/or places across time and space with respect to historical similarity and across canonical location with respect to literary similarity. Additionally, these literary and/or historical similarities also involve heightening; that is, each subsequent comparison points the reader forward toward the antitype, Christ.[33] Sometimes, these two avenues of similarity, literary and historical, are pitted against each other, so that typology is *merely* a literary trope used by the human author to compare a contemporaneous person, event, or place to a past person, event, or place, even if there is not an actual historical similarity that forms the basis for the comparison.[34] On the other hand, some might chalk up typological correspondence simply to historical coincidence; that is,

32. See Spellman, *Toward a Canon-Conscious Reading of the Bible*, 172–83.

33. See Collett, *Figural Reading and the Old Testament*, 46–47. For the classic work on typological writing and reading, see Goppelt, *Typos*. Goppelt includes this description of typology toward the end of the book, one that summarizes many of the themes I have been discussing in this and previous chapters:

> Each typology includes typological correspondence and heightening. Accordingly, every typology presupposes that the God of the OT is the Father of Jesus Christ and that Jesus of Nazareth is the Christ, the one who fulfills OT redemptive history. The OT is an entity in itself distinct from the history of religions and distinct from the fulfillment of salvation in Christ. The typological correspondence arises from the first presupposition and the typological heightening from the second. . . . The NT values the OT as a true, though merely provisional, redemptive history which in its literal meaning originated from God. . . . All typology proceeds through Christ and exists in him. (202)

While there are critiques to be made about Goppelt's argument, this short statement encapsulates the idea that typology understands biblical "persons, events, and institutions" (202) to correspond to and build toward Christ and his work.

34. While Hans Frei (*The Eclipse of Biblical Narrative*) was right to argue that certain aspects of modern interpretation (i.e., its obsession with historical background) have taken the focus of exegesis off the biblical literature itself and its attendant features, one wonders if this ahistorical understanding of typology is an

the literary similarity exists only because the human author happens to be describing a person, place, or event that is similar to something in the past, not because the author intended to compare the two.

Intertextuality and Typology in Theological Perspective

What are we to say about these phenomena from a *theological* vantage point? First, they are the products of both the Spirit's superintending inspiration and creation's ontological *telos*, its orientation toward the *Logos*. Just like every other created entity, the biblical text is *Logos*-centric, and in divine providence God orients this particular text, via the inspiration of the Holy Spirit, toward the Spirit's testimony to the Son and for the sake of his people.[35] Both historically and literarily, the biblical canon is oriented toward the revelation of the triune God in the person and work of Jesus Christ. This means that the entire Bible is a textual tapestry exhibiting interconnectivity textually and typologically due to its individual parts being oriented toward the same central point, the Word incarnate.[36]

Second, theologically speaking, typology is not an either/or phenomenon in terms of historical or literary correspondence.[37] Due to

---

effect of Frei's attempt to make this argument *without* simultaneously insisting on the historical character of the claims of Scripture.

35. So Vanhoozer, *Remythologizing Theology*, 376:

> Divine providence is best viewed in terms of triune authorship: *the Father rules by speaking Christ through the Spirit into the minds and hearts of the faithful*. "Christ" in this context is shorthand for what the law, prophets, and other biblical writings say about the new thing God is doing in Christ. This puts a new spin on canon as "rule." The canon is not only the norm that governs right Christian speech, thought, and action but also the means that God uses to direct his people as they seek to realize God's rule in their hearts and pursue God's mission in the world.

In other words, for our purposes here, God providentially authors the biblical text as a testimony to his Son by his Spirit, but notice also that there are implications for reception and reading (chaps. 6 and 8 of this book).

36. See Seitz, *Figured Out*, 6, 32, 43.

37. In this sense I disagree with Peter J. Leithart's conclusion that typological reading ought to be characterized mostly as a post hoc reading strategy, in which later events clarify the meaning of earlier ones and so later authors reflect that correspondence literarily (*Deep Exegesis*, 35–74). See especially, for instance, pp. 67, 74, and on the latter, this quote, which serves as a summary of the chapter: "The apostles

the inspiration of the Holy Spirit and the superintending providence of God, the literary correspondence between persons, places, and events is rooted in historical correspondence, providentially ordered by God, between those same persons, places, and events. Or, to say it the other way around, the human authors of Scripture, under the inspiration of the Holy Spirit, recognize the divinely ordered historical correspondence between persons, places, and events and describe them textually in such a way as to exhibit literary correspondence between canonical locations. Furthermore, both the literary and the historical correspondence are grounded in the centrality of Christ's person and work for all of creation and its history. In other words, both the Holy Spirit and the human author intend these intertextual and typological connections between individual texts, and in ways that accord with the divine author's and human author's order of knowing: infinite and eternal with respect to the divine author, finite and temporal with respect to the human author.[38]

Finally, because of the theological realities described in this chapter and the previous one, we can dispense with the handwringing about whether or not the human author consciously intended instances of intertextuality or typology. The truth is that we cannot get into the

---

teach us to recognize that 'how it turned out' exposes dimensions of the original event or text that may not have been apparent, *and perhaps were not even there*, until it turned out as it did. *Typological reading is simply reading of earlier texts in the light of later texts and events*" (emphasis added). At times, Leithart seems to give more credit to the human author (e.g., pp. 37–38, in reference to Hosea 11:1 and Matthew's later use of it), but the emphasis remains on the ability of later authors to pick up earlier texts in ways that fit the new context. While this understanding of typology may be true from the perspective of the human author (i.e., the truly typological significance of an earlier text/event becomes clear in their experience of contemporaneous events), it is not reflective of the more fundamental truth that God the Holy Spirit knows and intends the correspondence between every typologically related event, at both the historical and literary levels. Leithart is well aware of the Spirit's role in inspiration and readily acknowledges it, so I am not disagreeing here with his fundamental theological commitments about the nature of Scripture, or even some of his instincts for reading. I simply think that his definition of typological reading, especially with respect to the NT use of the OT, is truncated.

38. For an example of this kind of reading—one that takes seriously both the human author's intention and the Spirit's divine inspiration, and one that also takes seriously the eschatological, messianic thrust of the entire OT as a product of the human authors' intention—see Hamilton, "The Skull Crushing Seed of the Woman."

human author's mind and empirically verify an instance of intertextuality or typology. There are, of course, indications of likelihood regarding these instances,[39] but, in the case of allusions and echoes, we cannot *prove* that they are indeed intended by the human author. Even when direct quotations occur, there are still sometimes questions as to whether the author who quotes previous biblical material is doing so in a way that accurately and adequately accounts for the previous author's intent. Again, there are indications of whether this is likely.[40]

And many continue to labor to demonstrate that the human authors of Scripture carefully produced an interconnected textual tapestry in their quotation of and allusion to previous biblical material.[41] These labors matter because the human authors' intent matters in rightly interpreting Scripture. Vitally so. And they matter because they demonstrate that the Bible's human authors knew what they were doing, both literarily and theologically. We cannot, therefore, posit an interpretive leap of faith from what the OT text says according to the original intent of its human authors, on the one hand, to the NT authors' (surprising) citation of the OT text, on the other hand.[42] The human authors of both the OT and the NT were exegetically, literarily, and theologically savvy. Again, they knew what they

39. Most famously and fundamentally, perhaps, is the list of criteria given by Richard B. Hays in his *Echoes of Scripture in the Letters of Paul*, 29–32.

40. See Sailhamer, "Hosea 11:1 and Matthew 2:15."

41. I have been heavily influenced in this regard by G. K. Beale, and I remain grateful for and appreciative of his work. Most important to this point at hand are his *Handbook on the New Testament Use of the Old Testament*; *Hidden but Now Revealed* (coauthored with Benjamin Gladd); and *Commentary on the New Testament Use of the Old Testament* (coedited with D. A. Carson). But his commentaries on Revelation, as well as his *New Testament Biblical Theology*, demonstrate continued emphasis on the human authors' literary abilities and intentionality, to the extent that the NT use of the OT is imminently explicable from an exegetical standpoint. Another example from OT theology is Jason DeRouchie's *Delighting in the Old Testament*. Still, as we noted in the previous chapter (and I am not assuming that Beale or DeRouchie would disagree with what follows), we can affirm the human author's literary abilities and intentionality while also affirming that the Spirit's divine intention, imbued as it is with the Spirit's omniscience and Christ-centered trinitarian mission, does not contravene or disconnect itself from the finite intention of the human author.

42. I disagree, therefore, with the characterization of the NT use of the OT found in, for instance, Crump, *Encountering Jesus, Encountering Scripture*, esp. pp. 15–45. The following quote gives a good sense of Crump's understanding:

were doing. There is, in other words, sufficient exegetical warrant for affirming both the "eschatological messianic thrust" of the OT in its original setting and therefore also the NT's use of a given OT text. Inner-biblical allusions, or intertextuality within Scripture, is one such way that we see the whole Bible intentionally connected in terms of "the way the words go." Even so, while we continue to strongly affirm the human authors' abilities and intentions, we still cannot empirically *prove* what was in the mind of the human author, which means that there will be times where we cannot say with *empirical* certainty that a specific inner-biblical connection was consciously intended by the human author(s).

What we can do is recognize intertextual and figural—typological and allegorical—correspondence as a christologically oriented product of both the Spirit's inspiration and creation's *Logos*-centric reality. That is to say, perceived instances of intertextuality and typology are more likely to be, in fact, actual instances of such to the extent that they clearly testify to Christ and his work. Because of the Spirit's Christ-centered inspiration and creation's *Logos*-centric orientation, the rule for recognizing intertextuality and figuration—typology and allegory—is christological. We need to ask, "To what extent does this perceived instance testify to Christ?" not "To what extent can I prove that the human author had this in mind?" The latter is impossible to achieve with certainty. The former is the rule that Christ himself gives us.

> The specifics of Christ's accomplishments do not arise from the Old Testament, not even proleptically. Rather, they exist independently of that background and are imposed on it by gospel history. The claims of messianic fulfillment are highlighted most starkly when juxtaposed against the Old Testament literature, but their existence and visibility are not dependent on those writings. The messianic fulfillment of Jesus Christ is the gospel-tinted overlay placed on the Old Testament by the creativity of the New Testament writers who viewed life and their own sacred texts through a gospel-inspired imagination. (41)

Crump goes on to compare the NT writers' method to the *pesher* method applied at Qumran.

SIX

The Ruled Canonical List: Ecclesiology and Canon

Through Holy Scripture the risen Jesus Christ declares and exercises his kingly rule.

—John Webster[1]

Scripture is always the church's book, the church always the community under the Word.

—Brad East[2]

Along with intertextuality (chap. 5) and order (chap. 7), a predominant phenomenological concern in canon studies is that of manuscript inclusion and canonical lists. This chapter

1. Webster, *The Domain of the Word*, 46. Similarly, "An account of the canon and canonization is therefore an account of the extension of Christ's active, communicative presence through the commissioned apostolic testimony" (Webster, "The Dogmatic Location of the Canon," 36).

2. East, *The Church's Book*, 20. East's larger project is to analyze various attempts to coordinate the doctrines of ecclesiology and bibliology, and so is a further resource with respect to the topic of this chapter.

argues that the proper dogmatic location of that discussion is the doctrine of ecclesiology. Canonical lists, like canonical orders, are products, phenomenologically speaking, of the community of faith that receives the canon. Ultimately, the church is the creation of the Spirit of God in Christ, and so canonical decisions, evidenced in lists and manuscripts, are subject to evaluation via the ontological criteria given in chapters 2–4.[3] Differences between canonical lists and manuscripts, in other words, are not evidences of different canons in an *ontological* sense. These phenomenological differences must be measured (an intentional allusion to canon as "rule" or "measurement") against the trinitarian mission that serves as the source and context for the canon.

The People of God and God's Word

We begin with a brief theology of the people of God in the economy of salvation and in relation to Scripture.

Hearing, Receiving, Remembering, and Obeying

In both the Old and the New Testaments the called-out, covenanted, specially chosen people of God exists to glorify the triune God and display him to the nations around them. In the OT, the people of God is the nation of Israel, the descendants of Abraham, Isaac, and Jacob. All those from this family are part of this people. They await their Messiah, their deliverer, who will finally and fully fulfill God's promises to Abraham to make him fruitful and multiply his descendants, to bring kings from his line, to place him and his descendants securely in the land promised to him, and to dwell with him and his descendants forever.

In the NT, Jesus of Nazareth, God the Son in the flesh, fulfills these promises for Israel. The promises for Israel in the OT, though, are not

3. For an introduction to and analysis of the various lists in the early church, see Gallagher and Meade, *The Biblical Canon Lists from Early Christianity*. For an in-depth analysis of lists and manuscripts related to the OT, see Beckwith, *The Old Testament Canon of the New Testament Church*, esp. 16–62; for such a study in relation to the NT canon, see Parker, *An Introduction to the New Testament Manuscripts and Their Texts*.

just for Israel but for the world through Israel. Subsequently, all those who trust in Jesus are now part of True Israel, and it is by faith rather than by birth. The sign of inclusion in the covenant people of God therefore also shifts, from circumcision to baptism. Thus, while the distinction between Israel and the church is real, we need to be clear that it is not that the church replaces Israel, but that Jesus *is* Israel, and all those who are in him are in Israel. The church is thus grafted into Israel, and True Israel is made up of all those, Jew and gentile, who are united to Christ, the true and final and only faithful Israelite.

In both the Old and the New Testaments, the people of God are led by the Word of God given to them by the Spirit of God. This begins with Adam and Eve receiving instruction from God in the garden of Eden and continues throughout the biblical canon. In the OT, the proclaimers of God's Word are known as prophets. Israel hears God's Word from the prophets, an office that extends (at least) from Moses all the way through Zechariah (cf. Deut. 18:15–19; Matt. 23:35). Israel's role in this communicative act of the triune God is to hear (or receive) and obey. We will return to this concept of reception in a moment. For now, it is simply important to say that, in the OT, God's people received God's Word from God's prophets and were expected to obey it.

In the NT, the people of God is no longer only the nation of Israel but now is from all peoples, tribes, tongues, and nations. But God continues to give his Spirit-inspired Word to his people through his prophets. This time, though, they are not called prophets, but apostles. They are the ones appointed to hear and record God's Word, and their appointment to that role comes from Israel's last Prophet, Priest, and King, Jesus Christ. This is why the church historically has spoken of the prophets and apostles as a way to refer to the Old and New Testaments; God spoke to Israel through the prophets in the OT, while in these latter days he has spoken finally and fully through his Son, Jesus Christ, who in turn appointed apostles to proclaim his Word to his new covenant people, the church, in the NT. And, in both the OT and the NT, the people of God are to receive the Word of God that has been declared to them by the Spirit of God through the prophets and apostles.

The way that the Word is to be received is through hearing and obeying. Our focus here is on the former. The people of God are supposed to hear the Word of the LORD by receiving it (that is, recording it accurately and fully) and remembering it. This begins in the beginning, with Adam and Eve; they ought to receive God's Word to refrain from eating from the tree of the knowledge of good and evil. When confronted with temptation, however, Eve fails to recall the Word rightly, adding to it ("neither shall you touch it"), and Adam fails to remember it at all, remaining silent in the face of the serpent's attempted deception. Their failure to receive and remember God's Word leads to their failure to obey it.

Israel, too, is called to receive and remember God's Word. Immediately after they exit Egypt by way of the parted Red Sea, they complain about the lack of potable water. In response, God makes the bitter water sweet, but then we also learn that "there the LORD made for them a statute and a rule, and there he tested them, saying, 'If you will diligently listen to the voice of the LORD your God, and do that which is right in his eyes, and give ear to his commandments and keep all his statutes, I will put none of the diseases on you that I put on the Egyptians, for I am the LORD, your healer'" (Exod. 15:25–26).

God continues to give Israel rules and statutes through his prophet Moses throughout Israel's journey to Sinai (e.g., Exod. 16:16, 28; 17:14). This culminates with God's Word to them as they arrive at the holy mountain, when God tells Moses to say to them, "'Now therefore, if you will indeed obey my voice and keep my covenant, you shall be my treasured possession among all peoples, for all the earth is mine; and you shall be to me a kingdom of priests and a holy nation.' These are the words that you shall speak to the people of Israel" (Exod. 19:5–6). This refrain—"if you will obey my voice and keep my covenant"—punctuates the law-giving that happens in Exodus 19 all the way through Numbers 10. Of course, that legal material is also punctuated by Israel's repeated failures to listen and obey, most notably in the incident of the golden calf in Exodus 32.

Finally, though, Israel is prepared to depart Mount Sinai in Numbers 10. Instead of hearing and obeying God's Word, though, Israel continues to fail to receive and remember what has been said through the prophet Moses. God eventually declares that the entire first generation of Israel that came out of Egypt will not enter the promised land, and instead they die in the wilderness during forty years of wandering. Before the second generation enters, God gives them the law again, in the book of Deuteronomy. The book is again punctuated by commands to hear the Word of the Lord and obey it, to receive it and remember it (e.g., just in the first chapter, Deut. 1:1, 3, 6, 9, 19). The centerpiece of this command to hear and obey God's Word is found in Deuteronomy 6. It is worth quoting significant portions of the entire chapter to get the full impact and sense of God's expectation that his people will hear—receive and remember—his Word so that they will, in turn, obey it:

> Now this is the commandment—the statutes and the rules—that the Lord your God commanded me to teach you. . . . Hear therefore, O Israel, and be careful to do them, that it may go well with you, and that you may multiply greatly, as the Lord, the God of your fathers, has promised you, in a land flowing with milk and honey.
>
> Hear, O Israel: The Lord our God, the Lord is one. You shall love the Lord your God with all your heart and with all your soul and with all your might. And these words that I command you today shall be on your heart. You shall teach them diligently to your children, and shall talk of them when you sit in your house, and when you walk by the way, and when you lie down, and when you rise. You shall bind them as a sign on your hand, and they shall be as frontlets between your eyes. You shall write them on the doorposts of your house and on your gates.
>
> And when the Lord your God brings you into the land that he swore to your fathers, to Abraham, to Isaac, and to Jacob, to give you . . . , then take care lest you forget the Lord, who brought you out of the land of Egypt, out of the house of slavery. . . .
>
> When your son asks you in time to come, "What is the meaning of the testimonies and the statutes and the rules that the Lord our God has commanded you?" then you shall say to your son, "We were Pharaoh's slaves in Egypt. And the Lord brought us out of Egypt with a mighty hand. And the Lord showed signs and wonders, great and grievous, against Egypt and against Pharaoh and all his household, before our eyes. And he brought us out from there, that he might bring us in and give us the land that he swore to give to our fathers. And the Lord commanded us to do all these statutes, to fear the Lord our

> God, for our good always, that he might preserve us alive, as we are this day. And it will be righteousness for us, if we are careful to do all this commandment before the LORD our God, as he has commanded us." (Deut. 6:1, 3–10, 12, 20–25)

Notice that the primary command is to *hear*. But that is fleshed out as Israel receiving and remembering God's Word so that they will, in turn, *obey* God's Word. *This is the fundamental relation of the people of God to God's Word: They are to hear it by receiving it, remembering it, and obeying it.*

The command is clear enough. The question becomes, for Israel, "How do we know which words are God's Word?" Another way to ask that is, "Who is a true prophet, a true conveyor of God's Word, and who is a false prophet?" God addresses this in Deuteronomy 18:15–22:

> The LORD your God will raise up for you a prophet like me from among you, from your brothers—it is to him you shall listen—just as you desired of the LORD your God at Horeb on the day of the assembly, when you said, "Let me not hear again the voice of the LORD my God or see this great fire any more, lest I die." And the LORD said to me, "They are right in what they have spoken. I will raise up for them a prophet like you from among their brothers. And I will put my words in his mouth, and he shall speak to them all that I command him. And whoever will not listen to my words that he shall speak in my name, I myself will require it of him. But the prophet who presumes to speak a word in my name that I have not commanded him to speak, or who speaks in the name of other gods, that same prophet shall die." And if you say in your heart, "How may we know the word that the LORD has not spoken?"—when a prophet speaks in the name of the LORD, if the word does not come to pass or come true, that is a word that the LORD has not spoken; the prophet has spoken it presumptuously. You need not be afraid of him.

Which words are God's Word? Those that are (1) given by the LORD (2) from prophets like Moses and (3) demonstrably true ("if the word does not come to pass or come true"). Which prophets are true prophets? Those who speak words (1) given by the LORD (2) like Moses (3) that come true. Notice in both cases that the *source* of

God's Word, the words spoken by a true prophet, is God himself, and the *pattern* of the prophetic office is Moses. This ought to remind us that Moses receives his office and the words he is to speak from the Spirit of the LORD, and, in turn, he is told to "distribute" his spirit among the elders of Israel (Exod. 18). And, when God tells him to appoint Joshua as his successor, we are told:

> Moses spoke to the LORD, saying, "Let the LORD, the God of the spirits of all flesh, appoint a man over the congregation who shall go out before them and come in before them, who shall lead them out and bring them in, that the congregation of the LORD may not be as sheep that have no shepherd." So the LORD said to Moses, "Take Joshua the son of Nun, a man in whom is the Spirit, and lay your hand on him. Make him stand before Eleazar the priest and all the congregation, and you shall commission him in their sight. You shall invest him with some of your authority, that all the congregation of the people of Israel may obey." (Num. 27:15–20)

The true prophet, then, is the one who speaks God's Word in the power of God's Spirit for the edification of God's people and in the pattern of God's prophet to Israel, Moses. God's Word comes from God's Spirit to the prophet, and the prophetic Word is aligned with the words given to Moses. This is what Moses tells us in Deuteronomy 12:32, a passage already discussed in earlier chapters: "Everything that I command you, you shall be careful to do. You shall not add to it or take from it."[4]

Throughout Israel's history, this is the expectation of and standard for Israel's prophets. They must speak the words they hear from God's Spirit to God's people (e.g., 1 Kings 13; Jer. 28).[5] The prophet and the people know when it is God's Word—that is, it is from God's Spirit—when it is patterned after the Torah, God's first Word to his people through Israel's first prophet, Moses. They are to hear it—that is, receive it and remember it—and obey it. From

4. On the prophetic task and the identification of true and false prophets in relation to Deut. 12, see, e.g., Tully, *Reading the Prophets as Christian Scripture*, 57–89.

5. On the relation between Deut. 18, Jer. 28, and 1 Kings 13, and what that relation says about false prophecy, see Childs, *Old Testament Theology in a Canonical Context*, 133–44.

Joshua through Malachi (or, if you prefer the Tanakh order, through the Writings) Israel's prophets hear God's Word, receive it, remember it, and call Israel to obey it.

Israel never does obey it, though, at least not fully and consistently. The prophet like Moses, the one who leads God's people not only to hear God's Word but to "listen" to (obey) it (Deut. 18:15), never arrives in the OT. As Deuteronomy 34:10–12 tells us, "There has not arisen a prophet since in Israel like Moses, whom the LORD knew face to face, none like him for all the signs and the wonders that the LORD sent him to do in the land of Egypt, to Pharaoh and to all his servants and to all his land, and for all the mighty power and all the great deeds of terror that Moses did in the sight of all Israel." We are still waiting, at the end of Deuteronomy and at the end of the OT, for the New Moses, the prophet greater than Moses, who will lead God's people finally and fully into God's presence in the place that he has prepared for them.

This New Moses is Jesus of Nazareth, God the Son in the flesh, the son of Abraham and David, Israel's Messiah. In terms of titles, perhaps most importantly for our purposes, Jesus is the Word incarnate. He is the Word from whom all prophetic words originate and to whom all prophetic words point. According to his humanity, he is the last and greatest of Israel's prophets, the one greater than Moses and the one for whom Moses and the rest of Israel's prophets looked (1 Pet. 1:10–12). According to his divinity, he is God the Word, the origin of all true words and therefore the ground of Israel's prophetic words. It is in the person of Jesus of Nazareth that Israel's prophetic words are fulfilled. God the Father tells us this at Jesus's baptism and his transfiguration: "This is my beloved Son. . . . *Listen* to him" (Matt. 17:5, emphasis added). Because all of Israel's prophetic words point to him, Christ the incarnate Word is the last and final prophetic word.

But the incarnate Word does not keep his word to himself, nor does he limit his words' accessibility to his own earthly ministry. Instead, he appoints apostles, those to whom he gives authority to spread his word to Israel and the nations. He tells the disciples, immediately prior to his ascension, "You will receive power when the Holy Spirit has come upon you, and you will be my witnesses in Jerusalem and in all Judea and Samaria, and to the end of the earth" (Acts 1:8). This echoes his statement to them at the end of Luke 24:

> Then he said to them, "These are my words that I spoke to you while I was still with you, that everything written about me in the Law of Moses and the Prophets and the Psalms must be fulfilled." Then he opened their minds to understand the Scriptures, and said to them, "Thus it is written, that the Christ should suffer and on the third day rise from the dead, and that repentance for the forgiveness of sins should be proclaimed in his name to all nations, beginning from Jerusalem. You are witnesses of these things. And behold, I am sending the promise of my Father upon you. But stay in the city until you are clothed with power from on high." (Luke 24:44–49)

And again, we find similar comments in John's Farewell Discourse:

> I still have many things to say to you, but you cannot bear them now. When the Spirit of truth comes, he will guide you into all the truth, for he will not speak on his own authority, but whatever he hears he will speak, and he will declare to you the things that are to come. He will glorify me, for he will take what is mine and declare it to you. All that the Father has is mine; therefore I said that he will take what is mine and declare it to you. (John 16:12–15)

Jesus also commands the disciples to share the good news in a way that is dependent on his own words in the Great Commission, telling them, "Go therefore and make disciples of all nations, baptizing them in the name of the Father, Son, and Holy Spirit and *teaching them to observe all that I have commanded you*" (Matt. 28:19, emphasis added).

What Jesus does in his ministry, then, is fulfill the prophetic office as the New Moses. He also appoints apostles to declare his final word to Israel to both Israel and the nations, since the people of God is, in the new covenant, made up of people from every tribe, tongue, and nation. He gives these apostles his Spirit, through whom they speak (Luke 24:49) and by whom the church is birthed (Acts 2) and grown. In Acts, when the gospel is proclaimed, Luke says that "the Word of God was fruitful and multiplied" (Acts 6:7; 12:24; 19:20).[6] And when Jesus returns in glory, it is through his word, as God the Word in the flesh, that the new creation is made and secured (Rev. 21:5).

The words of the new covenant people of God, the words of the apostles, are once again judged by their faithfulness to the prophet of the New Israel, Jesus, the New Moses. John echoes Deuteronomy 12:32 in Revelation 22:18–19, when he says, "I warn everyone who hears the words of the prophecy of this book: if anyone adds to them, God will add to him the plagues described in this book, and if anyone takes away from the words of the book of this prophecy, God will take away his share in the tree of life and in the holy city, which are described in this book."

Likewise, in his first letter, John tells us, "Beloved, do not believe every spirit, but test the spirits to see whether they are from God, for many false prophets have gone out into the world. By this you know the Spirit of God: every spirit that confesses that Jesus Christ has come in the flesh is from God, and every spirit that does not confess Jesus is not from God. This is the spirit of the antichrist, which you heard was coming and now is in the world already" (1 John 4:1–3). In both Revelation and 1 John, the mark of a true Word from God is clear: It is in accordance with the Word of the New Moses, Jesus, and it affirms the true identity of Jesus, God the Son in the flesh.

At this point, it is important to say explicitly and clearly that the NT's judgment of apostolic words is not only parallel to OT Israel's judgment of prophetic words but also directly connected to and derivative from it. Israel's judgment was based on a particular word's continuity with the words of Moses. Jesus is the New and Greater Moses, the one who fulfills Moses's words. He appoints apostles who must declare his word to the nations, a word that is not only in continuity with Moses's words but also the fulfillment of them. Revelation 22:18–19 is not a plagiarism of Deuteronomy 12:32; it is the *terminus* of Moses's instructions. The OT and the NT, the prophetic and the apostolic words, are in continuity with each other precisely because both are derived from and point to the

6. Beale, *The Temple and the Church's Mission*, 266; see also Schreiner, *Acts*, 21–24.

person and work of Jesus Christ, God the Son in the flesh, God the Word incarnate.

To be a prophetic or apostolic word, then, means that the word in question is aligned not only with Moses but ultimately with the New Moses, to whom Moses points. It means that the word in question is from the Spirit of God, the Spirit who proceeds from the Father and the Son and who testifies to the Son in the economy of redemption. The task of the people of God, Israel in the OT and the church, the New Israel made up of both Jews and gentiles, in the NT is to hear God's Word, receive it, remember it, and obey it.

Christ the King and the King's Authoritative Word

A second important theological category that impinges on our understanding of the church's relation to the canon is that of Jesus's kingly authority, and especially as it relates to his ongoing reign prior to his return.[7] The church, Christ's body (Eph. 1:22–23) and temple (Eph. 2:21–22), is governed by Christ's Word. Of course, as in the previous discussion above, this is typologically patterned in the OT in God's rule over Adam and Israel through his Word. The church, as the New Israel constituted of Jew and gentile through their union by faith with the True Israel, Jesus Christ, is the outpost and sign of Christ's kingdom.

As Christ's body and temple, and as the sign of his kingdom, the church is governed by the King's authoritative Word. The church is entrusted with God's Word—that is, the church is to receive it and remember it—and is also called to follow it. We see this clearly in Paul's letters to Timothy and Titus. Paul's instructions are to "guard the good deposit" (2 Tim. 1:14; see also 1 Tim. 4:16; 6:20) by avoiding false teaching (1 Tim. 1:3; 6:2–4; Titus 1:9) and by passing down the sound teaching that they have received (2 Tim. 2:2; Titus 2:1). Timothy and Titus are to do this in the power and under the guidance of the Holy Spirit (2 Tim. 1:14) and in continuity with the teachings of Jesus Christ (1 Tim. 6:2–4; 2 Tim. 3:14–15). It is this Word that is the source of the church's growth in holiness by the Spirit (1 Tim. 4:16)

7. See Webster, *The Domain of the Word*, 46–47.

and the grounds for discipline and rebuke (1 Tim. 1:19–20; 4:1–3, 6–7; 6:1–5; 2 Tim. 1:15–18; 2:16–19; 4:1–5; Titus 1:9–16; 3:9–11).

The same pattern exists here that we saw in the previous section. The church is governed by the King's Word, a Word that is to be received from the Spirit, remembered faithfully, and obeyed by God's people. As with the suzerainty treaty of Deuteronomy, in which YHWH's kingship is declared and demonstrated through his kingly law, so for the church. The kingship of Christ, God the incarnate Word, is declared and demonstrated through his kingly Word, a Word that includes his Word to Israel but also the new covenant Word of the NT. This is not a departure or distinction from the OT, but rather its fulfillment in Christ and through his Word.

The Church and Canonical Reception

We have seen that Scripture speaks of Israel and the church, the people of God in the OT and NT, hearing God's Word, receiving it, remembering it, and obeying it. This gives us an indication of how to think about canonical reception theologically—namely, from the perspective of ecclesiology. To state it as succinctly as possible, *canonical lists—that is, lists of books that a person, church, or ecclesiastical body considers canonical—are fallible but continued attempts by the people of God to receive and remember the authoritative word given by the Lord.*[8]

To state this the other way around, canonical lists (and manuscripts) are *not* determinative of canonical status for particular books.[9] This kind of approach to canon, both in terms of the phe-

8. So Webster, *Holy Scripture*, 62: "The church's act with respect to the canon is an act of faithful *assent* rather than a self-derived judgment. The language of 'discipleship' is not incidental here: affirming the canon is a matter of the church 'obediently embracing' what comes from God, or of the sheep hearing the shepherd's voice; that is, it is an act of humble affirmation of and orientation towards what is already indisputably the case in the sphere of salvation and its communication in human speech."

9. For example, the following statement: "Advocates of a closed canon prevailed in the end, and an important function of the canonical lists they produced was to *suppress* texts now deemed to be non-canonical [e.g., those mentioned earlier in the essay: 1 Enoch, Jubilees, the Ascension of Isaiah, the *Epistula Apostolorum*, and the

nomenology of lists and manuscripts and in terms of the broader issue of authority in relation to canon, is pervasive in certain corners of the canonical conversation.[10] For example, Philip Davies says of the Hebrew Bible's canonical contents and the process of its authorization as Scripture:

> Canon and authority go hand in hand. Until or unless a canon is fixed, it operates as an arbiter, a definer, of *class* values. Its authority is enforced by the teacher and the group ethos. It is open, but it is also in the nature of canons to be self-referential: canonical works proclaim themselves as such by being quoted, rewritten, interpreted, and in the canon of the Jewish scriptures one can readily see how the parts refer to each other.

Apocalypse of Peter]" (Gebreananaye et al., *Beyond Canon*, 1, emphasis original). While the authors make clear that the word *suppress* is not necessarily intended to be pejorative, they also are clear from this quotation and from the remaining treatments in the book that, in their estimation, canon is a post hoc function of ecclesiastical determination. See also de Bruin, *Fan Fiction and Early Christian Writings*, e.g., 11–17, 24, 37, 63, 111, 119. For a survey of these kinds of sociologically and ecclesiologically oriented approaches, as well as theological critiques of those approaches along lines similar to my own, see Webster, "The Dogmatic Location of the Canon," 11–25.

10. From a theological perspective, see Allert, *A High View of Scripture?*, esp. 76, 82, 174–76. While Allert is clear that he believes Scripture is inspired by God and authoritative for the church, he makes a distinction between (1) Scripture and canon and (2) various aspects of the rule of faith that together end up placing canon in the category that we are trying to avoid here—namely, that it is an ecclesiastically determined set of books. I simply disagree with Allert that (1) various early church theologians' citations of books outside of the current canon means that, collectively, Scripture for them was separate from canon; and that (2) the various aspects of the rule of faith (e.g., canon, Christ as hermeneutical key, creedal summaries) were not viewed as synonymous with one another. Instead, canonical lists and even citations of extrabiblical books are *imperfect* attempts to receive God's Word by individuals and churches. The canon is Scripture, and Scripture is found in the canon and the canon alone. It would take another book to attempt to prove these points in response to Allert, so this footnote will have to suffice. For a succinct but sufficient critique of Allert's and others' articulation of the rule of faith along the same lines I am noting here, see Seitz, *The Character of Christian Scripture*, 192–94, esp. 192n2; see also 198–99, and note esp. this statement: "On this understanding, then, the canon [rule] of faith is not a pre-creedal (post-NT) digest that helps ground the authority of a two-testament canon, thus providing as it were the warrant for our recourse to Scripture as authoritative" (199). For a response to Allert's view, as well as others with similar approaches to canon (such as Lee McDonald), see Chapman, "The Canon Debate."

> Once a canon becomes a religious collection, the nature of its authority changes: divine sanction is invoked, even divine authorship can be claimed. . . . The *fixing* of a canon is a further step that both entails a political and religious authority capable of dictating and imposing uniformity, and also creates a dichotomy between canon and non-canon, making the canon itself a symbol of the distinction between human and divine knowledge. Thereafter the natural processes by which canons would grow are shut off, and the mode of interpretation takes over.[11]

To place canonical boundaries in the hands of the church first, rather than in God's hands, is to fundamentally misconstrue the nature and complexities[12] of the debates about this issue in the early church. Rather than various lists and categories indicating that certain books were not canonical until Irenaeus or Origen or Athanasius or a particular council listed them as such, we should understand differences between individual lists and categories as the church's attempt to rightly receive the Word of God.

The determining factor for canonical status, then, lies in a particular book's intrinsic nature as inspired by the Holy Spirit. In this sense, a particular biblical book is canonical at the time of its writing, or, holistically, at the time of the writing of the last book of the whole biblical canon. Canonical lists and manuscripts, as well as other paratextual phenomena like titles and the *nomina sacra*,[13] are

11. Davies, "The Jewish Scriptural Canon in Cultural Perspective," 51–52. See also McDonald's more recent treatment of the canonical process of the NT in *The Formation of the Biblical Canon*, 2:354–55, for a summary of his position on the ecclesiastical mechanisms that (in his telling) produced the NT.

12. One small example of how easy it is to oversimplify these complexities is Eusebius's use of "accepted," "debated," and "spurious" categories for the canonicity of certain NT books. Not only is it anachronistic to assume that these categories accurately reflect our twenty-first-century notion of canon and canonicity, but it is also the case that even within the early church there were debates about how exactly to understand what these categories mean and how to translate them from, e.g., Origen's Greek to Latin. See Gallagher, "Origen *via* Rufinus on the New Testament Canon," esp. 464–71.

13. Contra Allen, *Words Are Not Enough*. The kind of argument quoted in what follows occurs throughout the book: "Whenever we copy a text, frame it with paratexts, and select the materials on which we will write the words, we make the work anew. Bibles are the products of human choice. Sacred texts were never unassailable. . . . Paratexts

evidence of the people of God's continued attempts to rightly receive and remember those canonical books. The order of being precedes the order of knowing.[14] The canon *is* the canon at the time of writing; the canon *is acknowledged* as the canon through the historical process of the canon's reception by the people of God.[15]

The Church and Canonical Criteria

Israel's and the church's role in canonization is to hear, or recognize, the Word of the LORD as distinct from other words, and, upon hearing, to receive, remember, and obey it. Another way to put this is that Israel in the OT period and the church in the NT period and beyond are called to evaluate words about God for the ontological criteria of divine revelation discussed earlier in chapters 2, 3, and 4. A truly canonical book—that is, a book truly inspired by the Holy Spirit—will bear both intrinsic and extrinsic marks. Intrinsically, or ontologically, canonical books are known to be such because they (1) reveal the triune God (2) in the person and work of Jesus Christ (3) through the textually and conceptually unified inspiration of the Holy Spirit.

But there are also extrinsic marks. In the early church, these were commonly known as apostolicity, liturgy, ubiquity, and acceptance. A book was considered to be canonical if it was written by an apostle or someone closely associated with an apostle, if it was used in corporate worship, if it was used by churches throughout the geographical expanse of early Christianity, and if it was widely accepted as canonical by churches in the postapostolic period. The latter two criteria are,

---

give us new insights into our sacred texts, but they also tell us a lot about the people who made them" (34; see also 89, 98–99, 166–67). As is evidenced by the disjuncture between the point of the last sentence quoted above and the previous statements, Allen conflates throughout the book the *revelation* of Scripture with its *reception* and *production*. These are not the same.

14. See Collett, "Reading Forward," esp. 178–79, for this language.

15. So Gignilliat, *Reading Scripture Canonically*, 7: "To make matters clear, canon registers its proper theological force when it is understood first as an internal property of the biblical texts and second as an external decision or act." For a similar account from a dogmatic perspective, see Webster, "The Dogmatic Location of the Canon," 33–42.

effectively, what I've called in this chapter "lists and manuscripts." Not all evidence for ubiquity and acceptance is reducible to a list or manuscript, but those types of evidence are the predominant means by which we can now measure those criteria.[16] What, then, about apostolicity and use in worship?

I want to suggest that the criteria of apostolicity and liturgy are the early church's way of articulating that a book coheres with the rest of Scripture—that is, with the OT. At the time of the early church's reception of the NT, Israel's Scriptures were the measure by which the early church evaluated sound doctrine (e.g., 2 Tim. 3:14–15) and, in this case, canonical status. Apostolicity was a way to articulate that a NT book cohered with the authoritative Scriptures of the OT and, therefore and ultimately, with the authority of Jesus Christ, Israel's Messiah. Liturgical use was the sign of this coherence with established biblical authority.

This makes sense given the discussion of the church's role in the hearing the Word of the Lord in the first half of this chapter. To hear the Word of the Lord and receive it, we must recognize it as the Word of the Lord and not a false word. To "test the spirits" (1 John 4:1) is to test all words against the word of Moses, the Torah, and the Word incarnate, to whom Moses points, Jesus Christ. The early church's criterion of apostolicity was a way to articulate this task, and liturgical use was a sign of the authority recognized.

I want to suggest, though, that the canonical phenomena already discussed in chapters 4 and 5—intertextuality, typology, and Christ-centered narrative—are also intrinsic marks that may be used to evaluate canonicity. We can look at a particular book, whether the Didache or 2 Peter, and ask whether it bears those marks. Answering that question, in turn, helps the church to evaluate the book's

16. While I do not discuss the task of textual criticism at any length in this book, I believe it ought to be considered in this same set of categories: ecclesial reception of God's Word, tested and refined through the process of comparing manuscripts. For a theological account of textual criticism, see Gignilliat, *Reading Scripture Canonically*, 57–79. For a recent historical account of textual criticism and the transmission of the Bible that arises from many of the same fundamental theological commitments as those that ground this book, see Meade and Gurry, *Scribes and Scripture*. Regarding issues of the Septuagint and canon, especially as they relate to textual criticism and canonical reception of particular books, see Gallagher, "Suddenly and Then Gradually."

canonical status; it helps the church recognize the book's intrinsic nature either as merely a helpful human word or a divinely inspired Word given by the Spirit.

While these extrinsic and intrinsic marks were not called by these names, nor were they necessarily always even mentioned explicitly in discussions of a book's apostolicity or liturgical use, there is some indication that the early church paid attention to these phenomena in their evaluation.[17] These criteria were also related to the rule of faith. Apostolicity, for instance, is not merely a matter of knowing Jesus personally; it means that one has been entrusted to pass along faithfully Jesus's teaching—that is, the rule of faith. And the rule of faith is none other than the revelation of the triune God in the person and work of his incarnate Son, the content of Holy Scripture and the criterion by which all other Scripture is judged (e.g., chap. 2 of this book). Liturgical use and widespread acceptance are, relatedly, the church's recognition of Scripture and its accordance with the rule of faith, although, as I have said throughout this chapter, individual churches and theologians can err in their reception of the biblical text.

One example is Augustine's well-known list of canonical books in his *On Christian Teaching*. While Augustine lists books that Protestants would not affirm as canonical, it is important for our purposes here to note that he uses the criterion of widespread acceptance (i.e., catholicity) to adjudicate between canonical and noncanonical, but still useful, books. In other words, while he himself affirms certain extracanonical books, he also gives freedom for his readers to refrain from affirming those books because they are not widely accepted by all.[18] Augustine thus both (1) recognizes that his own opinion is not

17. On apostolicity as a theological category, rather than a purely historical or post hoc ecclesially declared marker, in relation to the Epistle to the Hebrews, see Webster, *God Without Measure*, 1:59–80. More broadly, see Webster, *Holy Scripture*, 50–52.

18. So Augustine, *On Christian Teaching* 2.24–25 (pp. 35–36):

> In the matter of canonical scriptures he should follow the authority of the great majority of catholic churches, including of course those that were found worthy to have apostolic seats and receive apostolic letters. He will apply this principle to the canonical scriptures: to prefer those accepted by all catholic churches to those which some do not accept. As for those not universally accepted, he should prefer those accepted by a majority of churches,

necessarily authoritative and (2) references a commonly used external criterion—widespread acceptance among churches—to allow for others to come to different conclusions.[19]

Conclusion

Ecclesial lists and other such canonical phenomena are products of the church's attempt to accurately recognize the Word that God inspired through his Holy Spirit. As Todd Billings notes, "The canonical process is one in which the church comes to recognize the ongoing voice of Jesus Christ through the Spirit in Scripture, not simply one in which a certain group of people exercise their own power."[20] Or, as Kevin Vanhoozer puts it, "The process of the church's gradual recognition of certain texts as canonical, which from the historical perspective appears both tainted and arbitrary, makes good theological sense when viewed in christological perspective. The proper dogmatic location of the canon may well be the prophetic office of Jesus Christ: 'You have heard that it was said, . . . But I say to you . . .' (Matt. 5:21–44)."[21]

> and by the more authoritative ones, to those supported by fewer churches, or by churches of lesser authority. Should he find that some scriptures are accepted by the majority of churches, but others by the more authoritative ones (though in fact he could not possibly find this situation) I think that they should be considered to have equal authority.

19. On this question see Provan, *The Reformation and the Right Reading of Scripture*, 77–78. Notice also that, in the quotation above, Augustine coordinates catholicity with apostolicity, another external criterion ultimately related to the intrinsic nature of the canon of Scripture.

20. Billings, *The Word of God for the People of God*, 96.

21. Vanhoozer, "The Apostolic Discourse and Its Developments," 203. I would adjust Vanhoozer's language here to say "*may* appear *to some* to be tainted and arbitrary." There is good historical reason to view the canonical process as logical and ordered, even from an entirely empirical perspective. See Provan, *The Reformation and the Right Reading of Scripture*, 55–80.

SEVEN

The Ruled Canonical Shape: Eschatology and Canon

The overall design of the Tanakh provides a hermeneutical lens through which its contents can be viewed.

—Stephen G. Dempster[1]

The significance of the New Testament canon lies, not in the presence of a great variety of perspective, but in its role as offering guidelines on how the variety was to be understood in the light of the unity of Christ.

—Brevard S. Childs[2]

This chapter and the two previous chapters move from the canon's ontology back to the phenomenology that so often dominates conversations about the canon. The discussions of order (chap. 7), lists (chap. 6), and intertextuality (chap. 5) are now couched in the broader ontology of the canon outlined in chapters 2–4. This particular chapter focuses on the shape, or order, of the

1. Dempster, *Dominion and Dynasty*, 42.
2. Childs, *The New Testament as Canon*, 30.

canon and argues that it is a function of the canon's Christocentric purpose. The canonical order, in all its variety, always evinces what John Sailhamer calls "eschatological messianic hope."[3] This chapter also returns to the concept of "final form" and relates it to the ontology of the canon outlined in the first half of the book. First, though, this chapter gestures toward the previous one, in that canonical order is related to the community of faith that receives the canon.

Order as Ecclesial Reception

Much like lists and manuscripts, different canonical orders are reflections of ecclesial reception of biblical books. Instead of acknowledging what is and is not Holy Scripture, however, different orders are primarily concerned with reading strategies. That is, while lists and manuscripts are concerned primarily with acknowledging what is and is not Holy Scripture, canonical orders are concerned primarily with how to read and understand Holy Scripture as a coherent and unified text.

Canonical Order in Recent Study

At least since Brevard Childs, and especially since the generation that followed him and adopted his approach, order as a canonical phenomenon has received much more attention than it did in previous generations, perhaps in the whole history of Christian hermeneutics. The discussion is wide-ranging, to say the least. There are a number of different approaches to and considerations of order, some of which overlap and some of which are completely contradictory to one another.

In a recent essay on the state of the question in NT canonical studies,[4] I have articulated three categories for approaching the issue of canonical shape. First, there are those who "see it as hermeneutically insignificant." Second, there are those who "see it as hermeneutically significant, but only in a *post hoc* fashion." Finally, there are those who "see it as hermeneutically significant because of

3. Sailhamer, *Introduction to Old Testament Theology*, 154–55.
4. Emerson, "The Canonical Shape of the New Testament."

its authorially- or editorially-intended compositional coherence."[5] For the first category, order plays no role in interpretation, either at the level of individual corpora or from a more macro-canonical perspective.[6] For the second category, order is a "paratextual"[7] phenomenon, one that is not part of the original authorship of the text but nevertheless plays a role in interpretation—namely, in a reader-oriented fashion.[8] Finally, certain canonically oriented interpreters argue that order is not merely a paratextual phenomenon but one that is embedded within the text in the process of the text's authorship. In other words, understanding the author's intent includes understanding how a particular corpus is ordered because authors within the corpus—or, perhaps, a "canonical editor" for the entire biblical corpus—embedded within the text features related to the particular corpus's "final form."[9]

Casey Croy has also recently articulated heuristic categories for different approaches to canonical shape from the perspective of OT studies: "compositional" and "compilational."[10] Compositional approaches argue, like my third category above, that there are features embedded within the texts of a particular corpus that are indicative of intentional canonical shaping. Compilational approaches, on

5. Emerson, "The Canonical Shape of the New Testament," 80.

6. So Metzger, *The Canon of the New Testament*, 300; Patzia, *The Making of the New Testament*, 182–83. James Barr provides some of the most fundamental and sustained critiques of so-called canonical approaches (Barr, *The Concept of Biblical Theology*, esp. 378–48, but also 307–11; Barr, *Holy Scripture*, 160–61).

7. Gregory Goswell has written extensively on this approach, especially in the *Journal of the Evangelical Theological Society*. Most recently, he has revised many of these essays and turned them into a single volume, *Text and Paratext*.

8. In addition to Goswell, see Gamble, *The New Testament Canon*, 67; D. Smith, *The Canonical Function of Acts*; Wall, "The Canonical View."

9. E.g., Lockett, *Letters from the Pillar Apostles*; Seitz, *The Goodly Fellowship of the Prophets*; Childs, *The Church's Guide for Reading Paul*; Spellman, *Toward a Canon-Conscious Reading of the Bible*, esp. 108–41; see also, on the notion of "canon consciousness" in the NT, Childs, *The New Testament as Canon*, 21–24.

10. Croy, *Sequencing the Hebrew Bible*. Croy's book was published prior to my T&T Clark essay, but unfortunately I submitted my essay for review prior to the publication of Croy's work and wasn't able to interact with it. In many ways our observations about the *status quaestionis* of OT and NT canonical approaches are complementary rather than contradictory. See also his definition of *canon* and *canonical approach*.

the other hand, acknowledge that certain aspects of shaping can be identified as a result of authorial intent embedded within particular texts, but also that certain shaping features may indeed be paratextual and post hoc. Sometimes it is difficult, maybe even impossible, to adjudicate between these options.

Additionally, Croy identifies "single arrangement" approaches as distinguished from "multiple arrangement" approaches.[11] The former argues for an "original arrangement" of the books within a particular corpus or testament, one that "best reflects the theological message of those who compiled the books within the Hebrew Bible together."[12] While not denying later alternative orders, this approach identifies one particular order as the first and therefore most fundamental in terms of hermeneutical significance. Multiple-arrangement approaches, on the other hand, argue that there are multiple, noncompeting orders to corpora and testaments, and that identifying and understanding each of these is important in order to "account for the theological message underlying the compilation of books."[13] Finally, Croy notes that there is variety among canonical interpreters as to the combination of these options. One can identify multiple-arrangement-compositional approaches, as well as multiple-arrangement-compilational approaches. The same is true for single-arrangement approaches; both compositional and compilational approaches exist within that larger single-arrangement model.[14]

Canonical Order as Ecclesial Reception

What, then, are we to do with these various options? One way to proceed is to examine carefully the textual and paratextual phenomena and make an argument for one of the above approaches. This is how much canonical conversation actually proceeds. Scholars argue for compositional evidence within particular corpora,[15] or for

11. Croy, *Sequencing the Hebrew Bible*, 4.
12. Croy, *Sequencing the Hebrew Bible*, 4.
13. Croy, *Sequencing the Hebrew Bible*, 4.
14. See the survey of scholarship in Croy, *Sequencing the Hebrew Bible*, 3–23.
15. E.g., Seitz, *The Goodly Fellowship of the Prophets*.

the historical priority of a particular order,[16] or for the theological fittingness of one shape among other options.[17] Others argue for strong compositional evidence at both the corpora and the macro-level, on the one hand,[18] and for the relative lack of importance of canonical shape at either level, on the other hand.[19] Perhaps someone someday will solve this exegetical and empirical riddle. I have my own doubts as to whether or not that is really possible. What, then, do we say about shape in the absence of a solution or, even if the future holds one, the presence of some yet-to-be-found answer key?

Here we return to the point made in the opening of this chapter, that shape as canonical phenomenon should be understood theologically in relation to the doctrine of ecclesiology. Specifically, canonical shape is evidence of the intentional arrangement of biblical books in order to facilitate understanding by the people of God. *At the very least*, this is a post hoc literary reality that cannot be ignored. Even if the authors of these books were entirely unaware of other biblical books (which is highly unlikely if not straight-out false), these individual books have been received, arranged, and circulated by the people of God as the collectively inspired Word of God. Both literary theory and the doctrine of ecclesiology demand that we acknowledge the significance of this fact.

Regarding the former, the order or shape of literary material always serves as a guide to interpretation. John Sailhamer refers to this as "con-textuality." In written, audial, and visual artistic productions, the arrangement of material, consciously intentional or otherwise, always aids the reader, hearer, or observer in understanding that material. This is no less true of the Bible. The people of God have received these books and arranged them in certain ways, and that

16. See Beckwith, *The Old Testament Canon of the New Testament Church*, 181–234.

17. See the discussion in Dempster, "A Wandering Moabite," and Stone, "The Search for Order."

18. See Chapman, *The Law and the Prophets*; Croy, *Sequencing the Hebrew Bible*; and Spellman, *Toward a Canon-Conscious Reading of the Bible*.

19. Most intractably, perhaps, James Barr. See *The Concept of Biblical Theology*, esp. 378–48, but also 307–11; and *Holy Scripture*, 160–61.

arrangement cannot help but impact the reader's interpretation of those texts.[20]

Consider again the shifting place of Ruth within the OT. It obviously resonates with Judges and Samuel on a number of levels. Historically, it is set during the period of the judges, which links it with the former book, and it also is the precursor to the rule of David, the subject of the latter book. Linguistically, it has ties to the formulas of Judges as well as to the opening chapters of Samuel. And, theologically, it is about God's faithfulness to his covenant to Abraham in the midst of Israel's failure.

But even given these resonances with Judges and Samuel and therefore Ruth's fittingness as an intervening book between the two, it also fits equally well in the third section of the Hebrew Bible, the Writings, whether as the first book because of its chronological preeminence in terms of David's life, and therefore followed by Davidic material (i.e., Psalms), or as a work adjacent to Proverbs and Song of Solomon because of its linguistic and theological resonances, with imagery of both the Davidic heir and the gentile virtuous woman (e.g., "the virtuous woman" who is "praised in the gates"; cf. Prov. 31:10, 31 and Ruth 3:11).

In both of these cases, the placement of Ruth helps the reader understand the book and identify certain themes within it. (Of course, we must hasten to add that order does not *add* meaning to a book, but merely prompts the reader to notice certain themes or parallels.) Literary theory acknowledges this role of shape, order, and arrangement in the reader's interpretation of a text.

But there is a more fundamental theological reality at play as well. The people of God have received these texts, arranged them, and circulated them for the purpose of discipleship. In that sense, order is not merely a function of literary theory but, more importantly, an aid to the ongoing catechetical task of the *ecclesia*. It is true that certain aspects of canonical order can be explained by simple empirical realities, like chronology and size. But this is not uniform (e.g., the Writings),[21] and it certainly is not the *exclusive* category by which to

20. See Sailhamer, *Introduction to Old Testament Theology*, 213–14; Goswell, *Text and Paratext*; Allen, *Words Are Not Enough*.

21. See Croy, *Sequencing the Hebrew Bible*, esp. 35–56, for exploration of this particular point.

understand shape. As we will see below, there are clearly exegetical, catechetical, and theological realities at play in the multiple arrangements of the canon.

Of course, all of this is what we have to say if order is a post hoc reality. Even more is at stake if there is not merely compilation and arrangement of individual books into a corpus but also composition of those individual books in order to be arranged as a particular corpus. In that case, order would be not merely a matter of reception, but of inspiration, which would bring us back to the discussion about intertextuality in chapters 4 and 5. For my part, I do believe that certain instances of arrangement are the result of the divine inspiration of human authors, and therefore should be understood along the lines of authorial intent that I have discussed previously. The point of this chapter, though, does not depend on where one lands on that question. Shape is, again, *at the very least*, the attempt of the people of God to understand the received Word of God and give disciples a guide to its interpretation via the arrangement of the collections.[22]

Given these relatively circumspect conclusions—order is a function of ecclesial reception and discipleship, and there are multiple received arrangements of individual corpora—what, then, can we say about that catechetical function of canonical arrangement? In other words, what are our spiritual forebearers attempting to teach us through these various shapes of the biblical material? In the section below, we will see that these multiple arrangements can each be explained as christological and, more particularly, eschatological.

Order as Christological and Eschatological Phenomenon

There are a few ways to address shape as a canonical phenomenon in relation to both Christology and eschatology. Most importantly, we need to address both the fact of the two-testament Christian Bible as well as the ordering within individual corpora. We also need to address these realities of shape as both compositional and compilational

22. This ought to prompt us to be circumspect about prioritizing one order over another. See Seitz, *The Elder Testament*, 119–29, as well as his treatment of the major OT corpora (Law, Prophets, Writings) in the subsequent chapters (pp. 131–75).

(interpretive grids related to ecclesial reception). First, though, we need to state briefly the relation between Christology and eschatology as theological loci.

A robust eschatology is rooted in Christology.[23] That is, the study of last things is a study of the culmination of the work of Christ at his return in glory. This is true narrowly of the four *novissima* (Latin: "last things") of eschatology: death and judgment (personal eschatology), and heaven and hell (cosmic eschatology). Death is crushed to death by Christ in his own death, descent, and resurrection, and will be thrown into the lake of fire at his return in glory. Additionally, because Christ has conquered death, every human being will be raised from death to either eternal life or eternal judgment at his return. Our own deaths and resurrections to final judgment are therefore intimately connected to and brought to finality by Christ's own death and resurrection and his authority to judge the living and the dead. Hell and heaven, as cosmic realities in which those eternal judgments are executed, are also realms of Christ's authority and governed by him in eternity. His vicarious life, substitutionary atoning death, descent to the dead, and resurrection from the dead are the means by which he secures (Rev. 1:18) and enacts (21:1–8) his earthly authority over those realms.

More broadly, eschatology as a reference not only to the four *novissima* but also to the *telos* of God's creation is centered on Christ's person and work as well. God's purposes for humanity—to be his image bearers who are fruitful and multiply and fill all the earth, who exercise dominion over his place, who cultivate and keep his place, who obey his word, and who dwell with him forever—are all fulfilled in the person and work of Christ. He is the New, Second, and Last Adam, and through his death and resurrection and at his return, he will dwell as the King among his people in the new heavens and new earth. In this sense, to say that canonical shape is eschatological is to affirm that, both doctrinally in the four *novissima* and narratively in the overarching story of Scripture, canonical shape is centered on the person and work of Jesus. What we see in order, then, is a canonical phenomenon rooted in the theological purpose of canon—namely, to be ruled toward Christ.

23. König, *The Eclipse of Christ in Eschatology*.

The Two Testaments of Scripture as Eschatological Phenomenon

The most basic fact of canonical shape is its two-testament character.[24] As we have noted throughout, Christopher Seitz, in particular, highlights this aspect of the biblical canon as its fundamental theological reality. As he puts it with respect to the NT's shape, "The NT takes form and derives its authority not only with respect to apostolic memory or eyewitnessing. . . . Crucial for the formation of the NT and its canonical logic is a proper understanding of the Law and the Prophets upon which this logic is based in the confession of Jesus Christ as the Son of God in accordance with the Scriptures."[25]

For our purposes in this chapter, I will highlight how this unified shaping of the two-testament Bible is an explicitly eschatologically oriented phenomenon.[26] This is true, first of all, through the compositional shape of the Christian Bible. That is, the NT's extensive quotations of, allusions to, and narrative mimetic repetition of the OT highlight the fundamental textual, narratival, and theological connection between the two. Further, this connection is explicitly eschatological, in the sense that the NT explicitly frames itself as the fulfillment of God's promises in the OT through the person and

24. While I emphasize in what follows the eschatological shape and unity of the canon, there is perhaps an even more fundamental point to be made relating to the canon's conceptual unity as indicated by its shape: The very fact of the two-testament Bible and the attendant shapes of its corpora are indications that the whole book shares one, unified message. This is the point that, e.g., Markus Bockmuehl makes in *Seeing the Word*, 108–13. Although he is speaking particularly of the shape of the NT, he makes clear that his assessment is in relation to Israel's Scriptures (e.g., noting that Matt. 1 provides a fitting introduction to the NT). Note also Childs, *Old Testament Theology in a Canonical Context*, 9: "I would suggest that careful attention to the shape of the Christian canon provides some initial guidelines for overcoming this dilemma [of pitting the "Jewish" OT against the "Christian" NT]. The Christian canon maintains the integrity of the Old Testament in its own right as scripture of the church. However, it sets it within a new canonical context in a dialectical relation with the New Testament. . . . The Old Testament functions within Christian scripture as a witness to Jesus Christ precisely in its pre-Christian form."

25. Seitz, *The Goodly Fellowship of the Prophets*, 35–36.

26. On the eschatological character of the Christian Bible and the eschatological context of its formation, see Work, *Living and Active*, 215–300. On the eschatological character of Scripture in general and in relation to the centrality of Christ's person and work, see Ratzinger, *The Word of the Lord*, 24–25.

work of Jesus Christ by his Spirit in his church. The canonical shape of the Christian Bible is therefore inescapably eschatological; God's promises to Adam and Israel have been fulfilled in the person and work of Jesus of Nazareth and will be consummated at his return in judgment and glory.

This brings us to a second way that the two-testament Christian Bible is explicitly eschatological in its shape: Both testaments end on a note of expectation. While there are multiple attested orders of each testament, each order in its own way brings with it the hope that God will soon fulfill his promises. With respect to the OT, both the Tanakh order and the Greek order end with expectation of Israel's coming Messiah and his restoration of God's people and God's place.[27] With respect to the NT, every attested order builds toward the expectation of the return of Christ, whether as promised in the book of Revelation or as highlighted in either the Catholic Epistles or the latter half of the letters of Paul.[28] I will discuss these various options for the orders of both testaments, along with their various corpora, below. Here, the primary point is that both at a compositional and a compilational level, the shape of the two-testament Christian Bible is fundamentally eschatological in its orientation toward the first and second comings of Israel's Messiah and the world's Savior, Jesus Christ.

Eschatological Ordering in Each Testament and in the Christian Bible

When we look closer at the ordering of each testament and the individual corpora within them, we see similar eschatological orientations. This is not to claim insight into the original authors', editors', and/or arrangers' thought processes, but rather is simply a hermeneutical claim about the interpretive effect of the orders as presented.[29] Additionally, it is a hermeneutical claim that is rooted not merely in the post hoc effects of order but, more fundamentally, in the compositional nature of the Christian Bible discussed above.

27. See Goswell, "The Old Testament as Prophecy and the Structure of the Canon."

28. This is the argument of Emerson, *Christ and the New Creation.*

29. See Sailhamer, *Introduction to Old Testament Theology*, 214–15.

The intertextual tapestry that is Christian Scripture demands that we read the whole Bible as a forward-looking testimony to the first and second advents of Israel's Messiah, Jesus Christ. What follows is thus an attempt to understand the phenomenon of canonical order from the perspectives of both composition and compilation.[30] The former is, at the very least, demanded by the fact of the two-testament Bible; the latter is warranted by the literary category of "con-textuality." While I will attempt to distinguish between the two in what follows, this is not always possible.

Regarding the OT, we can say that both at a macro-canonical level and within the individual corpora there is an eschatological thrust.[31] Indeed, one might characterize the entire OT as pushing toward an "eschatological messianic hope."[32] Again, this is true at both a compositional and a compilational level.[33] With respect to composition, we could mention the *protoevangelium* of Genesis 3:15 and its refrains throughout the remainder of the world's and Israel's story, or the narrative and textual interrelation between Moses, David, and Elijah, or the arrangement of the book of Psalms in intertextual harmony with other parts of the Hebrew Bible.[34] And, of course, there are many more instances of composition than these. The point here is that the OT is a textually and narratively interconnected whole, providentially[35] inspired by the Holy Spirit[36] and authorially intended

30. For another approach like this, see Croy, *Sequencing the Hebrew Bible*, and, similarly, Spellman, "Metaphors We Read Canonical Collections By."

31. So Seitz, commenting on early Christian reading of the OT: "So far as the New Testament was concerned, what was at stake was not prophecy's connection to Moses, which Jews and Christians both accepted, but rather the character of its future referentiality (and this was true not just of the prophets but of the Old Testament in its entirety). . . . Indeed, all of the Old Testament could be said to be prophetic" (Seitz, *Prophecy and Hermeneutics*, 67).

32. Sailhamer, *Introduction to Old Testament Theology*, 206.

33. For an example of reading the OT with canonical shape in mind, see Dempster, *Dominion and Dynasty*.

34. See Cole, *Psalms 1–2*.

35. On the relation of divine providence and "final form," see Gignilliat, *Reading Scripture Canonically*, 26–28.

36. On inspiration, composition, and "final form," see Seitz, *Convergences*, 39: "'Inspiration' refers then to a superintending of the entire canonical process. . . . The 'intent of the author' accords with the inspired movement through concrete history, culminating now in the achievement of the final form of the text."

by the human author, that builds in anticipation from Genesis 1 all the way through the exilic and postexilic literature. This is true regardless of the particular macro- or sub-corporal orders one prefers.[37]

With respect to the OT's macro-structure, we can say, at least, that there are some compositional realities at play between the three major sections—the Law, the Prophets, and the Writings. At the end of the Torah, in Deuteronomy 34, Israel awaits a "prophet like Moses." At the beginning of the Prophets, in Joshua 1, Joshua is portrayed as a prophet like Moses. But, under his leadership and the rest of the prophets, priests, and kings of Israel in the Former Prophets, Israel fails to obey YHWH's law, just as they failed under Moses's leadership. So too, at the end of the Prophets, in Malachi 4, Israel is once again looking for a prophet like Moses, another Elijah who will deliver Israel. In the Writings, whether they begin with Psalms or Ruth or Chronicles, we hear again of these same expectations: a new Moses and a new David, one who will save Israel and bring restoration to God's kingdom. These texts are not only thematically but also textually connected, helping us to see that the OT is an overtly eschatological book, awaiting a new Adam, a new Moses, a new David, Israel's Messiah, the world's Savior.

These compositional realities—of the OT as a whole, given each book's clear intertextual links to other OT texts, and of the macro-structure of Law, Prophets, and Writings—assist the reader of

37. For instance, Rolf Rendtorff says of the Hebrew Bible's orientation toward the future:

> First, the large part of the texts and writings [of the Hebrew Bible] are dominated by the consciousness that the present situation does not or does not yet correspond to what Israel hopes for and what it has been promised. So Israel must itself work towards the realization of that hope. Above all, this realization requires constantly hoping and praying for the help of God.
>
> Second, the Hebrew Bible texts look forward constantly to an anticipated "afterwards," i.e. to a time after the things that now stand in the way of the realization of the hopes and promises have been overcome. But this hope is not directed towards something that lies "beyond" present reality, but to a reformation or reshaping of this reality in line with the hopes and promises. Part of this reality is the firm certainty that, in the future too, God will never dissolve or break the covenant he has made with Israel. (Rendtorff, *The Canonical Hebrew Bible*, 714–15)

individual corpora and their shape.[38] We do not have space here to walk through each corpus of the OT and demonstrate the compositional realities that exist within, or to make extensive arguments about how to understand the shape of each given those intertextual links.[39] Suffice it to say that, when we study the order of the individual corpora, similar eschatological, messianic expectations emerge. The movement of the Torah from creation in Genesis 1–2 to the expectation of a new Moses who will lead Israel into the promised land is clearly one in which the end of the story is yet to happen. The Prophets begin with the Former Prophets telling the rest of Israel's story, which is not one of fulfillment of the Torah's promises of restoration but instead is one in which Israel experiences the punishment for disobedience. Adam's story is repeated in Israel's. For this reason, the Prophets end with the Latter Prophets, in which YHWH promises that, despite impending judgment on Israel's current generations, he will one day restore his people and his place.[40]

The most difficult and disputed section of the OT regarding order is the Writings. Despite these ongoing debates, however, we can still make modest observations about its shape, including, most importantly for our purposes, that there remains a similar eschatological expectation. Ruth, Psalms, and Chronicles, the three primary contenders for the beginning of the section, all end with notes of

38. While we should not overinterpret some of Childs's statements about final form and shape to indicate an affirmation of composition, he does make comments here and there that seem to suggest some kind of overall composition of the Hebrew Bible and its attendant shape. So, for instance, he says, "The canonical process involved the shaping of the tradition not only into independent books, but also into larger canonical units, such as the Torah, Prophets, and Writings" (Childs, *Old Testament Theology in a Canonical Context*, 13). On the ambiguity in Childs's work related to composition versus compilation, see Emerson, "The Canonical Shape of the New Testament," 84–86.

39. On textual association in the Prophets and the Writings and its relation to the final form of those corpora, see Seitz, *The Goodly Fellowship of the Prophets*, 77–104 and 105–25, respectively. Seitz also repeatedly makes gestures toward the canonical formation of both the Writings and the NT in light of the Law and the Prophets and with similar processes involving textual association (pp. 99–101 for the Writings, p. 103 for the NT).

40. On the interrelation of Torah to the Prophets and Writings, including with respect to the beginning and endings of those corpora, see Rendtorff, *The Canonical Hebrew Bible*, 5–6.

expectation and hope in Israel's future deliverance. Chronicles and Ezra–Nehemiah, the two main options for the end of the section, both end with unfinished business: the return from exile at the end of Chronicles and the continued disobedience of Israel at the end of Ezra–Nehemiah. These two features, the possibilities at the beginning and end of the corpus, give the section an eschatological flavor.

Looking at what comes in between, we find similar themes. Four of the five narrative books in the section—Esther, Daniel (1–6), Ezra–Nehemiah, and Chronicles—are set in the exilic and postexilic periods. Ruth is set during the period of the judges, but this is historically analogous. In all of them, Israel is waiting for deliverance from their enemies inside and outside the promised land. Job and Lamentations look for God to deliver his people from suffering. Ecclesiastes reminds its readers that nothing lasts except God and his works, and that wisdom is found in God alone. Proverbs awaits the son of the (Davidic) king who will walk in wisdom by the Spirit. Song of Solomon looks for that same king to return to the renewed land with his bride. Psalms looks for the wise king who will crush Israel's enemies with a rod of iron. Each of these latter three concerns David and his Son, the Son who will walk in wisdom, restore the land, and rescue his bride. In other words, these books are concerned with the same hope that is expressed narratively and prophetically in the Torah and in the Prophets. The middle of the Writings is filled with the same expectations that we find at its boundaries.

Before we leave the OT, we need to briefly address the order of OT books found in Greek translations of the Hebrew Bible. I do not intend here to solve any debates about priority or inclusion (or exclusion) of particular books. Rather, I need to state simply that the Greek order also demonstrates the fundamentally eschatological shape of the OT. The rearrangement of the Writings to be distributed throughout the rest of the OT in a way that prioritizes genre and chronology is not without its own theological impact. Here, we want to note that, at a basic level, the placement of the prophetic books at the end of the OT has a clearly eschatological and messianic thrust. The Greek OT ends with the hope that God will soon deliver Israel through the New Moses and New Elijah of Malachi 4 and, as seen more broadly in the other prophetic books, that he will restore the land, provide victory over his enemies, raise the dead, rebuild the temple, and send his Spirit through the Suffering Servant, Davidic king, and Anointed One.

Whether we consider the Hebrew or the Greek order, then, the shape of the OT is one of eschatological messianic expectation. The people of God have arranged the various books of the Word of God to communicate their hope in God's coming salvation through his Messiah.

The NT authors, both narratively and in epistolary fashion, indicate that Jesus of Nazareth, Israel's Messiah and the world's Savior, God the Son in the flesh, is the fulfillment of that eschatological hope articulated in Israel's Scriptures. The covenant promises to Abraham and David are brought to completion in the person and work of Jesus Christ. In the Gospels and Acts, the Evangelists (and Luke in particular in Luke and Acts) narrate Jesus's birth, ministry and miracles, passion and death, resurrection, ascension, gift of the Spirit, and ongoing mission through his church in order to show how he is the fulfillment of Israel's hopes. In the letters of the NT, Paul,[41] James, John, Peter, and Jude argue this point doctrinally and connect it to their ethical instructions to the churches under their care.[42] The Gospels, Acts, and Epistles also look forward to Christ's return

41. For an overview of theories regarding the compilation of the Pauline corpus from an historical perspective, see Porter, "When and How Was the Pauline Canon Compiled?," as well as Trobisch, *Paul's Letter Collection*, with which Porter interacts extensively in his essay. Finally, see Wall, "The Function of the Pastoral Letters in the Pauline Canon of the New Testament," who argues that the Pastoral Epistles are included in the Pauline Epistles canon in order to round out its emphasis on the church and good works. He summarizes his argument this way: "Only in consideration of this thirteen-letter whole, and not a fraction thereof, is a complete understanding of the Pauline *regula fidei* possible for Christian nurture" (36). This emphasis on a final, thirteen-letter Pauline collection is intended to provide contrast with Marcion's incomplete, ten-letter Pauline canon. Notice that Wall also places canonization at the end of an ecclesial process (see Wall, "Function of the Pastoral Letters," 27, as well as a multitude of other writings by him on the subject) rather than at the point of authorship. Canonization and shaping are first ecclesial—not pneumatological—functions for Wall, even though he would acknowledge the Spirit's role in that process.

42. As Richard Bauckham notes, James's canonical location, both in Eastern and Western orders, emphasizes not a disjunction between its message—or the message of the Catholic Epistles more broadly—and that of Paul, but instead their unity (*James*, 112–40). This is in contradistinction to, for instance, Luther's comments on the letter.

in glory and judgment. Finally, in the book of Revelation, John provides a fitting summary of the time between the times, from Jesus's first coming to his second coming, calling God's people to remain faithful to him in spite of the tribulation the world experiences prior to Christ's return. God has been faithful to us in Christ and will be faithful to the end, when Jesus returns in glory and judgment. At that point, he will consummate the work he completed in his first coming, bringing an end to death and sin, restoring his creation, and resurrecting his people to eternal life with him.

It is important to note that this eschatological shape of the NT, like that of the OT, is both compositional and compilational. That is, each of the NT books articulates its points about who Jesus is, what he has done, and how we should live through intertextuality, typology, and other modes of figuration that are explicitly and deliberately drawn from the OT. The NT is eschatologically shaped because it is composed as the articulation of the fulfillment of the eschatological hopes of the OT. And, like the OT, this eschatologically oriented composition gives warrant to understanding the canonical shape of the NT as eschatological as well.

While the shaping of the NT is not univocal in process or scope to the shaping of the OT, in large part due to the compact time frame of the composition of the NT as compared to the many centuries that it took to compose the OT, there are still evidences of shaping and shape. One of the most obvious is the circulation of different codices with distinct corpora of NT books: The Gospels circulated as one, the Pauline Epistles as another, and Acts with the Catholic Epistles and Revelation by itself circulated as the other two distinct corpora. These individual codices were also marked with particular text-critical notations marking them off as scriptural and circulated in relatively stable fashion in terms of internal order within each corpus (although there was, of course, some variation, especially among the epistolary corpora).[43]

43. For the manuscript tradition of the NT, see Parker, *An Introduction to the New Testament Manuscripts and Their Texts*. See also Hill and Kruger, *The Early Text of the New Testament*, which includes discussion of the composition of the NT, the manuscript (MS) tradition of various corpora, and the reception of the NT by early Christian writers (e.g., Justin Martyr, Irenaeus). For the compositional and

The point here is not to adjudicate debates about order within NT corpora, but to point out that, at a macro-level, and particularly by virtue of the whole NT's explicit textual and theological connection to the OT, we can say that the NT is eschatologically shaped. The whole NT, as well as its various corpora, serves as a fitting conclusion to the OT in its proclamation of Jesus as Israel's Messiah and also looks forward to the economy of redemption's conclusion in the return of Christ.[44]

The Gospels are primarily concerned with demonstrating how Jesus fulfills Israel's hopes in his life, death, and resurrection, but each Gospel also looks forward to the church's mission after Jesus's resurrection and, eventually, to his return in glory. Acts ends with the mission of the church still on the move, waiting for the gospel to be proclaimed to all nations even as it has already been proclaimed from Jerusalem to Judea and Samaria and the ends of the earth.

The Epistles each teach how Jesus's first coming fulfills Israel's hopes while they also look forward to his second coming. One could even argue that the Epistles are ordered in such a way that those that focus on Christ's first coming as a means of ethical exhortation (Romans through Colossians) precede those that focus on Christ's second coming as a means of ethical exhortation (1 Thessalonians through Jude).

And again, finally, Revelation is intertextually linked to the preceding epistolary corpus, to the narratives of the Gospels and Acts, to the OT prophetic literature, and, indeed, all the way back to Genesis 1–3. In this way, John's exhortation to the church to be faithful until Christ returns in glory and his depiction of Christ's second coming and establishment of the new creation are a fitting end to the NT and to the Bible as a whole. The canonical shape of the NT moves from Christ's first coming to his second coming, and the canonical shape of the Christian Bible moves from creation to new creation.

---

compilational evidence that the NT circulated as four distinct codices within the first century of the church's existence, see Trobisch, *The First Edition of the New Testament*.

44. On the canonical shaping of and connections between the Torah, the Prophets, and the NT canon, see Dempster, "The Prophets, the Canon, and a Canonical Approach," 310–13.

An example from the early church can be mentioned here.[45] Jerome famously listed the order of the Hebrew Bible in his preface to his Vulgate translation project.[46] While certain studies on canon emphasize the relation of Jerome's order to others (i.e., the Masoretic arrangement, Baba Batra 14b),[47] and while Roger Beckwith in particular says that Jerome's order is "purely chronological" (i.e., without hermeneutical basis or significance),[48] Jerome does make a few comments that indicate that he sees interpretive significance in the order of the OT.

First, he lists the order in its tripartite division: Law, Prophets, and Writings. Second, he notes the common refrain "Who will find a brave woman?," as well as the use of acrostics, throughout certain books of the Writings. Third, and drawing on his discussion of the use of acrostics in certain parts of the Hebrew Bible, he says, "As, then, there are twenty-two elementary characters by means of which we write in Hebrew all we say, and the compass of the human voice is contained within their limits, so we reckon twenty-two books, by which, as by the alphabet of the doctrine of God, a righteous man is instructed in tender infancy and, as it were, while still at the breast."[49] Fourth, Jerome compares the commonly acknowledged twenty-four-book order of the Tanakh with the twenty-four elders in the book of Revelation, focusing on their unified message that declares the identity of the one God.[50] Finally, Jerome notes that he has not included "the Apocryphal Writings," among which he lists Wisdom of Solomon, Sirach, Judith, and Tobit. His reason for not including them is that they are written not in Hebrew but in Greek.[51]

45. While I have limited the discussion here to Jerome, one could also mention, for instance, the Eusebian canon tables, paratextual guides to Gospel reading, which are studied at length in Crawford, *The Eusebian Canon Tables*.

46. Jerome, "Preface to Books of Samuel and Kings."

47. E.g., Croy, *Sequencing the Hebrew Bible*, 37–59; Beckwith, *The Old Testament Canon of the New Testament Church*, 181–234.

48. Beckwith, *The Old Testament Canon of the New Testament Church*, 200.

49. Jerome, "Preface to Books of Samuel and Kings," 489.

50. Cf. Hugh of St. Victor's similar comments about the harmony of the shapes of the OT and NT in "On Sacred Scripture and Its Authors," 218–19.

51. Jerome, "Preface to Books of Samuel and Kings," 490.

So, while Jerome's order within each OT corpus may be disputable in relation to other ancient orders, he notes the Hebrew Bible's tripartite shape, recognizes textual associative techniques between books within individual corpora, argues that its limited number of books is a synonym for how we should limit our talk of God to what he has revealed, acknowledges the relation between the OT and NT canonical shapes and their function as divine revelation, and makes canonical decisions about extrabiblical books based on their linguistic association with the acknowledged books (the Law, Prophets, and Writings). Shape, for Jerome, is both ecclesiological, in that it assists in the recognition of canonical books, and hermeneutical, in that it assists in understanding the book made up of these canonical books. While the eschatological element emphasized in this chapter is not immediately present in Jerome's preface, we might note his intentional connection to the last book of the NT, Revelation, in his attempt to relate OT shape to the NT.

This accords with what I have said over the last two chapters. Canonical shape, as evidenced in both textual association and book order, is a guide to reading. Textual association and book order are ultimately christological and (therefore) eschatological guides, urging readers to interpret the texts in front of them as testimonies to God the Son in the flesh and his epochal work in his life, death, resurrection, ascension, rule, and imminent return.

EIGHT

The Ruled Canon and the Rule of Faith: Illumination and Canon

Now if the ministry of death, carved in letters on stone, came with such glory that the Israelites could not gaze at Moses' face because of its glory, which was being brought to an end, will not the ministry of the Spirit have even more glory? For if there was glory in the ministry of condemnation, the ministry of righteousness must far exceed it in glory. Indeed, in this case, what once had glory has come to have no glory at all, because of the glory that surpasses it. For if what was being brought to an end came with glory, much more will what is permanent have glory.

Since we have such a hope, we are very bold, not like Moses, who would put a veil over his face so that the Israelites might not gaze at the outcome of what was being brought to an end. But their minds were hardened. For to this day, when they read the old covenant, that same veil remains unlifted, because only through Christ is it taken away. Yes, to this day whenever Moses is read a veil lies over their hearts. But when one turns to the Lord, the veil is removed. Now the Lord is the Spirit, and where the Spirit of the Lord is, there is freedom. And we all, with unveiled face, beholding the glory of the Lord, are being

> transformed into the same image from one degree of glory to another. For this comes from the Lord who is the Spirit.
>
> —2 Corinthians 3:7–18

This final chapter discusses how to read canonically. Here, the rule of faith will be discussed, and the focus will remain on Scripture's Christocentric content. Irenaeus's tools of hypothesis, economy, and recapitulation will be explained and put forth as proper tools for reading the canon in a Spirit-illumined or ruled fashion. The basic point of the chapter is that the theology of Scripture and in relation to canon articulated in the previous chapters necessitates a particular kind of hermeneutic, one that gives credence both to the canonical *ontology* and to the canonical *phenomena* of the preceding discussions.[1] Or, to say it slightly differently, if the Bible is one book by one author about one subject and one story, then we need modes of reading that give precedence to that fundamental unity.

As with the preceding chapters, these hermeneutical implications follow from both what canon *is* and how it is *formed*.[2] A canonical hermeneutic is ruled in two ways. First, the singular divine source and authorship of the canon—the triune God's Spirit-inspired testimony to himself in the person and work of Jesus Christ—demands a single subject: the person and work of Jesus Christ. This is the fundamental meaning of the *regula fidei* and of canon as theological rule. Second, and correspondingly, the single divine authorship of Scripture also demands reading Scripture as one book, whose parts are interconnected and mutually informative. This is the fundamental meaning of the *analogia fidei* and of canon as interpretive rule. To say this yet another way, and with reference to still more specific interpretive methods, the hermeneutical commitments of hypothesis, economy, and figuration follow from the canon's ontology as the revelation of the triune God in the person of Jesus Christ given by the Holy Spirit,

1. See Webster, "Hermeneutics in Modern Theology."

2. Swain, *Trinity, Revelation, and Reading*, 119–36. See also Chase, *40 Questions About Typology and Allegory*, for an introduction to the history of Christian interpretation, the nuances of defining allegory and typology, the relation of exegesis and figuration, and the biblical warrant for such readings.

while the commitments of *analogia fidei* and canonical reading follow from the phenomenological realities of canonical lists and shape. Or, as John Webster puts it,

> The Bible, its readers, and their work of interpretation have their place in the domain of the Word of God, the sphere of reality in which Christ glorified is present and speaks with unrivaled clarity. . . . Bibliology and hermeneutics are [therefore] derivative elements of Christian theology, shaped by prior Christian teaching about the nature of God and creatures and their relations. . . . [And] bibliology is prior to hermeneutics, because strategies of interpretation will be maladroit unless fitting to the actual nature of the text which they seek to unfold.[3]

I would add here only that canon and canonical hermeneutics are specific modes of addressing that to which Webster refers.

Finally, we will return to the original point of this book—that canon is the material, textual reality of divine revelation—in order to argue that a truly canonical reading is one that orients itself toward two primary ends: love of God and love of neighbor. With regard to the former, canonical hermeneutics is oriented toward theology, the right understanding of the triune God who gives the canon to us. With regard to the latter, love of God leads to imaging God, which means right living in God's world in relation to God, self, and neighbor. This twin goal is the goal of the canon—for its hearers to know God and be transformed into his image. For this reason, a truly canonical reading is akin to the ancient practices of the *quadriga* and *lectio divina*, wherein the reader orients himself toward love of God and neighbor, accomplished through meeting the triune God in the face of Jesus Christ by the power of the Spirit as revealed in the text of Holy Scripture.

Ruled Reading Considers What the Canon Is

We begin with reading strategies that arise from considering the canon's ontology.[4] These are framed largely along the lines proposed by

3. Webster, *The Domain of the Word*, viii.

4. For an overview of the kinds of hermeneutical commitments I cover in this chapter, see Malcolm, *From Hermeneutics to Exegesis*, 89–103; and, specifically

the church's original hermeneutician, Irenaeus of Lyons. Irenaeus, too, was deeply concerned with a right understanding of the church's canon of Scripture, given his ongoing debates with Gnostics and especially with Marcion of Sinope. Irenaeus's arguments for the Christian canon were at the same time arguments for the inclusion and exclusion of particular books and for the use of right reading strategies. These two commitments—canonical boundaries and canonical reading—were and are mutually reinforcing, as we have seen throughout the preceding chapters. It was no different for Irenaeus.

Irenaeus and Ruled Interpretation

In his refutation of the varieties of Gnosticism he encountered, Irenaeus argued, first, that Scripture must be understood in accordance with its own *hypothesis*. He did not mean by this term what we mean in, for instance, scientific experiments, but rather he meant, as the etymology of the word implies, that the Bible has its own foundational main point or underlying thesis (*hypo* + *thesis* = "underlying thesis"). The illustration Irenaeus uses to communicate this idea is that of a mosaic. The tiles must be placed, arranged, and understood in such a way that they reflect the overarching design of the intended picture. Otherwise, the individual tiles make no sense. With respect to the canon of Holy Scripture, the hypothesis is intended to portray a picture of "the handsome King" (Irenaeus's phrase), Jesus Christ (see chaps. 3–5; cf. Luke 16:31; 24:27, 44; John 5:46). A canonical reading acknowledges this fundamental intent of Scripture, to reveal the triune God in the face of Jesus Christ. This is not to say that any particular variety of Christ-centered readings is required, but it is to say that a truly Christian and canonically oriented reading will be one that has that fundamental Christ-centered, Trinity-revealing intent in mind.

A second and related reading strategy articulated by Irenaeus is *oikonomia*, or "economy." The canon of Scripture has one subject, Jesus Christ, and is structurally framed to center on that subject. Another way to put this is that the one story of the Bible centers on

---

with respect to the early church's similar commitments, B. Smith, *Taught by God*, esp. 13–120.

its one subject, the person and work of Jesus Christ. The conceptual center of Scripture is framed by its structure, which also has as its center, in terms of the canon's shape, Israel's Messiah and the world's Savior. To return to the illustration of the mosaic, the tiles must not only be understood as being intended to portray the "handsome King"; they must also be placed together and arranged in a way that actually accomplishes that goal. With respect to the Bible, if we want to understand the various parts of Scripture well, we need to read them both in light of Scripture's main idea, Jesus Christ, and with reference to any given text's place in the economy of Scripture, the storyline of the Bible.[5] As we saw in chapter 3, the Bible is structured as a metanarrative that climactically ends with the first and second advents of Jesus Christ. A canonical reading will therefore give adequate attention to what has been variously called the "grand narrative of Scripture," the "story of the Bible," and so on, when interpreting a particular passage.

Third, Irenaeus argued for a strategy called "recapitulation." Of the three concepts, this is the one most particularly focused on the details of individual texts, and by it Irenaeus means that any given text of Scripture is recapitulated in the person and work of Jesus Christ. This is especially true of narratives, each of which finds its climax, fulfillment, and culmination in the story of Jesus. To once again return to the mosaic, not only do the tiles collectively create an image of the "handsome King," but also each individual tile is in its own unique way an image of that same king. In order to understand individual passages of the Bible, therefore, we need to understand how they find their culmination in the story of Jesus. As we saw in chapters 4 and 5, the intertextual and figural connections of Scripture are a result both of the Bible's divine authorship by the Holy Spirit in his testimony to the incarnate Son and of the *Logos*-centric nature

5. For a representative example from the early church, see Athanasius, *Letters to Serapion on the Holy Spirit* 2.7.1 (p. 114), who says, regarding Prov. 8:22, "We must also demonstrate on the basis of this passage the extent to which they have erred through their ignorance of the plot of the Divine Scripture. . . . 'But,' our opponents say, 'isn't that what's written in the Scriptures?' Yes, that's what's written in the Scriptures! And it must be said. But what is well said is poorly understood by these heretics." See also the remainder of this section for use of the term *economy* combined with biblical quotations about the incarnation.

of creation, and therefore a canonical reading will give attention to the ways in which particular passages are connected textually and figurally to Jesus Christ.

Ruled Interpretation, the Biblical Canon, and Modern Hermeneutics

Having summarized Irenaeus's interpretive methods in light of a theology of Scripture, we can articulate some rules for modern hermeneutics. First, ruled interpretation will give precedence to the purpose of divine revelation: to reveal to us the triune God in the face of Jesus Christ. Second, ruled interpretation will give attention to the economy of Scripture, the storyline that moves from creation to new creation and centers on the person and work of Jesus Christ. Third, ruled interpretation will acknowledge the integral place of figuration in biblical writing, both as a result of the Spirit's inspiration of the whole canon and as consequence of the *Logos*-centric nature of creation. Further, figural reading acknowledges that figuration occurs in the biblical text in a variety of ways: typology, narrative recapitulation, intertextuality,[6] and, yes, allegory.[7] Each of these is, again, the direct result of divine inspiration and *Logos*-centric reality. Fourth, ruled interpretation will allow Scripture to interpret Scripture. That is, it will give attention to the *analogia fidei* due to the nature of the canon as a unified, Spirit-inspired testimony to the triune God in the person and work of Jesus Christ. Finally, ruled interpretation will give attention to the shape of the biblical canon, paying attention to the order of the material and the shape of the entire book.[8] Another way to say this is that ruled interpretation

6. Swain, *Trinity, Revelation, and Reading*, 124.

7. I do not intend to wade into debates about defining allegory. See the remainder of this chapter for discussion relevant to the topic at hand and for resources for further exploration of the topic more broadly.

8. For examples from the early church, see Melito of Sardis, *On Pascha*, 47–49; Gregory of Nyssa, "On the Final Subjection of Christ"; Gregory of Nazianzus, "Oration 38," 73. These orations are very typological, both in terms of Christology and ecclesiology, and many refer to the "analogical sense" (i.e., the summation of a type in the eschaton). For an example of such a reference, see Gregory of Nazianzus, "Oration 40," 132. See also Augustine, *Confessions*, books 12 and 13 (pp. 367–458).

will be canonical, recognizing a text's full literary context as the entire canon.[9]

Notice that each of these rules regarding ruled interpretation is directly tied to the conclusions reached in previous chapters. The first rule corresponds to the reality of the canon as theological rule—that is, as the locus and boundary of divinely inspired, textual divine revelation (chap. 2). The second rule corresponds to the reality of canon as economically centered on the person and work of Christ (chap. 3). The third rule corresponds to the reality of canon as a Spirit-inspired, *Logos*-centric textual unity (chaps. 4 and 5). The fourth rule corresponds to the reality of canon as an ecclesially received and bounded, pneumatologically unified book (chap. 6). And the fifth rule corresponds to the reality of canon as eschatologically (christologically) shaped, ordered toward the first and second comings of Christ both compositionally and compilationally (chap. 7).

Ruled Reading and Interpretive Method

Given these interpretive rules, how might we outline a corresponding interpretive method? There are at least three ways of proceeding. First, we need to consider the disposition of the reader. Second, we need to consider the method(s) by which a given text ought to be read. Finally, we need to consider how to interpret the text well, given its subject: the triune God and his work. In what follows, I am assuming the conclusions of the preceding chapters as well as what has been discussed already in this chapter in terms of the canonical realities at play. In other words, what follows is an attempt to construct an interpretive method based on a theological understanding of what the canon is and how it has been composed and compiled.

First, the nature of the canon as the locus and boundary of God's revelation of himself to his people demands a certain posture in reading—what has historically been called *lectio divina* ("divine [or spiritual] reading"). This posture entails the recognition that when we read the Bible, we are not reading just any other book; we are reading the exclusive, singular, divinely inspired text that is intended to help us

9. See R. Thompson, "Scripture, Christian Canon, and Community," esp. 262–65.

know and love God. While Benjamin Jowett's dictum that we should "read the Bible like any other book" may have had positive results in terms of modern readers' ability to discern literary features and excavate with greater clarity the sociohistorical background of particular texts, it should not be taken as an indication that the Bible is *merely* just another book.[10] Instead, while we should acknowledge the literary features and historical background of the text, we should also acknowledge the Bible's unique status as divinely inspired Scripture and its place in the economy of redemption and in God's covenant purposes for his people. In reading the Bible, we encounter God in the face of Christ by his Spirit. And, in doing so, we are transformed more and more into Christ's image (2 Cor. 3:17–18). In other words, God intends for our reading of the biblical canon to grow us in our love for him and in our love for our neighbor. Our posture in reading, then, should be one in which we expect to grow in that double love through encountering the God who is Love in the text of Holy Scripture. This is the heart of *lectio divina*.[11]

Second, along with a particular interpretive posture, the realities of canon, both ontologically and phenomenologically, demand a certain set of interpretive practices. Once more we start with the ontology of the canon, its status as divine revelation. Because God has chosen to reveal himself to his people, and because he does so in such a way that the divine missions reflect the divine processions, his revelation is conceptually and structurally centered on the person and work of Jesus Christ. Our expectation in reading is to see Jesus. For modern readers, this sounds like an affront to authorial intent. Modern hermeneutics (rightly) emphasizes that meaning is dictated by the author's intent.[12] But, as we saw in chapter 4, we should not pit the intent of the human author against that of the divine author. And, in terms of the category of divine inspiration, the Spirit's intent

10. While Jowett famously coined the dictum, Grant Osborne cites Friedrich Schleiermacher as the progenitor of this concept in modern hermeneutics. See Osborne, *The Hermeneutical Spiral*, 468.

11. On the interrelation of serious exegesis, a posture of *lectio divina*, and the liturgy of the Word in the context of the gathered church, see Bartholomew, *Introducing Biblical Hermeneutics*, 33–47.

12. For a theologically and philosophically rigorous defense of this understanding of meaning, see Vanhoozer, *Is There a Meaning in This Text?*

is to testify to the Son through the intent of the human author. We should expect, then, to see the Son by the Spirit in any given text.

Again, for modern readers, this feels strange. We tend to think of interpretation along inductive lines. By paying attention to the details of any given text, we can discern that text's (distinct, disparate) meaning. In my classes, I use math as an analogy here, noting that modern interpretation approaches the task of finding meaning like this:

> For Text^1, $x + y + z =$ Meaning^1 where x, y, and z are different exegetical details (e.g., original language grammar, vocabulary, and syntax; historical background; and genre-specific literary features).

One could multiply this for every distinct text in the Bible. So,

> For Text^2, $x + y + z =$ Meaning^2
> For Text^3, $x + y + z =$ Meaning^3
> For Text^4, $x + y + z =$ Meaning^4

And so on, *ad infinitum*, or at least *passim*, for every biblical text.

What I am arguing, and what the early church argued as well based on the ontology of the biblical canon, is that the right side of the equation, the text's meaning, does not change from one text to another. Rather, each text has as its meaning, its referent, the person and work of Christ. The math equation would look like this:

> For Text^1, $x + y + z =$ Jesus
> For Text^2, $x + y + z =$ Jesus
> For Text^3, $x + y + z =$ Jesus
> For Text^4, $x + y + z =$ Jesus

Of course, the unique ways that each text signifies Christ and his work will be particular to that text.[13] Even while their meaning is the

13. For entryways into how the early church understood the relation of the details of the text to its christological signification, see Simonetti, *Biblical Interpretation in the Early Church*; Young, *Biblical Exegesis and the Formation of Christian Culture*,

same, the ways in which they convey that meaning are as distinct as individual texts are from one another.[14] Still, the point here is that the first interpretive practice demanded by appropriate attention to the canon's ontology is a Christ-oriented interpretation of the details of the text.

As we noted briefly above, it is through the exegetical details of individual texts that we see Christ and him crucified. The canon is God's revelation of himself to his people, but it is God's revelation of himself *through the Spirit-inspired human authors*. The Bible is a book written by human beings under divine inspiration. The second interpretive practice demanded by attention to the reality of canon, then, is paying attention to the various linguistic, sociohistorical, semantic, and literary details of the text in order to understand well how the human author, under the inspiration of the Holy Spirit, intends to convey his intent.[15]

As we noted in chapter 4, the human author's intent is not in competition with the divine author's intent, and vice versa. Instead, it is through the human author's intent that the Spirit conveys his

---

119–216. See also Young, *Biblical Exegesis*, for examples of premodern exegesis with respect to the relation of the literal and allegorical or spiritual senses in, for example, Didymus (96–98), Diodore (255), Theodore (265–74), and Theodoret (338–40). While some would sharply distinguish the so-called Antiochene and Alexandrian schools on this issue, the differences between them (and between, broadly speaking, all premodern interpreters) are often exaggerated. See, e.g., Simonetti, *Biblical Interpretation in the Early Church*, 67–69; Levy, *Introducing Medieval Interpretation*, 9–19; Trigg, *Biblical Interpretation*, 23–47. Froehlich's summary statement is apt: "It must be pointed out . . . that the sharp antithesis [between Antiochene and Alexandrian approaches] is a construct" (Froehlich, *Biblical Interpretation in the Early Church*, 20). The question for all premodern interpreters is not necessarily *whether* the text points to Christ but *how* (i.e., exegetically speaking).

14. "The *telos* to which God has pointed the texts in the service of salvation is the ultimate criterion of exegetical validity, not the reading techniques used to retrieve it. . . . Because Christ is the content of Scripture, the confession of Christ is its only true hermeneutical canon" (Work, *Living and Active*, 204). See also Webster, *The Domain of the Word*, 45–49.

15. In this respect I find John Peckham's summary of a canonical approach to hermeneutics and theology helpful: "My approach to the canon includes three notable commitments regarding the nature of Scripture: (1) a high view of the revelation-inspiration of the canon, (2) the dual authorship (divine and human) of the canonical text, and (3) the grammatical-historical procedures of exegesis" (Peckham, *Canonical Theology*, 200).

own intent. Therefore, to understand what the divine author intends, we have to pay attention to the human author's intent, or what the early church called "the way the words go." A Christ-oriented reading is not at odds with close exegetical readings; just the opposite. Christ-oriented readings are most appropriate, helpful, and accurate when they give close attention to the exegetical, historical, and literary details of a biblical text. It is through these details that the text conveys its Christ-oriented meaning. As Christopher Seitz puts it, "The literal sense's pointing to the subject matter of Jesus Christ is more than economic referentiality. There is an ontological dimension that must be given proper scope and authority, because the subject matter Jesus Christ is himself 'God of God, Light of Light, very God of very God,' of one substance with the only true God, who speaks and lives and acts within the covenant life of Israel and is attested to on the pages of its sacred scripture."[16]

In other words, the literal sense of the OT does not speak of Jesus Christ *merely* or *only* in prophetic texts, or texts that are obvious fits in the progression of the messianic storyline. Rather, the literal sense of the whole OT is intended to reveal the triune God in the person and work of Jesus Christ. This means, once again, that being exegetically attuned to the details of particular texts is not antithetical to being simultaneously attuned to its theological purpose and dimension.

To be clear, then, none of what is stated above about the Spirit's role in authorship is intended to take us away from the human author's intention or to suggest that the human authors were merely puppets or pawns, ignorant of their own historical affirmations, literary devices, and theological frameworks, which are evident in the text itself and used by the Spirit. This is the exact opposite of what I am arguing. Rather, there is good reason to say that (1) sound hermeneutical theory, via a philosophy of language, can connect the dots between the historically situated author and the modern reader;[17] and (2) the OT authors really did know what they were doing, and

16. Seitz, *The Elder Testament*, 40.

17. Most notably, Vanhoozer, *Is There a Meaning in This Text?* See also Osborne, *The Hermeneutical Spiral*, 519.

they oriented their texts toward Israel's coming Messiah.[18] It is also to say, however, that we must account for the Spirit's divine attributes in articulating a theory of inspiration and meaning, even while we also account for the human author's intention, understood within its original context and with attendance to the details of the text.

Indeed, the bifurcation of the literal and spiritual senses in exegetical practice—a problem that becomes especially acute in the late medieval period—is at best an example of failure to properly use the fourfold method in the early church. It is not, in other words, an indication that premodern interpreters understood there to be an actual, conceptual break between the literal and spiritual senses. In theory, at least, the interpretive tradition, dating back to the earliest mentions of differentiating between the literal and spiritual senses, affirmed the unity of the four senses, their rootedness in the literal sense, and, therefore, the unity of the text's meaning explained across and via the four senses.[19] Seitz is correct in his description of the relation between the two:

> The spiritual sense that St. Thomas was talking about was in fact the literal sense, insofar as it had the capacity to extend signification at a later point in time. . . . At issue is not quibbling over what are two distinct areas of concern—exegesis of the literal sense and contemporary relevance—in terms of their possible significance, but rather the confounding of them. The spiritual sense, and other kindred extended senses, like figuration, were at work in the fathers and in the history of interpretation because they were held to be pressured forth

18. See, for instance, DeRouchie, *Delighting in the Old Testament*, and Cole and Kissling, *Text and Canon*, among many others, especially those cited in the later chapters of this book.

19. See de Lubac, *Medieval Exegesis*, 2:197–207, as well as vol. 1 on the development of the fourfold sense (and the conceptual understanding of the inherent unity of the senses) in the patristic period. Even in modern Roman Catholicism, in which some Protestant interpreters would assume such a bifurcation exists despite perhaps granting that it is not true in patristic or medieval theory, there are church leaders who continue to insist on the interrelation of the spiritual and literal senses. See Ratzinger, *God's Word*, 66–67, who makes an analogy between arbitrary allegorical interpretation and Gnosticism. In other words, to ignore the literal sense, or make it mean something detached from "the way the words go," is to participate in a kind of Gnostic dismissal of the "flesh" of the text's meaning.

> by the literal sense itself. An author said more than he knew, because the author was divinely inspired, and so redolent for a later divine purpose. Events had intelligibility and meaning in their own frame of reference, as divinely disclosed or ordered—the Passover of Israel—but their literal sense betokened a later-sense deliverance—the Passover of Jesus Christ—whose full significance is grasped in relationship to the first and in accomplishment of it.[20]

In other words, rigorous exegesis coupled with theological orientation gives rise to robust Christian readings[21]—that is, readings that recognize the inherently figural, prophetic, intertextual, and revelatory character of the entirety of the OT. Again, this figuration occurs *in the text itself* and is ascertained *through close study of the text.* But without recognizing first that God's revelation of himself gives rise to such figural writing (chap. 5), it is difficult to exegete accordingly, to allow figural writing to produce figural reading.[22]

Third, both ontologically (chap. 3) and phenomenologically (chap. 7), the canon is oriented eschatologically. In other words, because the canon is Christ-centered in its content (chap. 3), it is therefore also eschatological in its content. And because it is Christ-centered and therefore eschatologically oriented at a conceptual level, it is also eschatologically oriented at a phenomenological level

20. Seitz, *Convergences*, 101–2.

21. For a careful overview of the ways in which medieval interpreters, including and especially Thomas Aquinas, saw the literal sense as connected to the spiritual sense, as well the reactions to and interpretive adjustments of the Reformers in response to medieval use of the literal and spiritual senses, see Ballitch, *The Gloss and the Text*, 29–56. For a broader history of the fourfold sense, see de Lubac, *Medieval Exegesis*, esp. vol. 3. De Lubac covers the shifts in the late medieval period, and especially in the Victorine school, that led to some of the problems with allegory that prompted the Reformers' critiques. See 3:211–326 and how Hugh of St. Victor's *Didascalion* played a crucial role, although see Hugh's own statements regarding the importance of the letter in "On Sacred Scripture and Its Authors," 216–18. For instance, "To ignore the letter is to ignore what the letter signifies and what is signified by it" (217). On letter and spirit in the early church, see esp. de Lubac, *Medieval Exegesis*, 2:41–82, for the importance of the literal sense in early medieval exegesis, and 2:197–207 for the conceptual understanding of the unity of the four senses in that same period. Finally, see de Lubac, *History and Spirit*, for a classic study of the progenitor of the *quadriga* as a formal method.

22. See Seitz, *The Elder Testament*, 41n10, in which he refers to Frei, *The Eclipse of Biblical Narrative*, 35–36.

(chap. 7). And so a canonically informed hermeneutic will read individual texts in light of their *telos*.[23] It is not as though only certain texts, such as the OT Prophets or the Olivet Discourse, are about the future. The entire biblical canon is moving toward the center of God's economy, the person and work of Jesus Christ, and is composed in such a way that this movement from covenantal promise to covenantal fulfillment is the overarching structure of the book. Each text is a testimony to Christ, and therefore looks forward to Christ. In the OT, this predominantly means looking forward toward Christ's first coming (1 Pet. 1:10–14),[24] while in the NT this means looking forward toward Christ's second coming (e.g., 2 Pet. 3:10–18).[25]

Finally, the canon is God's *covenantal* revelation of himself to his people, meaning that the text has a desired response,[26] obedience to God's Word. We see this, for instance, in the end of the Torah, with the covenantal blessings and curses (Deut. 28–30), as well as at the end of Revelation, where Jesus, through John, calls for the nations to come to him for salvation (Rev. 22:17–21). The Word of God demands a response, and the expectation for God's people is that the response will be obedience. A canonically informed hermeneutic will, therefore, ask what kind of response is expected by each individual text in light of the vision of Christ portrayed in that text.

23. Again, this is a recognized hermeneutical approach in the early church. See, e.g., Emerson, "The Role of Proverbs 8." See also Kurz, "Patristic Interpretation of Scripture Within God's Story of Creation and Redemption," 36, who, of Irenaeus's and Athanasius's relative reluctance to deploy allegory in light of their opponents' misreading of Scripture, says that "the principal defense of Fathers like Irenaeus and Athanasius against heretical interpretations, whether of undisciplined allegorizers like Gnostics, or of proof-texting readers like Arians, was to interpret individual scriptural passages within the overarching biblical narrative from God's creation to redemption and ultimately to eschatological judgment and new creation."

24. However, we should recall that the OT's testimony to Christ is not *merely* predictive but revelatory in its own right; that is, the OT text testifies to Christ in its own idiom. See Collett, *Figural Reading and the Old Testament*, 46–47.

25. See Swain, *Trinity, Revelation, and Reading*, 35–60.

26. See Vanhoozer, *Is There a Meaning in This Text?*, 367–452. For some of the complexities involved with respect to the expected response of particular texts, and most notably the book of Lamentations, as well as how those expected responses relate to the overall meaning and theological message of Scripture, see Thomas, *Poetry and Theology in the Book of Lamentations*, esp. 247–48.

Additionally, and relatedly, a canonically informed hermeneutic will acknowledge that the original audience of the Word of God is the people of God throughout space and time. While attendance to "the way the words go" in terms of understanding the literal sense necessarily includes elements like study of the sociocultural background and attendant reception by the audience at the time of writing, neither the compositional nature of the human authors' strategy for writing nor the Spirit's superintending divine intent allows us to limit the original audience to some point in the past. The human authors, through composition of biblical books that stand in relation to wider corpora and through the correlated gathering of those books into distinct corpora and finally into the full biblical canon in its final form, signaled their intent for their book(s) to continue to speak to God's people beyond the spatial and temporal limits of their initial audience.[27]

Further, the Word of God is given to the people of God throughout space and time. It speaks to God's people "now" in the "day of salvation" (2 Cor. 6:2, after quoting Isa. 49:8). Paul reads the OT this way throughout his letters. For instance, he tells the Corinthian church that the events of the Exodus narrative "took place as examples for us" and were "written down for our instruction" (1 Cor. 10:6, 11). He tells the Roman Christians, similarly, that "whatever was written in former days was written for our instruction, that through endurance and through the encouragement of the Scriptures we might have hope" (Rom. 15:4). This comes after quoting Psalm 69:9 but is a general reference to the entire OT. Paul can say this (cf. also, e.g., 2 Cor. 8:15; 1 Tim. 5:18), and the other biblical writers can say similar things about the Scriptures that were written before their time, because the Spirit who inspires Scripture intends for Scripture to be read profitably by all believers (2 Tim. 3:16–17). The human authors,

27. So Childs on the Pauline corpus: "The letters of Paul, although retained in their discrete historical particularity, were always understood as universal in scope and not confined to a particular congregation. Paul's letters were never moored to a historical period in the past, but served as a continuing vehicle by which the church received new and fresh divine instruction, admonition, and a renewed understanding of faith through the presence of the Holy Spirit" (Childs, *The Church's Guide for Reading Paul*, 9).

through their canon-conscious form of writing, also intended their books to be read by believers beyond their own temporal horizon. There is thus a tropological immediacy to the entire biblical canon—the Scriptures are written for us, today.[28]

To summarize, a canonically informed reader will pay close attention to the details of the text in order to accurately ascertain its christological and eschatological orientation. In doing so, the reader will be exhorted to be conformed to the image of Christ in some way. One might even summarize it this way: The reader gives adequate attention to the literal sense of the text in order to discern its spiritual sense, which is at the same time christological, eschatological, and moral. My point here is not to advocate for the *quadriga* as a method. It is, however, to note that the *quadriga* captures what we have, in some ways, lost in modernity and postmodernity, which is a robust understanding of the text's meaning.[29] The phrase *original meaning* encapsulates those four aspects of the text's intent, because the text is intended to teach us about and bring us into the presence of the triune God in the face of Jesus Christ by the power of the Holy Spirit and, in doing so, transform us into Christ's image.

Ruled Reading and Theological Exegesis

The third aspect of canonically informed interpretation is theological exegesis.[30] Because the biblical text is intended to teach us about the

28. On how both individual biblical authors as well as the canonical process (i.e., compositional realities, "final form") indicate an "enduring" audience beyond the so-called original audience, see Gignilliat, *Reading Scripture Canonically*, 17, 30, 48–52.

29. On the basics of how the premodern church understood meaning, see de Lubac, *Medieval Exegesis*; on the shifts in how to understand the relation between the literal sense and the spiritual sense during the medieval period, see G. R. Evans, *The Language and Logic of the Bible: The Earlier Middle Ages*; G. R. Evans, *The Language and Logic of the Bible: The Road to the Reformation.*

30. This insistence on theologically and canonically informed and shaped rigorous exegesis has been a hallmark of the canonical approach ever since Brevard Childs's initial broadside fired at the Biblical Theology Movement (Childs, *Biblical Theology in Crisis*, 139–47). While I disagree with Childs at a number of important points, we should acknowledge that the fundamental motivation behind his comments aligns with what I am saying here: The status of the Bible as divine revelation and the historical processes related to the canon's formation require a particular

triune God and what he has done for us in creation and redemption, we must read it theologically. That is, we must read it in a way that renders accurate, coherent, and systematic judgments about who God is and what he has done.[31] Here again the canon's ontology and phenomenology help us.[32]

Theological exegesis is informed by the canon's ontology, in the first place, by its status as the revelation of the triune God to his creatures. The canon as communication is not from one like being to another like being, but rather from Creator to creature. This is another way of saying that acknowledgment of the canon's status as divine revelation is rooted in the Creator-creature distinction, a distinction that Scripture itself teaches (Gen. 1; Deut. 10:14; Neh. 9:6). At least one implication of this fact is that Scripture necessarily uses analogical language to describe God as he is in himself.[33] As creatures, we cannot ever fully comprehend who God is in his essence, but God does adequately and accurately reveal who he is, using language we can understand. These twin acknowledgments of accommodation and analogical language guard us from saying too much when we make theological judgments or from taking Scripture's own analogies about who God is too far, as though they were one-to-one correspondences.[34] (One thinks, for instance, of Scripture describing God as having a nose or being a shield.) The canon's status as God's revelation of himself to us reminds us that we have to read in ways that acknowledge the Creator-creature distinction.

A second way that theological exegesis is informed by the canon's ontology is vis-à-vis its christological shape.[35] The economy of

approach to exegesis, one that recognizes the unity of the Bible as both a literary and theological whole.

31. On the relation between biblical and systematic theology from the perspective of a biblical scholar, see Thomas, *Habakkuk*, 31–34.

32. On the interrelation of the canon's status as divine revelation, rigorous exegesis, and theological judgment, see Jamieson and Wittman, *Biblical Reasoning*, esp. 3–62.

33. See John of Damascus, *Three Treatises on Divine Images*, Treatise I (pp. 19–58); Athanasius, *Letters to Serapion on the Holy Spirit* 1.20.4 (p. 84).

34. Gregory of Nazianzus, "Oration 28."

35. In what follows on the christological and trinitarian teaching of Scripture, see again Jamieson and Wittman, *Biblical Reasoning*, 63–212. For a survey of the ways in which the early church read Scripture theologically and in relation to doctrinal

salvation, centered on the person and work of Christ, gives order to the canonical material.[36] Further, it gives order to the theological conclusions we make from the biblical material about who God is and what he has done for us in Christ. One such way it gives this kind of order is by telling us *who* this God is who reveals himself: the triune God—Father, Son, and Holy Spirit. We do not have space here to give a full-orbed defense of the doctrine of the Trinity from Scripture. Suffice it to say that the Bible is clear that there is one and only one God, YHWH, the God of Israel (e.g., Deut. 6:4), and that this one God is three in person, Father, Son, and Holy Spirit (e.g., Matt. 28:19, the one "name" of God is the name of Father, Son, and Spirit). These three persons are equal in essence. Because of the Creator-creature distinction, there is only God and not-God. Each person of the Trinity—the Father, Son, and Spirit—possesses attributes, performs actions, claims appellations, and receives adoration that belong exclusively on the divine side of the equation. Further, they are not three gods, but one; these attributes, actions, appellations, and adoration are one, just as God is one.[37] The God who reveals himself in Scripture, the God who creates and redeems, is not a generic deity but is the triune God, YHWH, the God of Israel, Father, Son, and Holy Spirit.

Another implication of the christological shape of the canon is that we ought to read passages about the Son in light of that shape. The economy of redemption is such that the Son takes on a human nature in the fullness of time. As Paul puts it in Philippians 2:6–8, "Though he was in the form of God, [he] did not count equality with God a thing to be grasped, but emptied himself, by taking the form of a servant, being born in the likeness of men. And being found in human form, he humbled himself by becoming obedient to the point of death, even death on a cross." Theological exegesis gives attention

development, see, most recently, Young, *Scripture in Doctrinal Dispute*. See also Young, *Biblical Exegesis and the Formation of Christian Culture*, and, with Andrew Neal, *From Nicaea to Chalcedon*; Behr, *The Way to Nicaea*; Anatolios, *Retrieving Nicaea*; Ayres, *Nicaea and Its Legacy*.

36. On the relation of the economy of Scripture to theological exegesis, see Rowe, "Biblical Pressure and Trinitarian Hermeneutics," esp. 310–12.

37. See Emerson, "Mark."

to the shape of the economy of redemption, which is mirrored in the shape of the biblical canon, and rightly distinguishes between speech about the Son "in the form of God"—that is, according to his divinity—and speech about the Son in "the form of a servant"—that is, according to his humanity. This distinguishing between divinity and humanity is an ancient practice of Christian hermeneutics and is known as partitive exegesis. It is warranted by Philippians 2:6–8 (among other texts), but it is also taught by the christological nature and shape of the biblical canon.

Third and finally, theological exegesis is informed by the ontology and phenomenology of the biblical canon by giving attention to its interconnectivity as a conceptually unified, divinely inspired, *Logos*-centric text. I have already referenced the *analogia fidei* in that regard. What I mean here is that theological exegesis ought to allow one biblical text to be theologically informed by other biblical texts. One such example is Proverbs 8:22–31. The pro-Nicene interpreters in the fourth century acknowledged that this is a reference to Christ because, according to Paul in 1 Corinthians 1:24, Christ is the "power of God and the wisdom of God." Who else would the writer of Proverbs be referring to when portraying Lady Wisdom, other than Wisdom himself, God the Son?

One can perhaps hear echoes of the judgments of Nicaea and Constantinople here. Indeed, the goal of the Niceno-Constantinopolitan Creed has been summarized as using appropriate conceptual language to render accurate theological judgments about patterns of biblical language.[38] This is another way to talk about "ruled" reading, one that is found in the early church.[39] The phrase *regula fidei* came to be used interchangeably in reference to the christological purpose of Scripture, the hermeneutical rules I have discussed above, and reading according to the judgments rendered by the Creed. It is important for us here to clarify that, while we acknowledge derivative authority of ecclesial statements, including but not limited to the three ecumenical creeds, *insofar as they are faithful to Scripture*, we do not place them

38. Yeago, "The New Testament and the Nicene Dogma." See also Rowe, "Biblical Pressure and Trinitarian Hermeneutics," esp. 307–9.

39. See Gregory of Nazianzus's discussion of the recitation of the "Credo" prior to baptism in "Oration 40," esp. 140–41.

on par with Scripture. The Bible alone is the *norma normans non normata*, the norming norm that cannot be normed. The creeds, as well as other forms of ecclesiastical judgment about the meaning and theological teaching of Scripture, are always, at least in theory, subject to correction by Scripture. Still, the creeds have stood the test of time, and in that sense can be considered a theological rule, or guide, for reading the Bible, even while they are not equal to the Bible itself.[40]

Conclusion

How, then, should we read? We read with an eye toward exegesis, a thick study of the literal sense, because we believe that the Spirit's inspiration of the human authors of Scripture and the *Logos*-centric character of all created reality (including texts, especially the inspired text) demand it. To put it slightly differently, we care about the human author's intent not merely because a twentieth-century atheist philosopher of language has provided a conceptual apparatus that helps us tether interpretation to authorial intent (although this is important), but because the doctrines of the Spirit and creation require it. In insisting on rightly understanding the human author's intent, E. D. Hirsch is reflecting something true, but his metaphysic is not sufficiently grounded in God, and so he cannot serve as the ultimate foundation of evangelical hermeneutics. But an ontologically aware and robust articulation of what Scripture is acknowledges Hirsch's point about authorial intent while also grounding it in wider metaphysical realities.[41]

These metaphysical realities mean that reading with an eye toward the literal sense will naturally also mean reading *figurally*. All kinds of

40. In this sense I disagree with Goldingay, "Old Testament Theology and the Canon," esp. 9–11, 17–20; see Seitz's response (in the same issue), "Canon, Narrative, and the Old Testament's Literal Sense."

41. So Collett, "Reading Forward," 181: "Christological meaning remains an affair of providence (Aquinas), rather than an affair of consciousness (E. D. Hirsch Jr.)." Note that neither I nor Collett (as indicated in the rest of the essay, as well as his other work) is denigrating the human author's intention to point to Christ, according to his own historical horizon and within the framework of his own literary style. Rather, the point is that, as we saw in chaps. 4 and 5, christological intent is ultimately grounded in divine inspiration and divine providence.

figuration are possible in the text of Scripture because all Scripture is a sign, a *signum*, of the reality, the *res*, that it reveals: the triune God in the face of Jesus Christ. The one God reveals himself through the inspiration of one book by one author, his Spirit, about one person, his Son Jesus Christ, and his work, the one work of salvation accomplished by Jesus.

This means that canonical reading is ruled reading. The canon is the rule, in terms of Christ as its content and goal (the *regula fidei*) and in terms of rightly bounding and interpreting that content and goal (the *analogia fidei*). Reading canonically means reading with an eye toward the unity of the Bible, which in turn is grounded in the unity of its subject, Jesus Christ, and its author, the Holy Spirit.

Bibliography

Alexander, T. Desmond. *From Eden to the New Jerusalem: An Introduction to Biblical Theology*. Kregel, 2009.

Allen, Garrick V. *Words Are Not Enough: Paratexts, Manuscripts, and the Real New Testament*. Eerdmans, 2024.

Allert, Craig D. *A High View of Scripture? The Authority of the Bible and the Formation of the New Testament Canon*. Evangelical Ressourcement: Ancient Sources for the Church's Future. Baker Academic, 2007.

Anatolios, Khaled. *Retrieving Nicaea: The Development and Meaning of Trinitarian Doctrine*. Baker Academic, 2011.

Athanasius of Alexandria. *Letters to Serapion on the Holy Spirit*. In *Works on the Spirit*, translated by Mark DelCogliano, Andrew Radde-Gallwitz, and Louis Ayres, 51–138. Popular Patristics Series 43. St. Vladimir's Seminary Press, 2011.

Athanasius of Alexandria. *On the Incarnation*. Translated by John Behr. Popular Patristics Series 44A. St. Vladimir's Seminary Press, 2011.

Auerbach, Erich. *Mimesis: The Representation of Reality in Western Literature*. Translated by Willard R. Trask. Princeton University Press, 1953.

Augustine. *Confessions*. Translated by Vernon J. Bourke. Fathers of the Church 21. Catholic University of America Press, 1953.

Augustine. *On Christian Teaching*. Translated by R. P. H. Green. Oxford University Press, 1999.

Auwers, J.-M., and H. J. de Jonge, eds. *The Biblical Canons*. Bibliotheca Ephemeridum Theologicarum Lovaniensium 163. Leuven University Press, 2003.

Ayres, Lewis. *Nicaea and Its Legacy: An Approach to Fourth-Century Trinitarian Theology*. Oxford University Press, 2006.

Baldermann, Ingo, et al. *Zum Problem des biblischen Kanons*. Jahrbuch für biblische Theologie 3. Neukirchener Verlag, 1988.

Ballitch, Andrew S. *The Gloss and the Text: William Perkins on Interpreting Scripture with Scripture*. Studies in Historical and Systematic Theology. Lexham, 2020.

Barr, James. *The Concept of Biblical Theology: An Old Testament Perspective*. Fortress, 1999.

Barr, James. *Holy Scripture: Canon, Authority, Criticism*. Westminster, 1983.

Barrett, Matthew. *Canon, Covenant, and Christology: Rethinking Jesus and the Scriptures of Israel*. New Studies in Biblical Theology 51. IVP Academic, 2020.

Barth, Karl. *Church Dogmatics*. Vol. I/1, *The Doctrine of the Word of God, Part I*. Translated by G. W. Bromiley. Edited by T. F. Torrance. T&T Clark, 1975.

Barth, Karl. *Church Dogmatics*. Vol. I/2, *The Doctrine of the Word of God, Part II*. Translated by G. T. Thomson and Harold Knight. Edited by T. F. Torrance. T&T Clark, 1956.

Bartholomew, Craig G. *Introducing Biblical Hermeneutics: A Comprehensive Framework for Hearing God in Scripture*. Baker Academic, 2015.

Bartholomew, Craig G. "Uncharted Waters: Philosophy, Theology, and the Crisis in Biblical Interpretation." In *Renewing Biblical Interpretation*, edited by Craig Bartholomew, Colin Greene, and Karl Möller, 1–39. Scripture and Hermeneutics Series 1. Zondervan, 2000.

Bartholomew, Craig G., and Michael W. Goheen. *The Drama of Scripture: Finding Our Place in the Biblical Story*. 3rd ed. Baker Academic, 2024.

Bartholomew, Craig G., Scott Hahn, Robin Parry, Christopher Seitz, and Al Wolters, eds. *Canon and Biblical Interpretation*. Scripture and Hermeneutics Series 7. Zondervan Academic, 2006.

Bartholomew, Craig G., and Heath A. Thomas, eds. *A Manifesto for Theological Interpretation*. Baker Academic, 2016.

Bauckham, Richard. *James*. New Testament Readings. Routledge, 1999.

Beale, G. K. "Did Jesus and His Followers Preach the Right Doctrine from the Wrong Texts? An Examination of the Presuppositions of Jesus' and the Apostles' Exegetical Method." In Beale, *The Right Doctrine from the Wrong Texts?*, 387–404.

Beale, G. K. *Handbook on the New Testament Use of the Old Testament: Exegesis and Interpretation*. Baker Academic, 2012.

Beale, G. K. *A New Testament Biblical Theology: The Unfolding of the Old Testament in the New*. Baker Academic, 2011.

Beale, G. K., ed. *The Right Doctrine from the Wrong Texts? Essays on the Use of the Old Testament in the New*. Baker Academic, 1994.

Beale, G. K. *The Temple and the Church's Mission: A Biblical Theology of the Dwelling Place of God*. New Studies in Biblical Theology 17. InterVarsity, 2004.

Beale, G. K. "The Use of Hosea 11:1 in Matthew 2:15: One More Time." *Journal of the Evangelical Theological Society* 55, no. 4 (2012): 697–715.

Beale, G. K., and D. A. Carson, eds. *Commentary on the New Testament Use of the Old Testament*. Baker Academic, 2007.

Beale, G. K., D. A. Carson, Benjamin L. Gladd, and Andrew David Naselli, eds. *Dictionary of the New Testament Use of the Old Testament*. Baker Academic, 2023.

Beale, G. K., and Benjamin L. Gladd. *Hidden but Now Revealed: A Biblical Theology of Mystery*. IVP Academic, 2014.

Beckwith, Roger T. *The Old Testament Canon of the New Testament Church and Its Background in Early Judaism*. SPCK, 1985.

Behr, John. "Scripture, the Gospel, and Orthodoxy." *St. Vladimir's Orthodox Quarterly* 43, no. 4 (1999): 223–48.

Behr, John. *The Way to Nicaea*. Vol. 1 of *Formation of Christian Theology*. St. Vladimir's Seminary Press, 2001.

Bell, Matthew T. *Ruled Reading and Biblical Criticism*. Journal of Theological Interpretation Supplements 18. Eisenbrauns, 2019.

Betz, John R. *Christ, the Logos of Creation: An Essay in Analogical Metaphysics*. Emmaus Academic, 2023.

Billings, J. Todd. *The Word of God for the People of God: An Entryway to the Theological Interpretation of Scripture*. Baker Academic, 2010.

Bockmuehl, Markus. *Seeing the Word: Refocusing New Testament Study*. Studies in Theological Interpretation. Baker Academic, 2006.

Boersma, Hans. *Scripture as Real Presence: Sacramental Exegesis in the Early Church*. Baker Academic, 2017.

Bokedal, Tomas. *Christ the Center: How the Rule of Faith, the Nomina Sacra, and Numerical Patterns Shape the Canon*. Lexham Academic, 2023.

Bovon, François. *New Testament and Christian Apocrypha*. Edited by Glenn E. Snyder. Baker Academic, 2011.

Brodie, Thomas L. *The Birthing of the New Testament: The Intertextual Development of the New Testament Writings*. New Testament Monographs 1. Sheffield Phoenix, 2004.

Bruce, F. F. *The Canon of Scripture*. InterVarsity, 1988.

Burke, Tony, ed. *New Testament Apocrypha: More Noncanonical Scriptures*. Vol. 2. Eerdmans, 2020.

Burke, Tony, ed. *New Testament Apocrypha: More Noncanonical Scriptures*. Vol. 3. Eerdmans, 2023.

Burke, Tony, and Brent Landau, eds. *New Testament Apocrypha: More Noncanonical Scriptures*. Vol. 1. Eerdmans, 2016.

Burridge, Richard A. *Four Gospels, One Jesus? A Symbolic Reading*. Eerdmans, 1994.

Carter, Craig A. *Interpreting Scripture with the Great Tradition: Recovering the Genius of Premodern Exegesis*. Baker Academic, 2018.

Chapman, Stephen B. "Brevard Childs as Historical Critic: Divine Concession and the Unity of the Canon." In *The Bible as Christian Scripture: The Work of Brevard S. Childs*, edited by Christopher R. Seitz and Kent Harold Richards, 63–82. Society of Biblical Literature, 2013.

Chapman, Stephen B. "The Canon Debate: What It Is and Why It Matters." *Journal of Theological Interpretation* 4, no. 2 (2010): 273–94.

Chapman, Stephen B. *The Law and the Prophets: A Study in Old Testament Canon Formation*. Baker Academic, 2020.

Chapman, Stephen B. "'The Law and the Words' as a Canonical Formula Within the Old Testament." In *The Interpretation of Scripture in Early Judaism and Christianity: Studies in Language and Tradition*, edited by Craig A. Evans, 26–74. Sheffield Academic, 2000.

Chapman, Stephen B. "The Old Testament Canon and Its Authority for the Christian Church." *Ex Auditu* 19 (2003): 125–48.

Chapman, Stephen B. "What Are We Reading? Canonicity and the Old Testament?" *Word & World* 29, no. 4 (2009): 334–47.

Charlesworth, James H., ed. *The Old Testament Pseudepigrapha*. Vol. 2, *Expansions of the "Old Testament" and Legends, Wisdom and Philosophical Literature, Prayers, Psalms and Odes, Fragments of Lost Judeo-Hellenistic Works*. Doubleday, 1985.

Chase, Mitchell L. *40 Questions About Typology and Allegory*. Kregel Academic, 2020.

Childs, Brevard S. *Biblical Theology: A Proposal*. Facets. Fortress, 2002.

Childs, Brevard S. *Biblical Theology in Crisis*. Westminster, 1974.

Childs, Brevard S. *Biblical Theology of the Old and New Testaments: Theological Reflection on the Christian Bible*. Fortress, 1993.

Childs, Brevard S. "The Canon in Recent Biblical Studies: Reflections on an Era." In Bartholomew et al., *Canon and Biblical Interpretation*, 33–57.

Childs, Brevard S. *The Church's Guide for Reading Paul: The Canonical Shaping of the Pauline Corpus*. Eerdmans, 2008.

Childs, Brevard S. *Introduction to the Old Testament as Scripture*. Augsburg Fortress, 1979.

Childs, Brevard S. *The New Testament as Canon: An Introduction*. Trinity Press International, 1984.

Childs, Brevard S. *Old Testament Theology in a Canonical Context*. Fortress, 1986.

Cole, Robert L. *Psalms 1–2: Gateway to the Psalter*. Hebrew Bible Monographs 37. Sheffield Phoenix, 2013.

Cole, Robert L., and Paul J. Kissling, eds. *Text and Canon: Essays in Honor of John H. Sailhamer*. Pickwick, 2017.

Collett, Don C. *Figural Reading and the Old Testament: Theology and Practice*. Baker Academic, 2020.

Collett, Don C. "Reading Forward: The Old Testament and Retrospective Stance." *Pro Ecclesia* 24, no. 2 (2015): 178–96.

Collins, John J., Craig A. Evans, and Lee Martin McDonald. *Ancient Jewish and Christian Scriptures: New Developments in Canon Controversy*. Westminster John Knox, 2020.

Corley, Bruce. "A Student's Primer for Exegesis." In Corley et al., *Biblical Hermeneutics*, 1–22.

Corley, Bruce, Steve W. Lemke, and Grant I. Lovejoy, eds. *Biblical Hermeneutics: A Comprehensive Introduction to Interpreting Scripture*. B&H Academic, 1996.

Crawford, Matthew R. *Cyril of Alexandria's Trinitarian Theology of Scripture*. Oxford Early Christian Studies. Oxford University Press, 2014.

Crawford, Matthew R. *The Eusebian Canon Tables: Ordering Textual Knowledge in Late Antiquity*. Oxford Early Christian Studies. Oxford University Press, 2019.

Croy, Casey K. *Sequencing the Hebrew Bible: The Order of the Books.* Hebrew Bible Monographs 94. Sheffield Phoenix, 2021.

Crump, David. *Encountering Jesus, Encountering Scripture: Reading the Bible Critically in Faith.* Eerdmans, 2013.

Cyril of Alexandria. *Commentary on the Twelve Prophets.* Vol. 1. Translated by Robert C. Hill. Fathers of the Church 115. Catholic University of America Press, 2007.

Cyril of Alexandria. *On the Unity of Christ.* Translated by John Anthony McGuckin. Popular Patristics Series 13. St. Vladimir's Seminary Press, 1995.

Davies, Philip R. "The Jewish Scriptural Canon in Cultural Perspective." In *The Canon Debate*, edited by Lee Martin McDonald and James A. Sanders, 36–52. Hendrickson, 2002.

de Bruin, Tom. *Fan Fiction and Early Christian Writings: Apocrypha, Pseudepigrapha, and Canon.* Library of New Testament Studies 673. Scriptural Traces 33. T&T Clark, 2024.

de Lubac, Henri. *History and Spirit: The Understanding of Scripture According to Origen.* Ignatius, 2007.

de Lubac, Henri. *Medieval Exegesis: The Four Senses of Scripture.* Translated by Mark Sebanc and E. M. Macierowski. 3 vols. Ressourcement: Retrieval & Renewal in Catholic Thought. Eerdmans, 1998–2009.

Dempster, Stephen G. *Dominion and Dynasty: A Theology of the Hebrew Bible.* New Studies in Biblical Theology 15. InterVarsity, 2003.

Dempster, Stephen G. "The Prophets, the Canon, and a Canonical Approach: No Empty Word." In Bartholomew et al., *Canon and Biblical Interpretation*, 293–332.

Dempster, Stephen G. "Torah, Torah, Torah: The Emergence of the Tripartite Canon." In *Exploring the Origins of the Bible: Canon Formation in Historical, Literary, and Theological Perspective*, edited by Craig A. Evans and Emmanuel Tov, 87–128. Baker Academic, 2008.

Dempster, Stephen G. "A Wandering Moabite: Ruth—a Book in Search of a Canonical Home." In *The Shape of the Writings*, edited by Julius Steinberg and Timothy J. Stone, with the assistance of Rachel Stone, 87–118. Siphrut 16. Eisenbrauns, 2015.

DeRouchie, Jason S. *Delighting in the Old Testament: Through Christ and for Christ.* Crossway, 2024.

Didymus the Blind. *Commentary on Zechariah*. Translated by Robert C. Hill. Fathers of the Church 111. Catholic University of America Press, 2006.

Didymus the Blind. *On the Holy Spirit*. In *Works on the Spirit*, translated by Mark DelCogliano, Andrew Radde-Gallwitz, and Louis Ayres, 143–228. Popular Patristics Series 43. St. Vladimir's Seminary Press, 2011.

Dolezal, James E. *All That Is in God: Evangelical Theology and the Challenge of Classical Christian Theism*. Reformation Heritage, 2017.

Driver, Daniel R. *Brevard Childs, Biblical Theologian: For the Church's One Bible*. Baker Academic, 2010.

Duby, Steven J. *Divine Simplicity: A Dogmatic Account*. T&T Clark Studies in Systematic Theology 30. Bloomsbury T&T Clark, 2016.

Dunn, James D. G. *Unity and Diversity in the New Testament: An Inquiry into the Character of Earliest Christianity*. 3rd ed. SCM, 2006.

East, Brad. *The Church's Book: Theology of Scripture in Ecclesial Context*. Eerdmans, 2022.

Elliott, Mark W. *The Song of Songs and Christology in the Early Church, 381–451*. Studien und Texte zu Antike und Christentum 7. Mohr Siebeck, 2000.

Emerson, Matthew Y. "The Canonical Shape of the New Testament." In *Canon Formation: Tracing the Role of Sub-Collections in the Biblical Canon*, edited by W. Edward Glenny and Darian R. Lockett, 79–100. T&T Clark, 2022.

Emerson, Matthew Y. *Christ and the New Creation: A Canonical Approach to the Theology of the New Testament*. Wipf & Stock, 2013.

Emerson, Matthew Y. "Land, Burial, and Temple: Deuteronomy 30:5, John 19–20, and Jesus' Burial as a Land Claim." *Journal of Theological Interpretation* 14, no. 2 (2020): 180–98.

Emerson, Matthew Y. "Mark." In *The Trinity in the Canon: A Biblical, Theological, Historical, and Practical Proposal*, edited by Brandon D. Smith, 115–48. B&H Academic, 2023.

Emerson, Matthew Y. Review of *Reading the Epistles of James, Peter, John and Jude as Scripture: The Shaping and Shape of a Canonical Corpus*, by David R. Nienhuis and Robert W. Wall. *Southeastern Theological Review* 6, no. 1 (2015): 142–45.

Emerson, Matthew Y. "The Role of Proverbs 8: Eternal Generation and Hermeneutics Ancient and Modern." In *Retrieving Eternal Generation*, edited by Fred Sanders and Scott R. Swain, 44–66. Zondervan Academic, 2017.

Emerson, Matthew Y. *The Story of Scripture: An Introduction to Biblical Theology*. Hobbs College Library. B&H Academic, 2017.

Emerson, Matthew Y., and Brandon D. Smith. *Beholding the Triune God: The Inseparable Work of Father, Son, and Spirit*. Crossway, 2024.

Enns, Peter. *The Bible Tells Me So: Why Defending Scripture Has Made Us Unable to Read It*. HarperOne, 2014.

Enns, Peter. "Inerrancy, However Defined, Does Not Describe What the Bible Does." In *Five Views on Biblical Inerrancy*, edited by J. Merrick and Stephen M. Garrett, 83–116. Counterpoints: Bible and Theology. Zondervan, 2013.

Enns, Peter. *Inspiration and Incarnation: Evangelicals and the Problem of the Old Testament*. Baker Academic, 2005.

Evans, C. Stephen. "Canonicity, Apostolicity, and Biblical Authority: Some Kierkegaardian Reflections." In Bartholomew et al., *Canon and Biblical Interpretation*, 146–66.

Evans, C. Stephen, ed. *Exploring Kenotic Christology: The Self-Emptying God*. Oxford University Press, 2006.

Evans, Craig A. "The Christian Apocrypha." In Collins et al., *Ancient Jewish and Christian Scriptures*, 145–66.

Evans, Craig A. "The Gospels of Peter and Thomas." In Collins et al., *Ancient Jewish and Christian Scriptures*, 167–93.

Evans, Craig A., and Emmanuel Tov, eds. *Exploring the Origins of the Bible: Canon Formation in Historical, Literary, and Theological Perspectives*. Acadia Studies in Bible and Theology. Baker Academic, 2008.

Evans, G. R. *The Language and Logic of the Bible: The Earlier Middle Ages*. Cambridge University Press, 1984.

Evans, G. R. *The Language and Logic of the Bible: The Road to the Reformation*. Cambridge University Press, 1985.

Fitzmyer, Joseph A. *The Biblical Commission's Document "The Interpretation of the Bible in the Church": Text and Commentary*. Subsidia Biblica 18. Editrice Pontifico Istituto Biblico, 1995.

Fowl, Stephen E. *Engaging Scripture: A Model for Theological Interpretation*. Blackwell, 1998.

Fowl, Stephen E., ed. *The Theological Interpretation of Scripture: Classic and Contemporary Readings*. Blackwell Readings in Modern Theology. Blackwell, 1997.

Frei, Hans W. *The Eclipse of Biblical Narrative: A Study in Eighteenth and Nineteenth Century Hermeneutics*. Yale University Press, 1974.

Froehlich, Karlfried, trans. and ed. *Biblical Interpretation in the Early Church*. Sources of Early Christian Thought. Fortress, 1984.

Gallagher, Edmond L. "Origen *via* Rufinus on the New Testament Canon." *New Testament Studies* 62, no. 3 (2016): 461–76.

Gallagher, Edmond L. "Suddenly and Then Gradually: The Growth of the Septuagint and Its Canon." *Journal of Biblical Literature* 143, no. 2 (2024): 303–22.

Gallagher, Edmond L., and John D. Meade. *The Biblical Canon Lists from Early Christianity: Texts and Analysis*. Oxford University Press, 2017.

Gamble, Harry Y. *The New Testament Canon: Its Making and Meaning; A Guide to Biblical Scholarship*. Augsburg Fortress, 1985.

Gathercole, Simon. *The Gospel and the Gospels: Christian Proclamation and Early Jesus Books*. Eerdmans, 2022.

Gebreananaye, Meron T., Logan Williams, and Francis Watson, eds. *Beyond Canon: Early Christianity and the Ethiopic Tradition*. Library of New Testament Studies 643. T&T Clark, 2021.

Gentry, Peter J., and Stephen J. Wellum. *Kingdom Through Covenant: A Biblical-Theological Understanding of the Covenants*. 2nd ed. Crossway, 2018.

Gignilliat, Mark S. *Reading Scripture Canonically: Theological Instincts for Old Testament Interpretation*. Baker Academic, 2019.

Goldingay, John. "Old Testament Theology and the Canon." *Tyndale Bulletin* 59, no. 1 (2008): 1–26.

Goppelt, Leonard. *Typos: The Typological Interpretation of the Old Testament in the New*. Eerdmans, 1982.

Gordon, Joseph K. *Divine Scripture in Human Understanding: A Systematic Theology of the Christian Bible*. Reading the Scriptures. University of Notre Dame Press, 2019.

Goswell, Gregory. "The Old Testament as Prophecy and the Structure of the Canon." *Journal of the Evangelical Theological Society* 66, no. 3 (2023): 495–508.

Goswell, Gregory. *Text and Paratext: Book Order, Title, and Division as Keys to Biblical Interpretation*. Lexham Academic, 2023.

Graves, Michael, ed. *Biblical Interpretation in the Early Church*. Ad Fontes: Early Christian Sources. Fortress, 2017.

Gregory of Nazianzus. "Oration 28." In *On God and Christ: The Five Theological Orations and Two Letters to Cledonius*, translated by Frederick Williams and Lionel Wickham, 37–68. Popular Patristics Series 23. St. Vladimir's Seminary Press, 2002.

Gregory of Nazianzus. "Oration 38: On the Nativity of Christ." In *Festal Orations*, translated by Nonna Verna Harrison, 61–77. Popular Patristics Series 36. St. Vladimir's Seminary Press, 2008.

Gregory of Nazianzus. "Oration 40: On Baptism." In *Festal Orations*, translated by Nonna Verna Harrison, 99–142. Popular Patristics Series 36. St. Vladimir's Seminary Press, 2008.

Gregory of Nyssa. "On the Final Subjection of Christ." In *On Death and Eternal Life*, translated by Brian E. Daley, 65–85. Popular Patristics Series 64. St. Vladimir's Seminary Press, 2022.

Hains, Todd R. *Martin Luther and the Rule of Faith: Reading God's Word for God's People*. New Explorations in Theology. IVP Academic, 2022.

Hamilton, James M., Jr. "The Skull Crushing Seed of the Woman: Inner-Biblical Interpretation of Genesis 3:15." *Southern Baptist Journal of Theology* 102 (2006): 30–54.

Hamilton, James M., Jr. *God's Glory in Salvation Through Judgment: A Biblical Theology*. Crossway, 2010.

Hasel, Gerhard F. *New Testament Theology: Basic Issues in the Current Debate*. Eerdmans, 1978.

Hasel, Gerhard F. *Old Testament Theology: Basic Issues in the Current Debate*. 4th ed. Eerdmans, 1991.

Hays, Richard B. *Echoes of Scripture in the Letters of Paul*. Yale University Press, 1989.

Hays, Richard B. *The Faith of Jesus Christ: The Narrative Substructure of Galatians 3:1–4:11*. 2nd ed. Biblical Resource Series. Eerdmans, 2002.

Hays, Richard B. *Reading Backwards: Figural Reading and the Fourfold Gospel Witness*. Baylor University Press, 2016.

Hengel, Martin. *The Four Gospels and the One Gospel of Jesus Christ*. Translated by John Bowden. Trinity Press International, 2000.

Hill, Charles E., and Michael J. Kruger, eds. *The Early Text of the New Testament*. Oxford University Press, 2012.

Hirsch, E. D., Jr. *Validity in Interpretation*. Yale University Press, 1967.

House, Paul R. *Old Testament Theology*. InterVarsity, 1998.

Hugh of St. Victor. "On Sacred Scripture and Its Authors." In *Interpretation of Scripture: Theory*, edited by Franklin T. Harkins and Frans van Liere, 213–30. Victorine Texts in Translation: Exegesis, Theology and Spirituality from the Abbey of St Victor 3. Brepols, 2013.

Irenaeus of Lyons. *Against Heresies*. Translated by Alexander Roberts and W. H. Rambaut. In *The Ante-Nicene Fathers*, edited by Alexander Roberts, James Donaldson, and A. Cleveland Coxe, 1:309–567. Hendrickson, 1994.

Irenaeus of Lyons. *On the Apostolic Preaching*. Translated by John Behr. Popular Patristics Series 17. St. Vladimir's Seminary Press, 2003.

Jamieson, R. B., and Tyler R. Wittman. *Biblical Reasoning: Christological and Trinitarian Rules for Exegesis*. Baker Academic, 2022.

Janowski, Bernd. "The Contrastive Unity of Scripture: On the Hermeneutics of the Biblical Canon." In *The Bible as Christian Scripture: The Work of Brevard S. Childs*, edited by Christopher R. Seitz and Kent Harold Richards, 37–62. Society of Biblical Literature, 2013.

Jenson, Robert W. *A Theology in Outline: Can These Bones Live?* Oxford University Press, 2016.

Jerome. "Preface to Books of Samuel and Kings, Addressed to Paula and Eustochium." Translated by W. H. Fremantle. In *Nicene and Post-Nicene Fathers*, Second Series, edited by Philip Schaff and Henry Wace, 6:489–90. Hendrickson, 1994.

John of Damascus. *Three Treatises on Divine Images*. Translated by Andrew Louth. Popular Patristics Series 24. St. Vladimir's Seminary Press, 2003.

Kaiser, Walter C., Jr. "The Single Intent of Scripture." In Beale, *The Right Doctrine from the Wrong Texts?*, 55–69.

Kaiser, Walter C., Jr. "Single Meaning, Unified Referents: Accurate and Authoritative Citations of the Old Testament by the New Testament." In *Three Views of the New Testament Use of the Old Testament*, edited by Kenneth Berding and Jonathan Lunde, 45–89. Counterpoints: Bible and Theology. Zondervan, 2008.

Klink, Edward W., III, and Darian R. Lockett. *Understanding Biblical Theology: A Comparison of Theory and Practice*. Zondervan, 2012.

Knox, John. *Philemon Among the Letters of Paul: A New View of Its Place and Importance*. Rev. ed. Abingdon, 1959.

König, Adrio. *The Eclipse of Christ in Eschatology: Toward a Christ-Centered Approach*. Eerdmans, 1989.

Koorevaar, Hendrik J. "Chronicles as the Intentional Conclusion to the Old Testament Canon." In *The Shape of the Writings*, edited by Julius Steinberg and Timothy J. Stone, with the assistance of Rachel Stone, 207–36. Siphrut 16. Eisenbrauns, 2015.

Kruger, Michael J. *Canon Revisited: Establishing the Origins and Authority of the New Testament Books*. Crossway, 2012.

Kruger, Michael J. *The Question of Canon: Challenging the Status Quo in the New Testament Debate*. IVP Academic, 2013.

Kurz, William S. "Patristic Interpretation of Scripture Within God's Story of Creation and Redemption." *Letter & Spirit* 7 (2011): 35–50.

Kynes, Will. *An Obituary for "Wisdom Literature": The Birth, Death, and Intertextual Reintegration of a Biblical Corpus*. Oxford University Press, 2019.

Laird, Benjamin P. *Creating the Canon: Composition, Controversy, and the Authority of the New Testament Canon*. IVP Academic, 2023.

Legaspi, Michael C. *The Death of Scripture and the Rise of Biblical Studies*. Oxford Studies in Historical Theology. Oxford University Press, 2010.

Leithart, Peter J. *Deep Exegesis: The Mystery of Reading Scripture*. Baylor University Press, 2009.

Lemke, Steve W. "The Inspiration and Truthfulness of Scripture." In Corley et al., *Biblical Hermeneutics*, 147–64.

Levering, Matthew. *Engaging the Doctrine of Revelation: The Mediation of the Gospel Through Church and Scripture*. Baker Academic, 2014.

Levering, Matthew. *Participatory Biblical Exegesis: A Theology of Biblical Interpretation*. Reading the Scriptures. University of Notre Dame Press, 2008.

Levy, Ian Christopher. *Introducing Medieval Interpretation: The Senses of Scripture in Premodern Exegesis*. Baker Academic, 2018.

Lieu, Judith M. *Marcion and the Making of a Heretic: God and Scripture in the Second Century*. Cambridge University Press, 2015.

Lim, Timothy H. "An Indicative Definition of Canon." In *When Texts Are Canonized*, edited by Timothy H. Lim, 1–24. Brown Judaic Studies 359. Brown University Press, 2017.

Lints, Richard. *The Fabric of Theology: A Prolegomenon to Evangelical Theology*. Eerdmans, 1993.

Lockett, Darian R. *Letters from the Pillar Apostles: The Formation of the Catholic Epistles as a Canonical Collection*. Pickwick, 2017.

Luther, Martin. "Avoiding the Doctrines of Men and a Reply to the Texts Cited in Defense of the Doctrines of Men." Translated by William A. Lambert. Revised by E. Theodore Bachmann. In *Word and Sacrament I*, edited by E. Theodore Bachmann, 125–53. Luther's Works 35. Augsburg Fortress, 1960.

Maier, Gerhard. *Biblical Hermeneutics*. Crossway, 1994.

Malcolm, Matthew R. *From Hermeneutics to Exegesis: The Trajectory of Biblical Interpretation*. B&H Academic, 2018.

Martens, Peter W. *Origen and Scripture: The Contours of the Exegetical Life*. Oxford Early Christian Studies. Oxford University Press, 2012.

Maximus the Confessor. "Ambiguum 7: On the Beginning and End of Rational Creatures." In *On the Cosmic Mystery of Jesus Christ*, translated by Paul M. Blowers and Robert Louis Wilken, 45–74. Popular Patristics Series 25. St. Vladimir's Seminary Press, 2003.

McCormack, Bruce L. *The Humility of the Eternal Son: Reformed Kenoticism and the Repair of Chalcedon*. Current Issues in Theology 18. Cambridge University Press, 2023.

McDonald, Lee Martin. *The Formation of the Biblical Canon*. Vol. 2, *The New Testament: Its Authority and Canonicity*. Bloomsbury T&T Clark, 2017.

McDonald, Lee Martin, and James A. Sanders, eds. *The Canon Debate*. Baker Academic, 2002.

Meade, John D., and Peter J. Gurry. *Scribes and Scripture: The Amazing Story of How We Got the Bible*. Crossway, 2022.

Melito of Sardis. *On Pascha*. Translated by Alistair Stewart-Sykes. Popular Patristics Series 20. St. Vladimir's Seminary Press, 2001.

Metzger, Bruce M. *The Canon of the New Testament: Its Origin, Development, and Significance*. Oxford University Press, 1987.

Mrozek, Eva. "The Hegemony of the Biblical in the Study of Second Temple Literature." *Journal of Ancient Judaism* 6, no. 1 (2015): 2–35.

Newport, John P. "Contemporary Philosophical, Literary, and Sociological Hermeneutics." In Corley et al., *Biblical Hermeneutics*, 133–46.

Nicklas, Tobias. *The Canon and Beyond: Collected Essays on the History and Hermeneutics of Biblical and Parabiblical Traditions*. Wissenschaftliche Untersuchungen zum Neuen Testament 525. Mohr Siebeck, 2024.

Nienhuis, David R. "The Letter of James as a Canon-Conscious Pseudepigraph." In *The Catholic Epistles and Apostolic Tradition: A New Perspective on James to Jude*, edited by Karl-Wilhelm Niebuhr and Robert W. Wall, 183–202. Baylor University Press, 2009.

Nienhuis, David R. *Not By Paul Alone: The Formation of the Catholic Epistle Collection and the Christian Canon*. Baylor University Press, 2007.

Nienhuis, David R., and Robert W. Wall. *Reading the Epistles of James, Peter, John and Jude as Scripture: The Shaping and Shape of a Canonical Corpus*. Eerdmans, 2013.

Nogalski, James D. *Redactional Processes in the Book of the Twelve*. Beihefte zur Zeitschrift für die alttestamentliche Wissenschaft 218. De Gruyter, 1993.

Oberman, Heiko A. *The Dawn of the Reformation: Essays in Late Medieval and Early Reformation Thought*. Eerdmans, 1992.

O'Keefe, John J., and R. R. Reno. *Sanctified Vision: An Introduction to Early Christian Interpretation of the Bible*. Johns Hopkins University Press, 2005.

Osborne, Grant R. *The Hermeneutical Spiral: A Comprehensive Introduction to Biblical Interpretation*. Rev. ed. IVP Academic, 2006.

Parker, D. C. *An Introduction to the New Testament Manuscripts and Their Texts*. Cambridge University Press, 2008.

Patzia, Arthur G. *The Making of the New Testament: Origin, Collection, Text and Canon*. 2nd ed. IVP Academic, 2011.

Peckham, John C. *Canonical Theology: The Biblical Canon, Sola Scriptura, and Theological Method*. Eerdmans, 2016.

Pennington, Jonathan T. *Reading the Gospels Wisely: A Narrative and Theological Introduction*. Baker Academic, 2012.

Porter, Stanley E. "When and How Was the Pauline Canon Compiled? An Assessment of Theories." In *The Pauline Canon*, edited by Stanley E. Porter, 95–128. Pauline Studies 1. Society of Biblical Literature, 2009.

Postell, Seth D. "Abram as Israel, Israel as Abram: Literary Analogy as Macro-Structural Strategy in the Torah." In *Text and Canon: Essays in Honor of John H. Sailhamer*, edited by Robert L. Cole and Paul J. Kissling, 16–36. Pickwick, 2017.

Presley, Stephen O. *Biblical Theology in the Life of the Early Church: Recovering an Ancient Vision*. Baker Academic, 2025.

Presley, Stephen O. *The Intertextual Reception of Genesis 1–3 in Irenaeus of Lyons*. The Bible in Ancient Christianity 8. Brill, 2015.

Prothro, James B. "The Christological Analogy and Theological Interpretation: Its Limits and Use." *Journal of Theological Interpretation* 14, no. 1 (2020): 102–19.

Provan, Iain. *The Reformation and the Right Reading of Scripture*. Baylor University Press, 2017.

Radner, Ephraim. *Time and the Word: Figural Reading of the Christian Scriptures*. Eerdmans, 2016.

Ratzinger, Joseph (Pope Benedict XVI). *God's Word: Scripture—Tradition—Office*. Edited by Peter Hünermann and Thomas Söding. Translated by Henry Taylor. Ignatius, 2008.

Ratzinger, Joseph (Pope Benedict XVI). *The Word of the Lord (Verbum Domini)*. Pauline Books & Media, 2010.

Reed, Annette Yoshiko. "Afterlives of New Testament Apocrypha." *Journal of Biblical Literature* 134, no. 2 (2015): 401–25.

Rendtorff, Rolf. *The Canonical Hebrew Bible: A Theology of the Old Testament*. Translated by David E. Orton. Tools for Biblical Study 7. Deo, 2011.

Reventlow, Henning Graf. *History of Biblical Interpretation*. Vol. 1, *From the Old Testament to Origen*. Translated by Leo G. Perdue. Resources for Biblical Study 50. Society of Biblical Literature, 2009.

Rowe, C. Kavin. "Biblical Pressure and Trinitarian Hermeneutics." *Pro Ecclesia* 11, no. 3 (2002): 295–312.

Sailhamer, John H. "Hosea 11:1 and Matthew 2:15." *Westminster Theological Journal* 63, no. 1 (2005): 87–96.

Sailhamer, John H. *Introduction to Old Testament Theology: A Canonical Approach*. Zondervan, 1995.

Sailhamer, John H. *The Meaning of the Pentateuch: Revelation, Composition, and Interpretation*. IVP Academic, 2009.

Schnittjer, Gary Edward, and Matthew S. Harmon. *How to Study the Bible's Use of the Bible: Seven Hermeneutical Choices for the Old and New Testaments*. Zondervan Academic, 2024.

Schreiner, Patrick. *Acts*. Christian Standard Commentary. Holman Reference, 2021.

Scobie, Charles H. H. *The Ways of Our God: An Approach to Biblical Theology*. Eerdmans, 2003.

Seitz, Christopher R. "Canon, Narrative, and the Old Testament's Literal Sense: A Response to John Goldingay." *Tyndale Bulletin* 59, no. 1 (2008): 27–34.

Seitz, Christopher R. "The Canonical Approach and Theological Interpretation." In Bartholomew et al., *Canon and Biblical Interpretation*, 58–110.

Seitz, Christopher R. *The Character of Christian Scripture: The Significance of a Two-Testament Bible*. Studies in Theological Interpretation. Baker Academic, 2011.

Seitz, Christopher R. *Convergences: Canon and Catholicity*. Baylor University Press, 2020.

Seitz, Christopher R. *The Elder Testament: Canon, Theology, Trinity*. Baylor University Press, 2018.

Seitz, Christopher R. *Figured Out: Typology and Providence in Christian Scripture*. Westminster John Knox, 2001.

Seitz, Christopher R. *The Goodly Fellowship of the Prophets: The Achievement of Association in Canon Formation*. Acadia Studies in Bible and Theology. Baker Academic, 2009.

Seitz, Christopher R. *Prophecy and Hermeneutics: Toward a New Introduction to the Prophets*. Studies in Theological Interpretation. Baker Academic, 2007.

Seitz, Christopher R. "Scriptural Authority and Canonical Prophet: The Theological Implications of Literary Association in the Canon." In *Essays on Prophecy and Canon: The Rise of a New Model for Interpretation*, 302–14. Forschungen zum Alten Testament 149. Mohr Siebeck, 2021.

Seitz, Christopher R. *Word Without End: The Old Testament as Abiding Theological Witness*. Baylor University Press, 2004.

Shepherd, Michael B. *An Introduction to the Making and Meaning of the Bible*. Eerdmans, 2024.

Simonetti, Manlio. *Biblical Interpretation in the Early Church: An Historical Introduction to Patristic Exegesis*. Edited by Anders Bergquist and Markus Bockmuehl. Translated by John A. Hughes. T&T Clark, 1994.

Smith, Brandon D. *Taught by God: Ancient Hermeneutics for the Modern Church*. B&H Academic, 2024.

Smith, David E. *The Canonical Function of Acts: A Comparative Analysis*. Liturgical Press, 2002.

Sparks, Kenton L. *God's Word in Human Words: An Evangelical Appropriation of Critical Biblical Scholarship*. Baker Academic, 2008.

Spellman, Ched. "Metaphors We Read Canonical Collections By: Exploring the Nature and Effect of Canonical Contextuality." *Journal of the Evangelical Theological Society* 65, no. 2 (2022): 261–76.

Spellman, Ched. *Toward a Canon-Conscious Reading of the Bible: Exploring the History and Hermeneutics of the Canon*. New Testament Monographs 34. Sheffield Phoenix, 2014.

Spellman, Ched. "Two Testaments to Tell: Biblical Theology and the Canonical Shape of the Gospel." *Journal of Theological Interpretation* 18, no. 2 (2024): 281–99.

Stein, Robert H. *A Basic Guide to Interpreting the Bible: Playing by the Rules*. 2nd ed. Baker Academic, 2011.

Steinberg, Julius, and Timothy J. Stone. "The Historical Formation of the Writings in Antiquity." In *The Shape of the Writings*, edited by Julius Steinberg and Timothy J. Stone, with the assistance of Rachel Stone, 1–58. Siphrut 16. Eisenbrauns, 2015.

Stone, Timothy J. "The Search for Order: The Compilational History of Ruth." In *The Shape of the Writings*, edited by Julius Steinberg and Timothy J. Stone, with the assistance of Rachel Stone, 175–87. Siphrut 16. Eisenbrauns, 2015.

Strawn, Brent A. "And These Three Are One: A Trinitarian Critique of Christological Approaches to the Old Testament." *Perspectives in Religious Studies* 31, no. 2 (2004): 191–210.

Stuhlmacher, Peter. *Historical Criticism and Theological Interpretation of Scripture: Toward a Hermeneutics of Consent*. Translated by Roy A. Harrisville. Pickwick, 2003.

Swain, Scott R. *Trinity, Revelation, and Reading: A Theological Introduction to the Bible and Its Interpretation*. T&T Clark Theology. T&T Clark, 2011.

Thiselton, Anthony C. "Introduction: Canon, Community, and Theological Construction." In Bartholomew et al., *Canon and Biblical Interpretation*, 1–32.

Thomas, Heath A. *Habakkuk*. The Two Horizons Old Testament Commentary. Eerdmans, 2018.

Thomas, Heath A. *Poetry and Theology in the Book of Lamentations: The Aesthetics of an Open Text*. Hebrew Bible Monographs 47. Sheffield Phoenix, 2013.

Thompson, Mark D. *A Sure Ground on Which to Stand: The Relation of Authority and Interpretive Method in Luther's Approach to Scripture*. Paternoster Biblical and Theological Monographs. Paternoster, 2004.

Thompson, Richard P. "Scripture, Christian Canon, and Community: Rethinking Theological Interpretation Canonically." *Journal of Theological Interpretation* 4, no. 2 (2010): 253–72.

Torrance, Alan. "The Trinity." In *The Cambridge Companion to Karl Barth*, edited by John Webster, 72–91. Cambridge University Press, 2000.

Trigg, Joseph W. *Biblical Interpretation*. Message of the Fathers of the Church 9. Michael Glazier, 1988.

Trobisch, David. *The First Edition of the New Testament*. Oxford University Press, 2000.

Trobisch, David. *Paul's Letter Collection: Tracing the Origins*. Augsburg Fortress, 1994.

Tully, Eric J. *Reading the Prophets as Christian Scripture: A Literary, Canonical, and Theological Introduction*. Reading Christian Scripture. Baker Academic, 2022.

Vanhoozer, Kevin J. "The Apostolic Discourse and Its Developments." In *Scripture's Doctrine and Theology's Bible: How the New Testament Shapes Christian Dogmatics*, edited by Markus Bockmuehl and Alan J. Torrance, 191–207. Baker Academic, 2008.

Vanhoozer, Kevin J. *Biblical Authority After Babel: Retrieving the Solas in the Spirit of Mere Protestant Christianity*. Brazos, 2016.

Vanhoozer, Kevin J. *The Drama of Doctrine: A Canonical-Linguistic Approach to Christian Theology*. Westminster John Knox, 2005.

Vanhoozer, Kevin J. *Is There a Meaning in This Text? The Bible, the Reader, and the Morality of Literary Knowledge*. Zondervan, 1998.

Vanhoozer, Kevin J. *Mere Christian Hermeneutics: Transfiguring What It Means to Read the Bible Theologically*. Zondervan Academic, 2024.

Vanhoozer, Kevin J. *Remythologizing Theology: Divine Action, Passion, and Authorship*. Cambridge Studies in Christian Doctrine 18. Cambridge University Press, 2010.

Vos, Geerhardus. *Biblical Theology: Old and New Testaments*. Eerdmans, 1948.

Wall, Robert W. "Acts and James." In *The Catholic Epistles and Apostolic Tradition: A New Perspective on James to Jude*, edited by Karl-Wilhelm Niebuhr and Robert W. Wall, 127–52. Baylor University Press, 2009.

Wall, Robert W. "The Canonical View." In *Biblical Hermeneutics: Five Views*, edited by Stanley E. Porter and Beth M. Stovell, 111–30. InterVarsity, 2012.

Wall, Robert W. "The Function of the Pastoral Letters in the Pauline Canon of the New Testament: A Canonical Approach." In *The Pauline Canon*, edited by Stanley E. Porter, 27–44. Pauline Studies 1. Society of Biblical Literature, 2009.

Wall, Robert W. "Romans 1.1–15: An Introduction to the Pauline Corpus of the New Testament." In *The New Testament as Canon: A Reader in Canonical Criticism*, edited by Robert W. Wall and Eugene E. Lemcio, 142–60. Journal for the Study of the New Testament Supplement Series 76. Sheffield Academic, 1992.

Wall, Robert W. *Studies in Canonical Criticism: Reading the New Testament as Scripture*. Library of New Testament Studies 615. T&T Clark, 2020.

Waltke, Bruce K., with Charles Yu. *An Old Testament Theology: An Exegetical, Canonical, and Thematic Approach*. Zondervan, 2007.

Walton, John H. *The Lost World of the Prophets: Old Testament Prophecy and Apocalyptic Literature in Ancient Context*. IVP Academic, 2024.

Walton, John H., and J. Harvey Walton. *The Lost World of the Israelite Conquest: Covenant, Retribution, and the Fate of the Canaanites*. IVP Academic, 2017.

Warfield, B. B. *The Inspiration and Authority of the Bible*. Edited by Samuel G. Craig. Presbyterian and Reformed, 1948.

Watson, Francis. *Gospel Writing: A Canonical Perspective*. Eerdmans, 2013.

Watson, Francis. *Text, Church and World: Biblical Interpretation in Theological Perspective*. Eerdmans, 1994.

Webster, John. "The Dogmatic Location of the Canon." In Webster, *Word and Church*, 9–46.

Webster, John. *The Domain of the Word: Scripture and Theological Reason*. T&T Clark Theology. Bloomsbury T&T Clark, 2012.

Webster, John. *God Without Measure: Working Papers in Christian Theology*. Vol. 1, *God and the Works of God*. T&T Clark Theology. Bloomsbury T&T Clark, 2016.

Webster, John. "Hermeneutics in Modern Theology: Some Doctrinal Reflections." In Webster, *Word and Church*, 47–86.

Webster, John. *Holy Scripture: A Dogmatic Sketch*. Current Issues in Theology 1. Cambridge University Press, 2003.

Webster, John. *Word and Church: Essays in Church Dogmatics*. T&T Clark, 2001.

Williams, Michael D. *Far as the Curse Is Found: The Covenant Story of Redemption*. P&R, 2005.

Williams, Rowan. *Christ the Heart of Creation*. Bloomsbury Continuum, 2018.

Wilson, Jonathan R. "Canon and Theology: What Is at Stake?" In *Exploring the Origins of the Bible: Canon Formation in Historical, Literary, and Theological Perspectives*, edited by Craig A. Evans and Emmanuel Tov, 241–54. Acadia Studies in Bible and Theology. Baker Academic, 2008.

Wilson, Mark. *Biblical Turkey: A Guide to the Jewish and Christian Sites of Asia Minor*. 4th ed. Istanbul: Ege Yayinlari, 2020.

Work, Telford. *Living and Active: Scripture in the Economy of Salvation*. Sacra Doctrina. Eerdmans, 2002.

Wright, N. T. *The Climax of the Covenant: Christ and the Law in Pauline Theology*. Fortress, 1992.

Wright, N. T. *The New Testament and the People of God*. Christian Origins and the Question of God. Fortress, 1992.

Yeago, David S. "The New Testament and the Nicene Dogma: A Contribution to the Recovery of Theological Exegesis." *Pro Ecclesia* 3, no. 2 (1994): 152–64.

Young, Frances M. *Biblical Exegesis and the Formation of Christian Culture*. Hendrickson, 1997.

Young, Frances M. "Divine Discourse: Scripture in the Economy of Revelation." In *The Oxford Handbook of Early Christian Biblical Interpretation*, edited by Paul M. Blowers and Peter W. Martens, 71–92. Oxford University Press, 2019.

Young, Frances M. *Scripture, the Genesis of Doctrine*. Vol. 1 of *Doctrine and Scripture in Early Christianity*. Eerdmans, 2023.

Young, Frances M. *Scripture in Doctrinal Dispute*. Vol. 2 of *Doctrine and Scripture in Early Christianity*. Eerdmans, 2024.

Young, Frances M., with Andrew Neal. *From Nicaea to Chalcedon: A Guide to the Literature and Its Background*. 2nd ed. Baker Academic, 2010.

Author Index

Scripture Index

Old Testament

Genesis

Exodus

Numbers

Deuteronomy

Joshua

Ruth

1 Kings

Nehemiah

Job

Psalms

Proverbs

1 John

Revelation